VIRTUOUS BANKERS

Virtuous Bankers

A DAY IN THE LIFE OF THE EIGHTEENTH-CENTURY BANK OF ENGLAND

Anne L. Murphy

PRINCETON UNIVERSITY PRESS

PRINCETON & OXFORD

Published by Princeton University Press
41 William Street, Princeton, New Jersey 08540
99 Banbury Road, Oxford OX2 6JX

press.princeton.edu

Library of Congress Cataloging-in-Publication Data

Names: Murphy, Anne L., author.
Title: Virtuous bankers : a day in the life of the eighteenth-century
     Bank of England / Anne Louise Murphy.
Description: Princeton : Princeton University Press, [2023] |
     Includes bibliographical references and index.
Identifiers: LCCN 2022030968 (print) | LCCN 2022030969 (ebook) |
     ISBN 9780691194745 (hardback ; alk. paper) | ISBN 9780691248431 (ebook)
Subjects: LCSH: Bank of England. | Banks and banking, Central—Great Britain—
     History—18th century. | Monetary policy—Great Britain—History—18th century.
Classification: LCC HG2994 .M87 2023 (print) | LCC HG2994 (ebook) |
     DDC 332.1/10942—dc23/enk/20220818
LC record available at https://lccn.loc.gov/2022030968
LC ebook record available at https://lccn.loc.gov/2022030969

British Library Cataloging-in-Publication Data is available

Editorial: Hannah Paul, Josh Drake
Jacket Design: Karl Spurzem
Production: Erin Suydam
Publicity: Kate Hensley, Charlotte Coyne

Jacket Credit: *The Great Hall, Bank of England* (*Microcosm of London*, plate 7).
Designed and etched by Thomas Rowlandson and Augustus Charles Pugin.
Courtesy of The Elisha Whittelsey Collection, The Elisha Whittelsey Fund, 1959 /
The Metropolitan Museum of Art.

This book has been composed in Miller

Printed on acid-free paper. ∞

Printed in the United States of America

10 9 8 7 6 5 4 3 2 1

For Philip Cottrell, in the hope that he would have approved

CONTENTS

Figures

Tables

ACKNOWLEDGEMENTS

THIS BOOK HAS TAKEN far too long to write, and along the way I have incurred many debts. The most important of these debts is to the late Professor Philip Cottrell, my mentor and former colleague, to whom this book is dedicated. Conversations with Phil shaped the early stages of this project and helped me think through the contents of the Minutes of the Committee of Inspection and consider their meaning. I shall always be grateful for those conversations and for Phil's capacity to critique and challenge with generosity, kindness and humour.

A conversation with David Kynaston convinced me that I could write this book as a 'day in the life'. Although there were many times I regretted the decision to follow that format, I was, in the end, pleased with the outcome and enjoyed the challenge of trying to make it work and make sense. I am grateful also to Natalie Roxburgh for many formative conversations about the Bank, its spaces and their meaning.

The Bank of England Archive and Museum were unfailingly attentive and supportive over the many visits and enquiries that were required for this project, even though I imagine they never thought it would actually see the light of day. I also owe a debt to the University of Hertfordshire and former colleagues in the History Group for research time, support and collegiality.

My thinking about the late eighteenth-century Bank was stimulated by conversations with many friends and colleagues including Ann Carlos, Julian Hoppit, Larry Klein, Inger Leemans, James Macdonald, Ciara Meehan, Renaud Morieux, Larry Neal, Malcolm Noble, Patrick O'Brien, David Ormrod, Helen Paul, Patrick Walsh, Carl Wennerlind, Koji Yamamoto, Nuala Zahedieh, and the always delightful participants of the Money, Power and Print Colloquiums. These conversations have certainly improved what follows, as did the suggestions of the anonymous reviewers of the manuscript. Any remaining infelicities and errors are mine alone.

Lastly, but certainly not least, I am grateful to Princeton University Press, and especially to Josh Drake, for their willingness to believe, on the slightest of evidence, that the manuscript eventually would be finished.

Introduction

ON 14 MARCH 1783, three Bank of England directors—Samuel Bosanquet, Thomas Dea and Benjamin Winthrop—embarked on a project to 'inspect' all aspects of the institution's work. The Committee of Inspection, as they were to be known, were to 'meet at such times as may be most convenient to themselves' and 'inspect the management of every Office together with all such Books & Papers as they may think necessary'.[1] To assist them in their work, they were permitted to call before them any of the clerks or other servants at the Bank. There was no interference implied from their fellow directors, but they were also asked to, 'from time to time', report their findings and recommendations to the Committee of Treasury and, thereafter, to the Court of Directors. Their final reports run to over 80,000 words and detail all aspects of the Bank's operation and management from the issue of banknotes to the recording of ownership of the public debt, from the opening of the gates at the start of each day to the locking away of the final ledger at the end of the day. They also demonstrate the Inspectors' confidence in the value and virtue of the Bank. When they presented their conclusions to the Court of Directors, they declared the institution to be of 'immense importance . . . not only to the City of London, in points highly essential to the promotion & extension of its Commerce, but to the Nation at large'. The Bank was, they stated, no less than 'the grand Palladium of Public Credit'.[2] It must 'necessarily excite care and solicitude in every breast . . . a religious Veneration for [its] glorious fabrick' and 'a steady and unremitting attention to its sacred Preservation'.[3]

1. Bank of England Archives (hereafter BEA), G4/23, Minutes of the Court of Directors, 14 April 1779–2 October 1783, fols. 352–353.
2. BEA, M5/213, Minutes of the Committee of Inspection, fols. 178–179. See appendix 7 for the full text of the Inspectors' final report.
3. Ibid.

One can scarcely imagine twenty-first-century bankers being so confident about their contribution to the public good. The popular imagination now often sees them dwelling in the bowels of hell rather than cathedrals of credit. The directors of the eighteenth-century Bank of England, however, had little trouble convincing themselves that the business they managed was essential to the smooth functioning of the national economy and worthy of the country's esteem. This book explores the basis of that conviction: the Bank's ability to deliver a set of services that were essential to the state and commanded the confidence of a wide public. It is a story that has not been told before. Sir John H. Clapham's *The Bank of England: A History*, published in 1944, remains the only monograph-length discussion of the institution's first century.[4] Other histories of the Bank are equally dated and add little to Clapham's account.[5] Even the most recent work on the Bank, David Kynaston's fascinating portrait *Till Time's Last Sand*, unfortunately does not linger long enough in the eighteenth century.[6] This book aims to rescue the eighteenth-century Bank from its relative obscurity.

The narrative ranges from the quiet mundanities of discounting bills and keeping ledgers via the noise and chaos of the financial market and the threat from rioting crowds to the aesthetics of one of London's finest buildings and the messages of creditworthiness embedded in that architecture and in the very visible actions of the Bank's clerks. Its focus is not the sweep of the Bank's activities during the long eighteenth century but rather a moment in time: the year that encompassed the ending and aftermath of the War of American Independence. This choice is partly practical. The Minute books of the Inspection conducted between 1783 and 1784 provide a unique opportunity to study the Bank's work in intimate detail. But there are also important reasons why this moment in time is an appropriate focus. The 1780s witnessed the beginnings of the age of reform, the earliest manifestation of which was the significant reorganisation of public finance.[7] The Bank of England has hitherto been excluded from

---

4. Sir John H. Clapham, *The Bank of England: A History*, 2 vols. (Cambridge, 1944).

5. Notably A. Andreades, *A History of the Bank of England* (London, 1909); W. D. Bowman, *The Story of the Bank of England: From Its Foundation in 1694 until the Present Day* (London, 1937); John Giuseppi, *The Bank of England: A History from Its Foundation in 1694* (London, 1966).

6. David Kynaston, *Till Time's Last Sand: A History of the Bank of England, 1694–2013* (London, 2017).

7. Arthur Burns and Joanna Innes, eds., *Rethinking the Age of Reform: Britain, 1780–1850* (Cambridge, 2003).

discussions of what was known to contemporaries as 'economical reform'.[8] Yet, what follows will demonstrate that the institution engaged willingly with the reforming agenda and emerged confident of its value to the public. An intimate study of the institution is also necessary. The Bank's value to the state and the public during the eighteenth century rested on the level and quality of its service. It is only by exploring in detail the nature of that service that we will be able to explain why the Bank owned by, and operated for the benefit of, its shareholders came to be thought of as 'a great engine of state' and how a private organisation became the guardian of the public credit upon which was based the economic and geopolitical success of Britain during the long eighteenth century.[9]

The Bank during the Long Eighteenth Century

The Bank of England had been in existence for nearly ninety years when the Inspectors began their work. Established in 1694 in borrowed premises and with just seventeen staff, the institution had grown significantly over the intervening period. By 1783 the Bank's buildings dominated Threadneedle Street, and more than 300 clerks were required to handle the expanding business.[10] The institution itself had become part of the everyday experience of many Londoners. It was a bustling environment, noisy and filled with people. As Bosanquet, Dea and Winthrop arrived on that March morning to begin their inspection, they would have walked through streets crowded with the City's businessowners, merchants and financiers going about their business, street sellers plying their trades and, in all likelihood, pickpockets on the lookout for the affluent and unwary. Once inside the Bank, the Inspectors would have observed clerks at their desks or conveying ledgers and papers between offices, and customers managing their accounts, exchanging banknotes and discounting bills of exchange. They would have seen brokers and jobbers buying and selling government debt to a wide variety of public creditors and that same variety of men and

8. The most important works relating to aspects of 'economical reform' are J.E.D. Binney, *British Public Finance and Administration, 1774–92* (Oxford, 1958); Philip Harling, *The Waning of Old Corruption: The Politics of Economical Reform in Britain, 1779–1846* (Oxford, 1996); David Lindsay Keir, 'Economical Reform, 1779–1787', *Law Quarterly Review*, 1 (1934), pp. 368–385; Earl A. Reitan, *Politics, Finance, and the People: Economical Reform in England in the Age of the American Revolution, 1770–92* (Basingstoke, UK, 2007).

9. Adam Smith, *An Enquiry into the Nature and Causes of the Wealth of Nations* (Oxford, 1976), p. 320.

10. A full staff list is reproduced in appendix 1.

women collecting their dividends. Porters would have been lingering in the hallways and in the banking hall to guide customers to their destinations. This was part of their job, but they still would have been hoping for a tip to reward their knowledge and diligence. The Inspectors had seen all this before, of course, but maybe that morning they looked with fresh eyes and started to formulate questions about the way in which the Bank functioned.

As the closing remarks of the Inspectors' reports suggest, whatever questions they had about processes, they remained confident about the importance of the Bank to the public. They also asserted the virtue of that work and the diligent and honourable behaviour of the majority of the Bank's employees. They would have fully understood the Bank's prominent role in the country's financial architecture, and they would have acknowledged that it rested upon the institution's intimate connection to the business of government through the provision of services in support of the creation and circulation of both short- and long-term public debt. Attaining that position had not been straight-forward. When the Bank was established in 1694 it had been a temporary solution to a pressing problem, that of financing the Nine Years' War (1689–1697). It had been granted a twelve-year charter and in return had lent the state £1.2 million, the totality of its initial capital.[11] The expectation was that this would be quickly repaid, and then the Bank, presumably, would have been left to develop its business in the service of the public. The repeated conflicts of the long eighteenth century ensured that repayment was not possible. Instead, the Bank's capital, all lent to the state, doubled and doubled again during its first decade through direct loans and the refinancing of existing debt.[12] The lucrative nature of this business meant there were early rivals to the Bank. The Land Bank was never a strong threat, although it may have appeared so when it was first proposed. The South Sea Company posed a much greater risk until it collapsed under the weight of its own ambition.

After 1720, the Bank was able to consolidate its position and develop its relationship with the state, and by the 1770s its loans to the government exceeded £11 million.[13] It also managed nearly 70 per cent of the

11. Clapham, *Bank of England*, 1:13–20.

12. Ann M. Carlos, Erin K. Fletcher, Larry Neal and Kirsten Wandschneider, 'Financing and Refinancing the War of the Spanish Succession, and then Refinancing the South Sea Company', in D. Coffman, A. Leonard and L. Neal, eds., *Questioning Credible Commitment: Perspectives on the Rise of Financial Capitalism* (Cambridge, 2013), p. 152.

13. Clapham, *Bank of England*, 1:171.

long-term public debt. This meant that for all but a relatively few funds, transfers were handled and interest payable at the Bank.[14] And this related to a significant amount of debt. By 1763, the combined total of the funded and unfunded debt stood at £133 million and, at the end of the war with America, at £245 million. By 1819, following the conclusion of the Revolutionary and Napoleonic Wars, the debt stood at £844 million.[15] The number of public creditors rose in tandem with the outstanding debt. By the mid-eighteenth century there were around 60,000 public creditors, and by 1815 that number had increased to an estimated 250,000.[16]

The Bank's services to the state also extended far beyond debt maintenance. From its earliest days it had been involved in remittances overseas to support the state's military operations. It managed the circulation of Exchequer bills in return for an allowance from the Treasury. This was ultimately to lead to what was essentially a monopoly over short-term lending to the government.[17] It also provided both deposit and borrowing facilities for government departments and offices, many in a formal capacity from the 1780s, and it lent to the army, navy and ordnance.[18] Moreover, although the Bank was not the only financial institution to issue paper money, the fact that its notes were not only accepted widely but also accepted in payment for tax liabilities meant that its paper was supported directly by the actions of the state.[19]

Absorbed as it was in supporting the public finances, the Bank never seriously pursued private business opportunities. Early in its history there had been some forays into private loans both through 'pawnes', advancing money against goods, and through mortgages.[20] This business soon fell away. By the mid-eighteenth century, private lending was concentrated on large and quasi-state institutions. Loans to the East India Company (EIC) dominated, and its outstanding debt to the Bank was seldom less

14. Clapham, *Bank of England*, 1:102–103.

15. B. R. Mitchell with Phyllis Deane, *Abstract of British Historical Statistics* (Cambridge, 1962), pp. 401–402.

16. P.G.M. Dickson, *The Financial Revolution in England: A Study in the Development of Public Credit, 1688–1756* (London, 1967), p. 285; Ranald Michie, *The Global Securities Market: A History* (Oxford, 2006), p. 53.

17. Dickson, *Financial Revolution*, p. 360.

18. H. V. Bowen, 'The Bank of England during the Long Eighteenth Century, 1694–1820', in R. Roberts and D. Kynaston, eds., *The Bank of England: Money, Power and Influence 1694–1994* (Oxford, 1995), p. 11.

19. Christine Desan, *Making Money: Coin, Currency and the Coming of Capitalism* (Oxford, 2014), pp. 312–318.

20. J. H. Clapham, 'The Private Business of the Bank of England, 1744–1800', *Economic History Review*, 11 (1941), p. 78.

than £100,000.[21] There were also constant, although more modest, credit lines offered to the South Sea Company, the Hudson's Bay Company and the Royal Bank of Scotland.[22] The Bank's bullion business likewise was limited and returned relatively insignificant profits. It did, however, ensure that the ratio of metallic reserves against notes issued was high throughout much of the eighteenth century. Clapham estimates that it stood above 50 per cent in much of the latter part of the 1700s and, prior to the Revolutionary and Napoleonic Wars, dropped lower only during the crisis years of 1763, 1772–1773 and 1783.[23]

Out of all the Bank's offerings, it was the discounting business that grew, especially from the 1760s onwards. However, it was not particularly lucrative, relative to the Bank's work for the state. Clapham estimates that, in its most profitable year prior to the Revolutionary Wars, the discounting business yielded £168,000, only enough to pay a quarter of the dividend for that period.[24] But by the later eighteenth century, this business had allowed the Bank to become integral to the management of the London economy. Its control was neither overt nor openly stated, but there is evidence that, at key points, the Bank's directors intervened to manage the credit market through its discounting policy. Thus, as Huw Bowen has asserted, it sat 'at the heart of the nation's credit structure' and contributed to the smoothing of the effects of financial upheaval.[25]

The Bank also commanded the trust and confidence of the business community. Indeed, as one measure of that trust, its stock stayed above par throughout the eighteenth century and was, for the most part, quite comfortably above par.[26] Moreover, the Bank's considerable and sound reputation underpinned the perception of London, and indeed Britain, as a site of financial stability and opportunity. As such, the Bank was a place where the business of financiers, merchants, producers and retailers was performed, noticed and recognized. It was a place to see the economy in action and to be seen as part of that economy. The Bank of England, therefore, was at the apex of Britain's financial architecture when the Inspectors started their work. With that power, however, there was also challenge.

21. Ibid., p. 87.
22. Ibid.
23. Ibid., p. 79.
24. Ibid., p. 81.
25. Bowen, 'Bank of England', p. 2.
26. Ibid., p. 14.

Criticism and Challenge

Although the Inspectors characterised the Bank as the 'grand Palladium of Public Credit', not everyone believed in the institution's integrity. The Bank had faced criticism from some factions throughout the preceding ninety years. Critics argued that the dependence of the state on funds either raised by or managed by the institution was unhealthy and created opportunities for corruption. The Bank, it was said and not without justification, meddled in politics and exerted 'undue influence in high political circles'.[27] Its monopoly was resented and the necessity of opening the business up to competition clearly stated. For much of the eighteenth century this criticism remained an undercurrent, creating little pressure on the Bank. The environment of the early 1780s, however, was increasingly febrile. Criticism of financiers grew as the War of American Independence rumbled on with few successes for Britain and growing tensions in other places of nascent empire: Ireland, India and the West Indies.[28] Disruption throughout the empire was matched by recession at home with the higher taxes needed to fund the rising tide of public debt eating into incomes and economic distress leading to industrial unrest and organised extra-parliamentary opposition to the government.[29] Solutions to these problems were elusive. In August 1779 Secretary to the Treasury John Robinson wrote to Secretary at War Charles Jenkinson, 'I shall not be surprised if the whole Administration blows up even before the Meeting of Parliament'. The Cabinet, Robinson believed, hated each other, and there was no plan for remedying the crises at hand. 'Nothing done, or attempting to be done, no Attention to the necessary arrangements at Home, none to Ireland, nothing to India, and very little I fear to foreign affairs'.[30] And Robinson was a supporter of the government.

Its critics attacked the poor handling of the war and the spiralling costs that had allowed financiers, particularly those responsible for managing debt issuance, and war contractors, those who supplied goods and services to the British war machine, to profit from the nation's misery.[31] To many of these critics, financial mismanagement seemed to be at the heart

27. Ibid., p. 7.

28. P. J. Marshall, *The Making and Unmaking of Empires: Britain, India and America, c. 1750–1783* (Oxford, 2005), p. 353.

29. Reitan, *Politics, Finance, and the People*, p. 1.

30. British Library (hereafter BL), Add. MS. 38212, Liverpool Papers, Volume XXIII, fol. 57.

31. Harling, *Old Corruption*, p. 33.

of the matter, and the solution was 'economical reform': the reform of the nation's seemingly corrupt financial systems. Economical reform was particularly directed at better management of state finances, the abolition of sinecures and the weakening of the influence of the crown. Although not central to these concerns, the Bank was presented as just another aspect of a sinister monied interest which prospered from the exigencies of war.[32] The debate about the renewal of the Bank's charter in 1781 best illustrates how such criticisms may have manifested into threats against the institution.

The limited charters granted to the Bank until the middle of the nineteenth century meant that, in theory, it could have been dissolved and replaced had the government chosen to do so. In reality, the balance of power was not so one-sided, especially since charter renewals were generally negotiated during periods of fiscal emergency.[33] This was also the case in 1781 when the existing charter had more than six years remaining. Who prompted the discussion—the state in need of additional funds or the Bank's directors seeking to exploit that need—is not known.[34] However, the terms of the renewal were negotiated in secret, and the deal, renewal until 1812 in return for a loan of £2 million, was brought to the Commons with no notice. Factions both within and outside of Parliament were vehement in their opposition. Former Member of Parliament (MP) David Hartley argued that it needed to be seen as a matter of basic economy, and he chided Lord North that he should spend a 'morning or two . . . shopping with the maids of honour, till he has learnt that the best way to make a bargain is by going to more shops than one'.[35] Hartley argued that the Charter had a value, one that he put at £120,000 per annum.[36] Supposing fourteen years' purchase, therefore, the Bank should owe £1.68 million to the state, whereas Lord North was simply requiring a loan of £2 million at 3 per cent interest.[37] If other providers of the services offered by

---

32. Bowen, 'Bank of England', p. 9.

33. J. Lawrence Broz and Richard S. Grossman, 'Paying for Privilege: The Political Economy of Bank of England Charters, 1694–1844', *Explorations in Economic History*, 41 (2004), p. 70.

34. Clapham, *Bank of England*, 1:177.

35. Hartley lost his seat as member for Hull in 1780. He returned to Parliament in 1782 and was defeated again in 1784, whereupon he retired from politics. Christopher F. Lindsey, 'David Hartley (1731–1813), Politician', *ODNB*, accessed 7 January 2018, https://doi.org/10.1093/ref:odnb/12495; David Hartley, *Considerations on the proposed renewal of the Bank Charter* (London, 1781), p. 17.

36. Hartley, *Considerations*, p. 19.

37. Clapham, *Bank of England*, 1:179.

the Bank could be found, then the charter could be offered to the highest bidder, not given away to the Bank. Rockinghamite MP Sir George Savile agreed.[38] The 'public had an estate to sell', he raged, but it was being sold 'damned cheap'.[39]

North's counter, that he 'could not imagine there was one man living, who, after the long experience of its utility, would deny that it was the duty of parliament to cement and strengthen the connection and union between the Bank and the public as much as possible', is often used to demonstrate Parliamentary support for the Bank.[40] But North was not praising the institution; he was coming to its defence against a powerful and well-supported opposition. Ultimately, his arguments were successful and the Charter was renewed. Almost a century of accumulated experience could not be dispensed with lightly. Moreover, the most powerful argument against replacing the Bank was that the state owed it many millions of pounds, which it could not afford to repay in return for removal of the institution's privileges. But we should not suppose that the choice was merely between continuing with the Bank of England and dissolving it. There was more than one potential way of curbing the Bank's power and securing a better deal for the country. Establishing a rival public bank would have been possible. Indeed, this was the remedy most often called for.[41]

Likewise, it would have been feasible to place the Bank of England under rigorous Parliamentary scrutiny or even bring it under some form of state control, as the case of the EIC demonstrated. The EIC, also a private company, was from the late 1760s onwards under regular scrutiny. In 1773 a Regulating Bill was passed which limited the dividends the Company could pay, restricted the participation of its employees in private trade and made provisions for state interference in its affairs, especially in the governance of India. George III said of the Bill, 'It lays a foundation for a constant inspection from Parliament into the affairs of the Company which must require a succession of Regulations every year'.[42] The EIC came under further scrutiny during the economical reform period. In 1781 a Secret Committee was established under the chairmanship of Henry Dundas. Its ostensible purpose was to investigate the causes and

38. J. Cannon, 'Savile, Sir George, Eighth Baronet (1726–1784), Politician', *ODNB*, accessed 5 May 2018, https://doi.org/10.1093/ref:odnb/24736.

39. Clapham, *Bank of England*, 1:181.

40. Speech of 13 June 1781, in William Cobbett, ed., *The Parliamentary History of England, from the Earliest Times to the Year 1803*, 36 vols. (London, 1806–1820), 22:517.

41. Bowen, 'Bank of England', pp. 8–9.

42. Quoted in Lucy S. Sutherland, *The East India Company in Eighteenth-Century Politics* (Oxford, 1962), p. 261.

consequences of the recent war in the Carnatic with Haider Ali, the sultan of Mysore.[43] The Bill proposed by Dundas as a consequence of the Committee's investigations was primarily concerned with India and would result in the establishment of the Board of Control in 1784.[44] One of its key points, however, was reorganisation of the EIC in London so as to prevent shareholders from interfering in India and to allow the British government to exercise greater power over the Company's affairs.[45]

The actions that led to the Board of Control violated not only the EIC's rights as a private company but also its shareholders' rights. Arguably, this was done in the pursuit of a greater good, but it must have been a concern for the other monied companies. It certainly set a precedent for interference in the Bank of England's business, and the institution's intimate connections to the financial stability of the state would undoubtedly have provided a valid excuse for that interference had its performance been less than satisfactory. The timing of Dundas's Bill is also significant. It was introduced to the House of Commons in mid-February 1783. The debate would be postponed until later that year because of the fall of the Shelburne administration, but that could not be known in the early spring. It was under these circumstances that, in March 1783, the Bank of England's directors took decisive action. They appointed their own Committee of Inspection, empowered to 'inspect & enquire into the mode & execution of the Business as now carried on in the different departments of the Bank'.[46]

In taking this action, the Bank's directors were, in all likelihood, seeking to put a halt to any plans to impose the kinds of control seen at the EIC on their own institution. Their means of doing so were, seemingly, intelligently conceived. They appear to have replicated the response of Lord North to Parliamentary criticism of the government's handling of its finances. To head off his critics, North had formed a statutory commission to examine the public accounts. The Commissioners were asked to establish the real state of the public finances, identify defects in the systems for managing the public finances and propose solutions.[47] It is key to our story that three of their number were bankers: George Drummond, Samuel

43. M. Fry, 'Dundas, Henry, First Viscount Melville (1742–1811), Politician', *ODNB*, accessed 6 January 2018, https://doi.org/10.1093/ref:odnb/8250.

44. H. V. Bowen, *The Business of Empire: The East India Company and Imperial Britain, 1756–1833* (Cambridge, 2008), p. 73.

45. Ibid.

46. BEA, M5/212, fol. 1.

47. Reitan, *Politics, Finance, and the People*, p. 64.

Beachcroft and Richard Neave.[48] Beachcroft and Neave were directors of the Bank of England—Beachcroft had been governor from 1775 to 1777, and Neave was to become governor in April 1783.[49] Although the Minutes of the two bodies with oversight at the Bank, the Court of Directors and the Court of Proprietors, do not confirm the reasons for the appointment of the Committee of Inspection, both the timing of its appointment and the probable influence of Beachcroft and Neave allow us to assume a direct connection between the Committee and the cause of economical reform.[50]

Economical Reform at the Bank

The working practices of the Committee of Inspection closely matched those of the Commission for Examining Public Accounts, suggesting the precedent set by models for economical reform was being followed. The Bank's Inspectors, like the Commission, had wide-ranging powers and not just to inspect but also to recommend any necessary changes to improve working practices and eliminate corruption. Each body pursued a similar mode of inspection. They both visited one department after another and published interim findings and recommendations as their work continued.[51] Similarities existed between the practical agendas of the two bodies. Both were concerned chiefly with the effectiveness of working systems, the nature of the work and the integrity of the post-holder with regard to job performance and remuneration, including gratuities and perquisites. In this respect, the Commissioners, of course, were faced with problems somewhat different from those of the Bank's Inspectors. The Commissioners were dealing with a long-established system mired in tradition and dependent on sinecure posts. The Bank's Inspectors were faced with a system that was, on the whole, fit for purpose but had grown out of all proportion in the years running up to the Inspection. The result of this was systems that relied upon shortcuts and had grown lax to accommodate much higher volumes of work. Equally, the Bank's Inspectors found no obvious sinecures. Each post at the Bank was associated with a specific set

48. Ibid., p. 66.

49. George Drummond was the more junior partner in the family banking business, but Drummonds was a prosperous and influential firm. Anon., *Drummond Bankers: A History* (Edinburgh, 1993?); Philip Winterbottom, 'Henry Drummond (c. 1730–1795)', *ODNB*, accessed 6 January 2018, https://doi.org/10.1093/ref:odnb/48025.

50. BEA, G4/23, fols. 352–353.

51. J. Torrance, 'Social Class and Bureaucratic Innovation: The Commissioners for Examining the Public Accounts, 1780–1787', *Past and Present*, 78 (1978), p. 66; BEA, M5/212; BEA, M5/213, passim.

of duties and held by a working post-holder. On the other hand, as we will discover, there were poor working practices and lapses in security aplenty.

One significant difference between the Commission and the Bank's Inspectors was that the latter were appointed from within. No external views were to be brought to bear on the situation at the Bank, and this was, undoubtedly, a calculated response. It demonstrated that the Bank, unlike the EIC, could, and was willing to, put its own house in order. Yet, we should not assume that this made the Inspection a toothless process. The Commissioners appointed to examine the public accounts were arguably sympathetic to the reform agenda at hand. Thus, Neave and Beachcroft's apparent role in the establishment of the Committee of Inspection makes it likely that they followed this model and appointed men sympathetic to the cause to inspect the Bank.[52] Bosanquet, Winthrop and Dea were directors of relatively short standing. Bosanquet had first been elected as director twelve years previously, in 1771.[53] Dea had been elected in 1775 and Winthrop only in 1782.[54] Both Bosanquet and Winthrop were merchants, and both went on to serve as Governors of the Bank and thus were clearly very capable individuals. Very little is known about Dea. All three had served on the Bank's Committee for House and Servants, as did the majority of directors. As its name suggests, the Committee was responsible for various aspects of the maintenance of the Bank's premises and the pay, employment and disciplining of the clerks. The reports of the Committee for House and Servants, which met every three months, tend to suggest a rather formulaic agenda. There were warrants to approve and sign for the payment of tradesmen and suppliers and decisions to be made regarding any changes. Reports were received on the behaviour of the staff, although very few direct complaints were made and usually the various heads of department noted only absences.[55] Nevertheless, Bosanquet, Dea and Winthrop's service on this committee suggests that they were broadly familiar with the day-to-day running of the Bank and of the rules governing the working practices of the clerks and had encountered instances of how those rules could be circumvented.

52. Torrance, 'Social Class and Bureaucratic Innovation', p. 64.

53. Bosanquet continued to serve as a director until his death on 5 July 1806. He was elected deputy governor in 1789 and 1790 and governor in 1791 and 1792. BEA, M5/436, Directors Annual Lists, fol. 25.

54. Dea served as a director on and off until 1798. Winthrop served with occasional breaks until his death on 7 October 1809. He was elected deputy governor from 1802 to 1803 and governor from 1804 to 1805. BEA, M5/436, fols. 26–27.

55. BEA, M5/376, Minutes of the Committee for House and Servants, passim.

The Inspectors spent a little over a year pursuing their business. Their work stopped from the end of July to 24 September 1783 because 'some of the Committee were going out of Town', but they took no other significant breaks. They submitted interim reports throughout their tenure and submitted their conclusions in March 1784 but continued to deal with lingering business for several months after that.[56] Their work was recorded by a secretary, Mr Aslett, who, when his task was finished, received the commendation of the Inspectors as having been 'very diligent in his Duty, & in his attendance on us'.[57]

Reading between the lines of the reports allows us to make some assumptions about how the Inspection was conducted. When working, the Inspectors adopted a procedure that combined observation of the clerks with interviews and other enquiries. Notice was given of their itinerary in order to allow the senior men time to prepare their testimonies.[58] Observations appear to have taken place during business hours, and thus the process of the Inspection was obvious to all the clerks and to any astute customers of the Bank who were in the offices at that time.[59] Other than this, there is no indication that the Inspection was made public in any way.

It appears that the Inspectors' behaviour was not overtly intrusive or forceful. Indeed, on a number of occasions they consulted with staff about proposed changes. This suggests that they had respect for accumulated knowledge and an understanding that they were engaging in the alteration of physical activities and processes of which the Inspectors had less understanding than men who had been working in the same capacities for many years. Yet, while periods of consultation point to a cooperative process, perhaps we should not underestimate the possible negative effects of such operations. The milieu of criticism of public finance and public servants cannot have escaped the attention of men who would undoubtedly have frequented the coffee houses of London. Equally, the process of being observed and questioned might have led to feelings of unease. Some of the Bank's clerks must have felt intimidated by the Inspection, although, as we shall see, others used it for promotion of their own interests and to settle scores.

It seems likely that the Committee of Inspection was appointed primarily to demonstrate the value and virtue of the Bank, and this aspect of its role is acknowledged throughout the chapters that follow. But for the

56. BEA, M5/212, fols. 175–176; M5/213, fol. 180.
57. BEA, M5/213, fols. 177–178.
58. See, for example, BEA, M5/213, fol. 21.
59. See, for example, BEA, M5/212, fols. 102, 209.

historian, the Inspectors' reports offer much more than an opportunity to study the practical consequences of the economical reform movement. They provide us with an analysis of all aspects of the Bank's business and intimate details about the nature of the work undertaken by the clerks in the service of the public and of the state. Of course, the details preserved in the Committee of Inspection's Minute books cannot all be taken at face value. Undoubtedly compliance with the standing rules of the Bank was higher when the Inspectors visited a particular office.[60] Moreover, the year-long establishment of the Committee taught both supervisors and junior clerks what to expect from the Inspectors' visits and interviews. Practices were certainly adapted in advance of their visits.

Nonetheless, the diligence with which the Inspection was conducted and the systematic cross-examination of certain clerks suggest that the Inspectors, for the most part, uncovered the realities of the Bank's inner workings. Numerous other extant sources are available to supplement the information in the Minutes. Various rule books have been preserved which offer rich detail about how certain offices were supposed to operate. Diaries of the Bank's governors and Minute books from the various committees that managed the Bank also survive, as do the Minutes of the Courts of Directors and Proprietors. Details of the clerks' working lives, pay, conditions and career progression can be reconstructed from various records. And, most interestingly, one of the Inspectors, Samuel Bosanquet, kept a notebook in which he recorded his personal musings on the clerks and their work as the Inspection proceeded. Drawing on all of these records, the chapters that follow will reconstruct life and work at the late eighteenth-century Bank.

Historiographical Contexts

The narrative follows a day in the life of the Bank, beginning as the gates opened at dawn and continuing through a twenty-four-hour cycle. This is more than a conceit. As in John Brewer's discussions of the Excise in *Sinews of Power*, the 'heroes' of this story are clerks—in this case, those who managed the business of banking.[61] For them, as a general rule, every day was the same. The quest for control of a vast amount of business in a manner

60. Bartrip suggests a similar effect after the establishment of a full-time professional agency for factory inspection. P.W.J. Bartrip, 'British Government Inspection, 1832–1875: Some Observations', *The Historical Journal*, 25 (1982), p. 613.

61. John Brewer, *The Sinews of Power: War, Money, and the English State, 1688–1783* (London, 1989), p. xvi.

that gained public confidence necessitated a regimented system which depended upon specific tasks done at specific times. It will also be argued below that it was the seeming reliability and regularity of the systems at the Bank that helped make it an indispensable part of the apparatus of public credit and one which lent credibility to the state's financial promises.

The chapters that follow consider how work was organised at Britain's primary financial institution, but they represent more than just a discussion of the management of eighteenth-century money. By the 1780s the Bank's operations and numbers of staff employed were considerable. It employed more than 300 permanent clerks, and its work was supported by numerous supernumeraries, porters and watchmen. This was more than double the number of white-collar workers of the EIC, ten times the numbers employed by large insurance companies such as the Royal Exchange and Sun Assurance companies and five times the numbers employed by the Admiralty and the Treasury.[62] The Bank of England's clerks dealt with thousands of customers and thousands of transactions a month. They were employed in specialised capacities and required to develop specific skills. Because of the nature and the scale of the work, they had to coordinate with their fellows to ensure that work was completed in a timely fashion. There was seldom any leisureliness about this business and little room for error.

Indeed, work at the Bank could be thought of as an industrial process: complex; requiring specific equipment, spaces and skills; time-defined; specialised and coordinated. It was also one of the more precocious sites of labour management in the eighteenth century. Long before Samuel Greg began managing Quarry Bank Mill by the clock, the Bank of England regulated its business by strict clock time, kept an appearance book and imposed rules about hours and modes of working. Thus, from a discussion of the Bank's work we can learn something about the stock and value of human capital available to eighteenth-century employers. Focusing on the potential industrial workforce, Joel Mokyr has argued for the existence in eighteenth-century Britain of a 'class of able and skilled people, larger and more effective than anywhere else', with abilities that made Britain into the workshop of the world.[63] Robert Allen's rather more pragmatic take

62. Bowen, *Business of Empire*, p. 139; H. M. Boot, 'Real Incomes of the British Middle Class, 1760–1850: The Experience of Clerks at the East India Company', *Economic History Review*, 52 (1999), p. 639. The EIC employed a total staff of over 1,700, if warehouse labourers and dock workers are included in the count. B. Supple, *The Royal Exchange Assurance: A History of British Insurance, 1720–1970* (Cambridge, 1970), p. 70; Stephen Conway, *War, State and Society in Mid-Eighteenth-Century Britain and Ireland* (Oxford, 2006), p. 39.

63. Joel Mokyr, *The Enlightened Economy: An Economic History of Britain, 1700–1850* (New Haven, CT, 2009), p. 111.

does not ignore the endowment of 'human capital', but it stresses that the incentive to innovate was a result of the high costs of labour.[64] The contested nature of these arguments need not detain us for long. More important in this context is the neglect of the service sector in such accounts.[65] Yet, the scale of the Bank's business necessitated forms of 'industrial' organisation, and although there was little mechanisation, innovation in its practices was substantial and wide-reaching. And if a key factor in the development of the British economy was the quality and productiveness of labour, as is suggested by Kelly et al., then the neglect of white-collar work in this debate is inexplicable.[66] Our understanding of the contribution of human capital to 'precocious Albion' will only be enhanced by exploring the eighteenth century's primary site of clerical labour.

The main beneficiary of the Bank of England's organisational skill was the state. It is hoped that one outcome of this book will be to encourage scholars to place the Bank at the heart of debates about the nature of British power during the long eighteenth century. Thus, one of its key contributions will be to extend the discussion of 'credible commitment'. As expounded by Douglass North and Barry Weingast, credible commitment posited a direct connection between the political change brought about by the Glorious Revolution and the ability of the British state to raise public funds.[67] North and Weingast argued that although seventeenth-century Stuart monarchs had been unreliable, and thus were constrained, the Glorious Revolution placed decisions about borrowing in the hands of Parliament. Parliament had the right to veto government borrowing and the right to audit spending that had been approved.[68] For North and Weingast, the fundamental institutions of representative government created 'multiple veto points' supported by the protection of property rights in the courts. This operated to create a credible commitment on the part of the government to honour its financial promises over the long term.[69]

---

64. Robert Allen, *The British Industrial Revolution in Global Perspective* (Cambridge, 2009), pp. 238–271.

65. A useful summary and extension of the debate is offered by Morgan Kelly, Joel Mokyr and Cormac Ó Gráda, 'Precocious Albion: A New Interpretation of the British Industrial Revolution', *Annual Review of Economics*, 6 (2014), pp. 363–389.

66. Ibid.

67. Douglass C. North and Barry Weingast, 'Constitutions and Commitment: The Evolution of Institutions Governing Public Choice in Seventeenth-Century England', *Journal of Economic History*, 49 (1989), pp. 803–832.

68. Ibid., p. 816.

69. Ibid., p. 829.

North and Weingast's arguments have been contested and extended by numerous scholars.[70] It has been decisively demonstrated that credible commitment was not in evidence until the latter part of the eighteenth century, and indeed property rights remained insecure throughout the period.[71] The fate of the EIC is, of course, a case in point. Yet, the people, from the aristocracy to their servants, were still willing to lend to the British state, and, despite more than thirty years of debate on the topic, we are not any closer to understanding why. In the chapters that follow, I will argue that the answer lies, in great part, in understanding the operations of the Bank of England. The Bank functioned to underpin the rights of lenders through its administrative processes and its willingness to review those processes. The Inspection was a strong symbol of that commitment. The institution itself was also an enforcement mechanism which operated, through the actions of its directors, to hold the government to account and allowed the public creditors to associate and act in defence of their own rights. In addition, the Bank was a visible symbol of credible commitment through its buildings and the openly displayed actions of its clerks as they maintained the record of ownership of the national debt.

The importance of the visible bureaucracy at the Bank of England also connects this book directly to the work of John Brewer. Brewer's 'fiscal-military state' was one that was capable of operating a central bureaucracy dedicated to securing substantial taxation and borrowing which could then be employed in the prosecution of war. Brewer's exemplary bureaucratic processes were those of the Excise. His reasons for making this choice were clear. Eighteenth-century Britain's sizeable debt was underpinned by tax funds allocated to pay the interest. The connections are logical ones: commitment is linked to the ability to pay, and efficient taxation was the cornerstone on which the ability to pay was built. One of the consequences of Brewer's work, however, is that taxation and its

70. G. Clark, 'The Political Foundations of Modern Economic Growth: England, 1540–1800', *Journal of Interdisciplinary History*, 26 (1996), pp. 563–588; Gary W. Cox, *Marketing Sovereign Promises: Monopoly Brokerage and the Growth of the English State* (Cambridge, 2016); Anne L. Murphy, 'Demanding Credible Commitment: Public Reactions to the Failures of the Early Financial Revolution', *Economic History Review*, 66 (2013), pp. 178–197; N. Sussman and Y. Yafeh, 'Institutional Reforms, Financial Development and Sovereign Debt: Britain, 1690–1790', *Journal of Economic History*, 66 (2006), pp. 906–935; Mark Dincecco, *Political Transformations and Public Finances: Europe, 1650–1913* (Cambridge, 2011). See also Daron Acemoglu and James A. Robinson, *Why Nations Fail: The Origins of Power, Prosperity and Poverty* (London, 2013).

71. Julian Hoppit, 'Compulsion, Compensation and Property Rights in Britain, 1688–1833', *Past and Present*, no. 210 (2011), pp. 93–128.

bureaucratic underpinnings have been the subject of much scholarship, while the question of how the state borrowed, and from whom, has been neglected.[72] Yet, although taxation was essential, borrowing provided the immediate funds needed in emergent situations like war. Taxation, to a great extent, could be enforced; lending was voluntary. To understand the geopolitical success of the eighteenth-century British state, it is necessary to understand much more fully the bureaucratic processes that supported its borrowing.

Brewer also argued that the 'fiscal-military' state 'produced a military strength out of all proportion to population and domestic natural resources'.[73] Recent scholarship has qualified his findings.[74] Brewer's assertion of a strong, centralised state has been tempered by a better understanding of the wide dispersion of powers through British society and persistent weaknesses in national defence.[75] In particular, Conway accepts that the state operated with increasing efficiency but asserts that this was the result of symbiotic relationships with both private interests and local authorities. The centralised power of the state operated in partnership with other entities, and it was those partnerships that were 'key to Britain's ultimate success in mobilizing such impressive quantities of manpower, material, and money'.[76]

A particularly informative account of how those partnerships worked can be found in Roger Knight and Martin Wilcox's work on the British navy's victualling service. Knight and Wilcox offered an alternative to the 'fiscal-military state' in the 'contractor state', a shift that focuses attention on the way 'Britain expended the taxes and loans which the government

72. See, for example, William J. Ashworth, *Customs and Excise: Trade, Production, and Consumption in England, 1640–1845* (Oxford, 2003).

73. Quoted in Richard Harding and Sergio Solbes Ferri, 'Introduction', in Richard Harding and Sergio Solbes Ferri, coords., *The Contractor State and Its Implications, 1659–1815* (Las Palmas de Gran Canaria, Spain, 2012), p. 8.

74. For a useful starting point, see the volumes produced by the Contractor State Group and its predecessors: H. V. Bowen and A. González Enciso, eds., *Mobilising Resources for War: Britain and Spain at Work during the Early Modern Period* (Pamplona, Spain, 2006); Rafael Torres Sánchez, ed., *War, State and Development: Fiscal-Military States in the Eighteenth Century* (Pamplona, Spain, 2007); Stephen Conway and Rafael Torres Sánchez, eds., *The Spending of the States: Military Expenditure during the Long Eighteenth Century: Patterns, Organisation and Consequences, 1650–1815* (Saarbrücken, Germany, 2011); Harding and Solbes Ferri, 'Introduction'. See also A. González Enciso, *War, Power and the Economy: Mercantilism and State Formation in 18th-Century Europe* (Abingdon, UK, 2017).

75. Paul Langford, *Public Life and the Propertied Englishman, 1689–1798* (Oxford, 1991); J. E. Cookson, *The British Armed Nation, 1793–1815* (Oxford, 1997).

76. Conway, *War, State and Society*, p. 34.

collected'.[77] The concept of the contractor state is generally applied to the process of converting financial strength into military power, but, at its heart, it denotes a system that turned to 'agents outside the government, for procuring goods and services to enable it to carry out its functions'.[78] Although not previously written of in these terms, I would like to assert that the Bank of England was, in fact, the most successful and long-lived of all the contractors employed by the British state. Indeed, it survived as a private firm, owned by its shareholders and controlled by a directorate elected from among those shareholders, from its establishment in 1694 to nationalisation in 1946. It was a contractor because it received fees to manage the state's debts. It was a contractor because the collective mind of its directors understood and could negotiate with markets for money to which the state did not have easy direct access. It was a contractor because it connected public and state in that profitable relationship which delivered funds to the British war machine while rewarding the public creditors with regular dividends. It was a contractor because it delivered the efficiency that state machinery can seldom achieve.

A central part of what follows, therefore, is directed at understanding the Bank's connections with the British state not at the level of high politics but at the level of service-provider, particularly through the prolonged periods of war that punctuated the long eighteenth century. This will involve an assessment of the bureaucratic and organisational effectiveness of the institution and the value for money that it represented for the state. Here we must consider much more than simply the costs of the services the Bank provided. There were also intangible savings offered by the Bank becoming the face of public credit. Equally, the Bank was not just the primary intermediary between the state and the public creditors; it also provided an interface between the state and the money market.[79] As O'Brien asserts, given the level of debt issued during the wars of the eighteenth century, this was a function not to be taken lightly. The pathways from debt issuance to public uptake of the debt operated mostly through loan contractors, and the Bank facilitated that relationship.[80]

77. Roger Knight and Martin Wilcox, *Sustaining the Fleet, 1793–1815: War, the British Navy and the Contractor State* (Woodbridge, UK, 2010), p. 10.

78. González Enciso, *War, Power and the Economy*, pp. 187, 186.

79. Patrick K. O'Brien, 'Mercantilist Institutions for the Pursuit of Power with Profit: The Management of Britain's National Debt, 1756–1815', in Fausto Piola Caselli, ed., *Government Debts and Financial Markets in Europe* (London, 2008), p. 185.

80. Ibid.

Finally, focus on the Bank as one of the state's key contractors allows a further exploration of a central platform of Brewer's thesis: the efficiency of state administration. Brewer's view of Britain as the paradigm of state effectiveness has been tempered by scholars who point to Aylmer's more realistic assessment that British administration was an 'extraordinary patchwork' of efficiency and incompetence.[81] What follows will reveal that there were numerous failings in the Bank's systems, many of them the result of human error and some the result of the mendacity of clerks who knew the failings in their systems and how to exploit them. Yet, the Bank got the job done and could be seen to get the job done. In the end, whatever the criticisms of the Bank, few doubted the veracity of Lord North's praise of its 'prudent management'.[82] The achievements of the institution and its workers, therefore, offer powerful new evidence that adds to our understanding of how bureaucratic processes underpinned the geopolitical success of the British state during the long eighteenth century.

Outline of the Book

The chapters that follow will re-create a day in the life of the Bank. Its gates opened early in the morning. There was much to do before the customers arrived, including the domestic work of cleaning the building, lighting lamps, winding clocks and laying fires. The clerks, many of whom arrived early to work, also had the task of readying the offices. This included the disgorging of the safes and vaults and the preparation of the ledgers and paperwork needed by the clerks whose daily business took them outside of the Bank. Chapter 1 discusses these routines and demonstrates their importance to the maintenance of order. It also situates the Bank in its surroundings in the City through an exploration of what the clerks saw when they arrived at work. Thus, it details the development of the Threadneedle Street site, noting the Bank's aggressive protection of its own space and its concern to create an aesthetic that combined security, transparency and integrity.

Chapter 2 focuses on the business that dominated the early morning at the Bank, that of the management of London's payment systems. The

---

81. For an overview, see Rafael Torres Sánchez, 'The Triumph of the Fiscal-Military State in the Eighteenth Century: War and Mercantilism', in Torres Sánchez, *War, State and Development*, p. 20. See also G. E. Aylmer, 'From Office-Holding to Civil Service: The Genesis of Modern Bureaucracy', *Transactions of the Royal Historical Society*, 30 (1980), pp. 91–108; Philip Harling and Peter Mandler, 'From "Fiscal-Military" State to Laissez-Faire State, 1760–1850', *Journal of British Studies*, 32 (1993), pp. 44–70.

82. Cobbett, *Parliamentary History*, 22:518.

primary focus of this chapter is the Cashiers Department, one of the two great departments of the Bank. It will outline the offices that could be found in this department and give examples of the management of their work and its risks and rewards. The business conducted by the Cashiers Department embedded the Bank in the wider economy through the issuance of banknotes and the discounting of bills of exchange. Thus, chapter 2 will explore the Bank's developing role as an institution and its acceptance of, and resistance to, taking responsibility for regulating the British economy.

During the late morning the Bank shifted gears as the market in government debt opened in the Brokers' Exchange, bringing with it the noise and confusion of an open outcry market and a significant flurry of activity as brokers, jobbers and ordinary investors sought to confirm their transfers and collect their dividends. Chapter 3 negotiates the confusion of the market to present a picture of public finance at work. It demonstrates the importance of the Bank to the process of maintaining the public credit and situates it as the primary embodiment of the credible commitment to honour the financial promises made by the state. This was work which involved both administration and demonstration. This chapter will argue that the Bank, being seen to deliver secure and well-ordered public credit, was just as important as its administrative service to the public. But it will also show that the transfer clerks consistently violated the Bank's rules by acting as brokers and jobbers sometimes to the aid, and sometimes to the hindrance, of the investors.

Early afternoon was viewed by the Inspectors as one of the times during which the Bank was at its most vulnerable. This was because most of the senior men would leave for the day at around three o'clock, some to pursue second jobs and others to take advantage of the leisure 'earned' by their seniority. It was an action that the Inspectors regarded as 'very extraordinary' and certainly not what was expected from men in positions of responsibility.[83] Chapter 4 will explore how the routines of the Bank echoed those of the wider City and why they allowed the Bank to be left in the charge of some of the most junior clerks. It will then explore the hierarchies at the Bank, noting who held responsibility, how the senior men achieved their positions and how the committees of directors interacted with the chiefs and supervisors of the Bank's offices. The chapter will also explain the 'sticks and carrots' mechanism that was used in an attempt to keep clerks honest in an environment where they often were not closely supervised.

83. BEA, M5/213, fol. 173.

The Bank of England essentially operated a pattern of shift work. The first, in the early morning, revolved around the preparation for the day. The second was the period during which the public had access to the Bank. That period generated a very significant amount of paperwork. Thus, the final shift of the day, during the late afternoon and into the evening, involved a number of workers updating ledgers and accounts. Chapter 5 details the work of the Accountants Office and traces the bookkeeping procedures and checks and balances that ensured the maintenance of accurate accounts and records of ownership of the national debt and Bank stock. It explores in detail the risks of this system, which placed the most junior men in charge of vast sums. And it discusses the instances when the system failed and allowed some clerks to use their knowledge of the Bank's processes to commit fraud.

During the late evening and night the Bank was most at risk from intruders, from acts of revolt and from fire. As a consequence, its precautions against those risks were elaborate and significant. The final chapter traces the processes of locking up the Bank and securing it from risk. It explores the failures in the technologies of security employed by the Bank, including a system where keys had proliferated, safes and treasure chests were inadequate to the task and the gates stood open late into the evening, allowing people to enter the Bank without being noticed by the watchmen. But it will also demonstrate that the Bank was innovative and active in its own defence using its political leverage to remove the physical threats in its environs, funding its own fire prevention systems and, from the time of the Gordon riots of 1780, having the advantage of a military guard at night, in violation of the City's privileges but much to the appreciation of shareholders and public creditors, both domestic and foreign.

CHAPTER ONE

Opening the Gates

THE BUSINESS OF the Bank of England started early. At six in the morning in the summer and seven in the winter, William Watkins, the principal gate porter, took a set of keys from where they hung near the kitchen in his apartment in the Bank, unlocked the main gates and set them open for the day.[1] As he opened the gate, Watkins would find two groups of workers waiting to be let in: the out-tellers and the house porters. The former were clerks whose job it was to negotiate bills due with customers in their own homes or places of business. The out-tellers collected their bills and set out early so that they could complete their work before midday. The porters were charged with arriving early to clean and set up the offices to which they were assigned.

These men would have risen between five and six o'clock and may have had a long walk to work. The clerks had most likely woken in furnished rooms for which they paid a rent of around 2 shillings 6 pence a week from a starting salary at the Bank of £50 a year.[2] Although, as we shall see, a long career at the Bank held the prospect for advancement and significantly improved remuneration, few luxuries were available to the junior men. The author of a 1767 pamphlet advocating a raise in wages for clerks described their living conditions. He offered a view of furnished rooms, which would have contained

> a half-tester bedstead, with brown linsey woolsey furniture, a bed and
> bolster, half flocks, half feathers, a green glazed Chamber-pot, a small
> wainscot table, two old chairs with cane bottoms, a small looking glass
> six inches by four in a deal frame, painted red and black, a red linsey

1. BEA, M5/212, fol. 190.
2. M. Dorothy George, *London Life in the Eighteenth Century* (Chicago, 2000), p. 100.

woolsey window curtain, an old iron stove, poker, shovel, tongs and fender, an iron candlestick mounted with brass, a tin extinguisher, a quart bottle of water, a tin pint pot, a vial for vinegar and a stone white tea cup for salt. Also two large prints cut in wood and coloured, framed with deal but not glazed.[3]

Having little capacity for preparing food in their rooms, they may have breakfasted on their way to the Bank. A variety of street food would have been available in the City, although tea and bread would have been a common meal for many. Benjamin Franklin, while working as a printer in London during the 1720s, noted that some had 'a pint of beer before breakfast followed by a pint with bread and cheese for breakfast'. His more abstemious repast was 'a good basin of warm gruel, in which was a small slice of butter, with toasted bread and nutmeg'.[4]

The collection of men waiting at the Bank would have been noticeable at that time in the morning. The surrounding streets would have been relatively empty. Christian Goede, a German visitor to London, observed that few people were around before 8:00 A.M. Thereafter, the streets filled rapidly with people starting work and going about their business. The 'city shops are opened . . . hackney coaches begin to rattle' and by nine o'clock the City's streets were 'crowded in the extreme'.[5] London was a city full of people and full of noise, 'the broadcasting of municipal news, canvassing, debate and conversation. Doorstep tittle-tattle blended with rowdy banter and marketplace barter'.[6] It was busy and everyone was in a hurry. Arriving in London in 1762, James Boswell noted the 'hurry and splendour . . . the noise, the crowd, the glare of shops and signs'.[7] The effect, he found, was 'agreeably confus[ing]'.[8]

This chapter will situate the Bank within these bustling City streets emphasising both its distinctiveness as a site of commerce and public credit and its embeddedness in the day-to-day life of the City. It will introduce the men whose work started early and trace their routines prior to the commencement of office hours. Before the doors were opened

3. Anon., *Considerations on the Expediency of raising at this Time of general Dearth, the Wages of Servants that are not Domestic, particularly Clerks in Public Offices* (London, 1767), p. 6.

4. Dan Cruikshank and Neil Burton, *Life in the Georgian City* (London, 1990), p. 29.

5. Ibid., p. 23.

6. Emily Cockayne, *Hubbub: Filth, Noise and Stench in England* (New Haven, CT, 2007), p. 155.

7. Quoted in ibid., p. 158.

8. Quoted in ibid.

to customers at 9:00 A.M., the Bank and its surroundings needed to be cleaned. Stoves were lit to heat the offices; ledgers, cash and banknotes were retrieved from the overnight stores; and the notes, papers and equipment were prepared for the men whose work took them, early each morning, elsewhere in the City.

Threadneedle Street

The porters and clerks waiting to be let into the Bank at the Threadneedle Street gates, had they chosen to look around, would have seen an impressive building set in a wide thoroughfare. Like any modern City worker, they would have been aware of a constantly changing environment and been able to see building work going on all around them. In 1783 the London Bridge Water Works were laying new water pipes in Threadneedle Street.[9] As a consequence, the clerks may have needed to watch where they stepped. The water company's work would have created hazards underfoot, both during and after construction, as companies sometimes left pipes exposed or back-filled pavements with inferior materials.[10] The church of St Christopher le Stocks, which stood directly adjacent to the Bank, was being pulled down between 1781 and 1784, and new buildings were being erected on the site to accommodate the institution's ever-expanding work.[11] These works were just the latest of many. The area on which the Bank stood, 'formerly covered with taverns and slums, with low tenements and mean shops', had been systematically dismantled over many years.[12] The demolition and rebuilding work fundamentally changed the character of the area around Threadneedle Street in order to not only provide space for the growing Bank but also accommodate its directors' desire to shape their environment for the purposes of both security and profit.

In order to better understand how the Bank's building would have appeared to City dwellers and visitors, it is worth taking a longer view of its development.[13] The Bank had moved to Threadneedle Street in 1734. Before that it had been sited in rented accommodations in Grocers' Hall,

9. BEA M5/748, Committee for Building Minutes, fol. 97.

10. Cockayne, *Hubbub*, p. 163.

11. BEA, M5/748, fol. 97; BEA, 13A84/2/19, "An Account of the Architectural Progress of the Bank of England" (c. 1857), p. 24.

12. BEA, 13A84/2/19, "Architectural Progress," p. 3.

13. For a comprehensive architectural history of the Bank of England, see Daniel M. Abramson, *Building the Bank of England: Money, Architecture, Society, 1694–1942* (New Haven, CT, 2005). Further work on the architectural development of the City and its meaning includes Iain S. Black, 'Spaces of Capital: Bank Office Building in the City of London,

inconspicuously tucked away in Grocers' Alley, a small street off Poultry.[14] The Threadneedle Street site of the new Bank placed it opposite the Royal Exchange and closer to Exchange Alley, the location of much of the activity in London's stock market. The move also brought the Bank closer to East India House and South Sea House, the other great monied companies of the long eighteenth century. Threadneedle Street was, and is, a major thoroughfare close to other important London streets, notably Cheapside and Cornhill, which were important commercial and shopping districts; Leadenhall Street, dominated by its marketplace; and Old Jewry and Lombard Street, traditionally areas where financiers had operated.

The transfer to Threadneedle Street was a significant step in the Bank's history, but it was not a straight-forward one. The land had been in the Bank's possession for a decade before the decision was taken to move. Purchased at a cost of £15,000 in 1724, the estate was primarily residential, and in the years that followed, the directors gradually bought out the tenants' leases. The plan was to erect purpose-built premises in time for the expiring of the Bank's lease at Grocers' Hall in 1734.[15] The necessity of some form of change was obvious. Grocers' Hall was too small for the Bank's expanding business, access to the building was awkward and the premises were not as secure as they should have been. Yet, there was disagreement among the directorate about the prospective move, with four of the most senior directors—Sir Gilbert Heathcote, John Hangar, William Joliffe and Thomas Cooke—dissenting when asked to confirm the decision to leave Grocers' Hall.[16] Abramson argues that those most against the move had seen the institution through the worst of times. Heathcote had been one of the original directors, appointed in 1694, and thus had witnessed the battle to establish the Bank of England against those who believed that a public bank might be bent to the needs of politicians or monarchs. He had seen challenges from the Land Bank during the 1690s, the seeming opposition to the financial system from a new Tory government in 1710 and the threat posed by the South Sea Company over the period from 1711 to 1720.[17] Men like Heathcote may

---

1830–1870', *Journal of Historical Geography*, 26 (2000), pp. 351–375; John Booker, *Temples of Mammon: The Architecture of Banking* (Edinburgh, 1990).

14. Ralph Hyde, ed., *The A to Z of Georgian London* (London, 1981), 13 Ba.

15. Abramson, *Building the Bank*, p. 28.

16. Ibid., p. 29.

17. Dennis Rubini, 'Politics and the Battle for the Banks, 1688–1697', *English Historical Review*, 85 (1970), pp. 693–714; B. W. Hill, 'The Change of Government and the "Loss of the City", 1710–1711', *Economic History Review*, 24 (1971), pp. 395–413; On the South Sea Company, see Dickson, *Financial Revolution*, pp. 90–156; L. Neal, *The Rise of Financial Capitalism: International Capital Markets in the Age of Reason* (Cambridge, 1990),

have remained wary about flaunting the Bank's position in the economy and political system and may have seen an advantage from maintaining the low profile afforded by residence in Grocers' Hall. Heathcote and his fellow dissenters were also hard-headed businessmen with, perhaps, little interest in the aesthetic and may have regarded investment in a permanent building a waste of capital.[18] But those old men were living past battles.

The building of a new Bank of England was representative of a significant change in the institution's fortunes. Following the bursting of the South Sea Bubble in late 1720 and the consequent disgrace of the South Sea Company, the Bank's relationship with the state became 'smooth and easy' and the institution began to be seen as the safe hands into which the nation's finances were entrusted.[19] Its role in discounting bills of exchange and providing banking services to London's business and mercantile communities, discussed in the next chapter, also embedded the institution in the management of the economy. The Bank's acquisition of a permanent home, its physical expansion and its relocation to a visible spot at the heart of London's business district were part of that process of change. The building made a statement about its central place in the country's economy and the management of its finances.

A further measure of the Bank's changing position was the strength of the competition to design its new buildings. Designs were received from John Tracy, the City of London surveyor; Theodore Jacobsen, amateur architect, businessman and designer of East India House; and Roger Morris, renowned architect of country houses. The Bank's chief accountant, Zerubbabel Crouch, also submitted a design.[20] The Committee for Building, formed to oversee the construction of the new building, were, however, persuaded by practicality rather than fame. They selected designs submitted by Henry Joynes and George Sampson as the finalists in the competition. Both men were government clerks of the works. Joynes was working as surveyor to the Commissioners of Sewers for Westminster. Sampson had been clerk of the works for the Tower of London and Somerset House. These men, thus, brought not only competent design skills but experience of such large-scale public building works. Sampson's and Joynes's designs were similar, and there was no consensus among the Committee about which design should win. Each, apparently, had much to commend it but also

---

pp. 62–117; Helen J. Paul, *The South Sea Bubble: An Economic History of Its Origins and Consequences* (Abingdon, UK, 2011).

18. Abramson, *Building the Bank*, p. 31.

19. Clapham, *Bank of England*, 1:91.

20. Abramson, *Building the Bank*, pp. 35, 39.

contained elements that were objected to. The final decision was eventually turned over to the Court of Directors, a committee of the Bank's governor, deputy governor and twenty-four elected directors. They selected George Sampson's as the winning design. They may have been persuaded by Sampson's social connections, but his plan was also more practical than Joynes's, incorporating, as it did, three separate entrances, a spacious courtyard and more central and accessible Pay Hall.[21] However, the Court also retained Theodore Jacobsen as advisor to the Committee for Building, perhaps as a way of ensuring sufficient attention was also paid to the sophistication and taste required for such a prestigious building.[22]

As soon as Sampson's Bank of England was completed, it was too small to house the Bank's growing business, and the directors were forced to rent extra office space from as early as 1737.[23] Moreover, the business of the Bank continued to increase in line with the growing economy and the rapidly expanding national debt. In 1734 the total debt, funded and unfunded, stood at £49.1 million. By the end of the Seven Years' War in 1763 it stood at £132.6 million and by the end of the War of American Independence at £231.8 million.[24] The Bank handled the majority of this business on the government's behalf, and its staff base increased accordingly, from 96 in 1734 to over 300 when the Committee of Inspection started their work in 1783.[25] In response to the expansion of the Bank's business, between 1764 and 1766, three Acts of Parliament enabled the directors to acquire more property around Threadneedle Street.

In their expansion plans, the directors desired not just an increase in office space but also the removal of the tightly packed alleys and courtyards that surrounded the Bank and created a fire risk.[26] This had been an ongoing project but clearly remained a concern. When the issue was raised during the 1760s, it was observed that the roads around Threadneedle Street were still too narrow and other property remained too close to the Bank, with the risk that, especially in case of a fire, 'buildings, papers and property . . . may be in danger of being destroyed to the irretrievable loss of the publick'.[27] Restricted space around the Bank was a concern for other reasons also. London had expanded considerably over the course

21. Ibid., 1:47.
22. Ibid., 1:45.
23. Ibid., 1:59.
24. Mitchell with Deane, *Abstract*, pp. 401–402.
25. Clapham, *Bank of England*, 1:103.
26. Abramson, *Building the Bank*, p. 60.
27. W. M. Acres, *The Bank of England from Within*, 2 vols. (London, 1931), 1:191.

of the eighteenth century, as had the amount of traffic and numbers of people on the move. The problem was particularly bad around the Threadneedle Street area because it encompassed both the Bank and the Royal Exchange. Hackney carriages, carriages for private hire, plied their trade around the area in such numbers that their presence was regularly complained of to the Cornhill wardmote inquest, a meeting of elected male householders convened to hear complaints and punish offenders.[28] The press of traffic was not just a nuisance. Horse-drawn vehicles are not easy to manoeuvre, they do not reverse, they need a wide turning-circle and horses do not always come to a stop at command.[29] The danger this posed to pedestrians in the vicinity was significant, and fatalities from traffic accidents were a regular happening on London's streets.[30]

In response to these concerns and the requirement for additional space, more than an acre was added to the Bank's footprint from the middle of the eighteenth century, and the thoroughfares around the site were widened significantly. The Bank was not alone in undertaking this kind of clearance. London was notorious for its closely packed streets and alleyways and the poor quality of its buildings. In 1760 the City Corporation's Committee of the City Lands embarked on an extensive improvement scheme for clearing dilapidated areas and widening thoroughfares.[31] The City was slow in its work, however, whereas the Bank's directors pursued a rapid process of change. Their actions pushed out the area's previous residents, including a plumber, a diamond cutter, a schoolmistress and a doctor. Also removed were a number of taverns and coffee houses.[32] With the destruction of the latter, some of the tangle of informal spaces where businessmen, merchants, brokers and jobbers met were lost.[33] They were replaced by new office blocks, known as Bank Buildings. Into these blocks moved the bankers James and Fordyce, the bullion dealer Solomon Da Costa, a lottery office and the Sun Fire Insurance Office, along with a couple of coffee houses. These spaces represented not just a significant shift in the institution's control of its environs but also an important diversification of its business. The cost of constructing Bank Buildings was around £18,500, and the space eventually yielded rents of around £2,000 per annum.[34]

28. Cockayne, *Hubbub*, p. 169.
29. Ibid.
30. Ibid.
31. George, *London Life*, p. 107.
32. Abramson, *Building the Bank*, p. 61.
33. Ibid.
34. Ibid., p. 78.

During this period, building work at the Bank was overseen by the architect Robert Taylor. Taylor was the son of one of London's leading mason contractors. He had an early career as a sculptor, undertaking work for the Bank, including the figure of Britannia, which sat over the entrance to the Pay Hall. He turned to architecture in the 1750s, taking advantage of a London building boom, and soon found himself in great demand.[35] He began work at the Bank in 1764 and was responsible for all aspects of its expansion. Under his direction, wings on both sides of Sampson's façade and a four-storey, fire-proof library building, the most important function of which was housing the Bank's ever-expanding archive, were added to the Bank. Taylor also built a grand Court Room, three times the size of the previous one, and a suite of parlours, committee rooms, writing rooms, a private office for the Bank's secretary and a coffee room.

These new spaces were situated behind the church yard of St Christopher le Stocks and largely segregated from the day-to-day business of the Bank but were accessible through the banking hall and a grand lobby to accommodate the meetings of customers with the Bank's directors.[36] The most important addition to the Bank during this period, however, was the Rotunda, or Brokers' Exchange, and four new Transfer Offices. The Rotunda was a domed and circular space, around sixty-two feet high and wide, which filled each day with a 'cacophonous crowd' of investors, brokers and stockjobbers jostling for space and for the best deals.[37] It was this addition that brought the secondary market in the government's debt onto the Bank's premises. As we shall see, this offered many advantages to brokers, jobbers and public creditors. But the presence of the market, which seemed so often to undermine the value of public credit in an institution regarded as its guardian, also posed a challenge. It is possible to argue that one response to that challenge was the messages of integrity communicated to the public through the Bank's architecture.

The Meaning of the Bank

Indeed, the spaces created by Sampson and then Taylor were redolent with strong messages to the state and to the public. Figure 1.1 depicts the Bank during the early nineteenth century flanked by similar structures, but in the 1780s its Palladian façade in Portland stone stood in physical contrast

35. Ibid., pp. 61–66.
36. Ibid., pp. 66–67.
37. Ibid., pp. 70–71.

FIGURE 1.1. *A View of the Bank of England* (1816), Daniel Havell, printmaker, after a drawing by Thomas Hosmer Shepherd.
Source: Rijksmuseum, CCO.

to the high and narrow brick, wood and stucco buildings that surrounded it.[38] Thus, the Bank stood out in its environment and attracted attention. It was mentioned in tourist guides and traveller's memoirs.[39] Thomas Malton found it to be designed to a 'tolerable good style, and the parts are simple and bold'.[40] M. de Colonne, 'a foreigner of the first taste', thought it 'with no exception but St Paul's, to be the first architecture in London'.[41] According to Sir John Fielding in his *Brief Description of the Cities of London and Westminster*, the Bank exceeded East India House and South Sea House in appearance. The former was described as too small with 'not much to praise or much to censure', and the latter was 'large but plain', whereas the Bank was a 'noble Structure' of around eighty feet in length

38. Ibid., p. 57.
39. See, for example, Anon., *The Ambulator; or the Stranger's Companion in a tour round London* (London, 1774), ix; T. Malton, *A Picturesque Tour through the Cities of London and Westminster* (London, 1792–1801).
40. Malton, *Picturesque Tour*, p. 76.
41. Quoted in Booker, *Temples of Mammon*, p. 5.

'of the Ionic Order, raised on a Rustic Base, and by judges it is held to be well-executed'.[42]

The impression that the building made upon these commentators was intentional. The expensive building work that had been undertaken in the wake of the South Sea Bubble had been part of a process of rebuilding confidence in finance. It was a strategy pursued not only by the Bank but also by the East India Company (EIC) and the South Sea Company.[43] In the case of the Bank, the building work created an exterior view that, in the words of Clare Walcot, conveyed a 'polite, public image appropriate for a city street and the self-identity of a corporate institution'.[44] There can be no question that the educated would have recognised those messages. Contemporary commentators certainly linked architecture, especially Palladian architecture, with business integrity. Walcot notes that in contemporary architectural theory, the appearance of a building equated to the appearance of an individual 'in its potential to reveal character'.[45] Thus, in Roger North's late seventeenth-century architectural treatise, he argued the following: 'I can shew you a man's character in his house. If he hath bin given to parsimony or profusion, to judge rightly or superficially, to deal in great matters of small, high or low, his edifices shall be tincted accordingly, and the justness or imperfection of his mind will appear in them'.[46] The architect John Gwynn likewise argued for the 'political and moral advantage' of magnificence in public building and called upon his fellow countrymen to 'employ our riches in the encouragement of ingenious labour, by promoting the advancement of grandeur and elegance'.[47] Equally, the quality of public buildings was linked in architectural theory to the strength of the state and of its commerce. Thus, Robert Morris in *An Essay in Defense of Ancient Architecture* argued that 'the Decay of the State and government of a Kingdom, is dependent upon the Decay of publick Buildings'.[48] A flourishing state, on the other hand, was demonstrated, and promoted, through its public buildings.

42. John Fielding, *A Brief Description of the Cities of London and Westminster* (London, 1776), p. 2.

43. Clare Walcot, 'Figuring Finance: London's New Financial World and the Iconography of Speculation, circa 1689–1763' (unpublished PhD thesis, University of Warwick, 2003), p. 86.

44. Ibid., p. 98.

45. Ibid., p. 93.

46. Roger North, *Of Building* [c. 1695–1696], quoted in Walcot, 'Figuring Finance', p. 93.

47. John Gwynn, *London and Westminster Improved* (1766), quoted in Miles Ogborn, *Spaces of Modernity: London's Geographies, 1680–1780* (New York, 1998), pp. 98–99.

48. Robert Morris, *An Essay in Defense of Ancient Architecture* (1728), quoted in Walcot, 'Figuring Finance', p. 102.

The conflation of Bank and state would have become more obvious as staff and visitors walked through the front gates and into the courtyard. Here was located the entrance to the Pay Hall, where general banking business was conducted. On the pediment of that building they would have seen Robert Taylor's statue of Britannia depicted pouring out the fruits of commerce from her cornucopia, while also carrying the shield and spear which symbolised the defence of the nation.[49] Britannia was adopted as the Bank's symbol at its foundation. On 30 July 1694, just a few days after the Bank was established, the Minutes of the Court of Directors recorded that they had decided their Common Seal should depict 'Britannia sitting and looking on a bank of mony'.[50] As we shall see, she appeared not just on the exterior of the Bank but on numerous objects inside the institution, including all the ledgers used for registering the ownership and transfer of the national debt. Britannia was also a symbol carried outside the Bank as the letterhead on all its correspondence and as a visible image on all the Bank's notes.

Britannia's importance as the symbol which most represents the Bank is brought into sharp focus by contrasting her with another dominant female allegory of the eighteenth century, that of Lady Credit. Britannia remained an exemplary figure and was always above reproach. Lady Credit, on the other hand, was intensely volatile: one moment she was your friend and the next she was turning away from you. Borrowers were warned to be 'very tender of her for if you overload her, she's a coy mistress—she'll slip from you without any warning, and you'll be undone from that moment'.[51] Joseph Addison also depicted the 'quick Turns and Changes in [Credit's] Constitution' and her tendency to 'fall away from the most florid complexion . . . and wither into a Skeleton'.[52] Sherman shows that Lady Credit quickly became depicted as a whore at the fall of a speculative market.[53] This inconstancy was applied not only to the imaginary Lady Credit but to the very real South Sea Company in the wake of the Bubble's bursting in 1720. Thus, one commentator raged,

the Chief Managers of a certain Stock may dress up their Darling Mistress once more, and send her into the World not without a tempting

49. Fielding, *Brief Description*, p. 2.

50. BEA, ADM 30/59, Britannia and the Bank, 1694–1961.

51. Cited in T. Mulcaire, 'Public Credit: Or the Feminization of Virtue in the Marketplace', *PMLA*, 114 (1999), p. 1031.

52. Cited in Mulcaire, 'Public Credit', p. 1033.

53. S. Sherman, *Finance and Fictionality in the Early Eighteenth Century, Accounting for Defoe* (Cambridge, 1996), p. 157.

Aspect; but People who have already been Sufferers by their Schemes, will look upon her with a cautious Eye. A fine Lady, who had deceiv'd a Man once, will for the Future be treated as a common Prostitute.[54]

Another depicted the South Sea Company as having 'bewitch'd thousands to fall in Love with her . . . yet her Lust is not one bit abated; and She runs a whoring after new Lovers every day'.[55] But Britannia did not fall in the way that Lady Credit and the Lady of the South Sea fell. Nor did the Bank. In James Milner's *Three Letters, Relating to the South Sea Company and the Bank*, the great monied companies, all written of in feminine form, were assessed with regard to their behaviour during the speculative boom of 1720. The Bank, in the final letter, was judged to be run by a 'Body of Men not addicted to the Scandalous Tricks of Stock-Jobbing'.[56] Following the South Sea Bubble, the 'Lady Credit as whore' image was used frequently, while the Bank's Britannia ultimately matured into the inviolable 'Old Lady of Threadneedle Street'.

In the image of Britannia, therefore, the behaviour of the Bank and the integrity of public credit became inextricably and productively linked, and the message would have been apparent to many users of the Bank. Moreover, Britannia became ubiquitous in eighteenth-century Britain, repeatedly appearing as an emblem of the Protestant nation and in connection to the monarchy.[57] She was also used frequently to depict the state of the nation. Although this sometimes rendered Britannia vulnerable, especially in the latter part of the eighteenth century as the threat from the loss of the American colonies grew, in the Bank's depictions she was an icon that spoke of strength and stability. With her warlike iconography and close associations with trade, industry and profit, she offered a clear statement of the conflation of the Bank's aims with the goals of the British state. Indeed, Abramson argues that the use of Britannia as the Bank's emblem 'might even be read as implying the identity of the Bank of England *itself* as the nation's protector and provider'.[58]

The Bank's exterior view held another set of messages for the public. Although of fashionably classical design, the Bank was an imposing and, some might have said, intimidating structure. Because of the need

---

54. *The South-Sea Scheme Detected* (1720), quoted in Sherman, *Finance and Fictionality*, p. 53.

55. Quoted in Walcot, 'Figuring Finance', p. 82.

56. Ibid.

57. Emma Major, *Madam Britannia: Women, Church, and Nation, 1712–1812* (Oxford, 2012), p. 1.

58. Abramson, *Building the Bank*, p. 54.

for security, there were no windows facing the street at the ground-floor level. Thus, passers-by were presented with an elegant but essentially blank façade. Iain Black labels those windowless walls 'exclusionary', linking them to the Bank's aggressive protection of its privileges and monopoly position.[59] Abramson likewise has argued that the very structure and architecture of the Bank were strongly symbolic of the erosion of people's traditional rights and liberties. It was enclosed and secretive, an embodiment of economic and political forces that were undermining the lives of the City's lower sorts of people.[60] As we have already seen, some contemporaries regarded the Bank as part of a corrupt and dangerous financial system. Moreover, the directors' actions underlined the messages of exclusivity and secrecy. They were aggressive and ruthless in their command of the Bank's physical environment. Many people in London would have been excluded from its environs either incidentally, by having no business to conduct there, or deliberately. Indeed, the Bank's porters were charged with monitoring those who entered the Bank during business hours and ensuring that undesirables were removed from its public spaces.[61] These attempts at exclusion should not, however, be read solely as undermining the rights of the people. For the Bank's customers and for the public creditors, they were an important part of establishing the reputation and security of the Bank. In particular, they helped embed the message that the Bank's architecture offered to those who used its services: capital invested here will be safe.

The question of how we interpret the Bank's physical presence is a complex one, and it will be returned to in the chapters that follow. We will see how both the exterior and the interior represented corporate virtue, security and probity and emphasised the institution's connections to the state and its usefulness to country and government.[62] It will also be shown that the employees as well as the customers of the Bank, through their actions, had the power to contribute to the performance of virtuous banking. They also had the power to undermine that message. What follows will emphasise that the more polite spaces within the banking hall offered something quite different to the chaos of the market in the Bank's Rotunda and Transfer Offices. While there is no doubt that accommodating the business of stockjobbers and brokers within the Bank's environs was a convenience to many, it posed a threat to the institution's integrity as

59. Black, 'Spaces of Capital', p. 357.
60. Abramson, *Building the Bank*, p. 85.
61. BEA, M5/607, Old Book of Orders for Porters and Watchmen, fols. 2–3.
62. Abramson, *Building the Bank*.

the guardian of public credit. The secondary market had the power to support but also to undermine the state's efforts to raise funds. It was also a target for those who saw high finance as synonymous with speculation and even dishonesty. And the Bank's transfer clerks, by virtue of their access to the market, found it all too easy to step into the role of broker and stockjobber and cross from supporting to exploiting the public creditors. Disorder and dishonesty were sometimes closer than the Bank's directors cared to acknowledge.

Cleaning and Making Ready

Attention to the Bank's appearance did not end with its buildings. The routines at the start of the day included cleaning of the institution's public and private spaces and the streets on which it stood. Before dawn some of the institution's night watchmen ceased their guard duties or woke from a few snatched hours of sleep to begin the tasks of cleaning, fetching coal and lighting fires so the buildings would be ready when the clerks arrived for work.[63] The job of cleaning certain offices would be taken on by the porters, who were directly responsible for the maintenance of the spaces to which they were assigned.

The Bank was large by the end of the eighteenth century, and cleaning was a significant undertaking but one which was time constrained. The watchmen aimed to complete their tasks promptly, as many of them had day jobs elsewhere. Some were EIC labourers, who would have needed to make their way to the warehouses for an eight o'clock start.[64] The porters had other jobs in addition to cleaning, and everything needed to be ready before the admittance of customers at nine o'clock. The cleaning routines were overseen by the Bank's housekeeper, the institution's only recorded female employee. The wife of the head gate porter was generally appointed housekeeper, and from 1771, when the new Stock Offices were opened in the Bank, she was paid £50 per annum.[65] The housekeeper at the time of the Inspection was Jane Watkins. Her specific duties are not made clear in the Bank's records but, given that the watchmen and porters did much of the heavy work, it is likely that the housekeeper's role, as in a private home, was primarily supervisory. Mrs Barker's *The Complete Servant Maid*, published in 1711, advised that the housekeeper be first up in the morning

63. BEA, M5/212, fols. 186–187.
64. Acres, *Bank of England from Within*, 1:249.
65. Ibid., 2:386.

and that all her employer's belongings be kept in good order, since 'all the goods in the house are committed to her care'. She was to provision the house prudently with 'every sort of necessaries for the family' and to direct the cleaning of rooms, carpets, furnishings, stoves and hearths.[66] Given that the Bank contained public spaces, parlours for private meetings and office space for the directors, there is no reason not to assume that Mrs Watkins would have been responsible for the kinds of elegant furnishings and decorative pieces that might be found in a private home. Further, it is likely she would have contributed to provisioning the Bank, although not with regard to the larger-scale purchases of coal and candles, which would have been necessary to heat and light the offices and were taken care of by the Committee for House and Servants. Mrs Watkins undoubtedly had an unenviable task dealing with a cleaning force who were not under her direct supervision and a public space that was large, was complex and attracted hundreds of people through its doors each day.

The cleaning work undertaken by the porters and watchmen would have been heavy and potentially tiring. Stone floors had to be swept and washed. Wooden floors required additional maintenance; washing and scouring with sand was the norm. Furniture needed to be dusted and polished. Furniture and fabrics also needed upkeep and mending, where appropriate.[67] Clocks needed to be wound. Offices were lit by candles, probably of tallow in all spaces except those used regularly by the governor and directors. Tallow candles were smelly, burned poorly and required maintenance to prevent guttering.[68] The offices were heated by 'large open stoves' and fires. They were probably too cold in winter and too warm in summer.[69] Cleaning hearths and stoves and laying new fires was dirty work. Coal was the primary means of heating in eighteenth-century London. It was observed that it did not always give off much heat but did create thick black smoke and 'caustic vapours'.[70] Another of the porters' less enviable early-morning tasks was removing waste from the Bank. This may have included leftovers from meals, cinders and ashes from the Bank's various fires, and other waste from the Bank's activities, including discarded and broken items.[71] At Grocers' Hall there had been a 'dunghill

66. Quoted in Paula Humfrey, 'Introduction', in Paula Humfrey, ed., *The Experience of Domestic Service for Women in Early Modern London* (Farnham, UK, 2011), p. 16.

67. Humfrey, 'Introduction', p. 17.

68. Cruikshank and Burton, *Georgian City*, p. 74.

69. *The Old Lady of Threadneedle Street*, 7, p. 6.

70. Cruikshank and Burton, *Georgian City*, p. 5.

71. Cockayne, *Hubbub*, p. 188.

in the foreyard' where the waste was deposited.[72] It would have stunk, especially in summer, and rain would have turned the dunghill into a quagmire of filth. Later in the eighteenth century, waste removal was more efficient. There were carters, dustmen and chimney sweeps who would take away accumulated waste, including waste from cesspits. The latter had, by law, to be done at night. It was an unpleasant and laborious business. The night watchmen had to dig out the deposited matter and carry it in buckets to their carts.[73] But it was necessary since London's sewerage system was ill equipped to cope with solid waste during the eighteenth century.

Although not obviously evident in the plans, the Bank undoubtedly had privies on site for the use of customers, staff and the individuals who lived within its environs. Privies were built external to the main building or house, usually in the rear yard. They were likely to be located over a cesspit and might have been little more than wooden benches with holes over a pit or tub. Some would have had lids to cover the holes when not in use.[74] All would have been malodorous in the extreme. Cesspits were not intended to be watertight, and thus the liquid waste drained away while the solid matter remained to be removed by the night watchmen.[75] Although no evidence can be found, it is likely that the Bank also had water-closets, located inside the buildings. Most fashionable town-houses would have included at least one by the 1780s, and thus the directors and the Bank's more illustrious customers may have expected this convenience.[76] The water-closet was generally a lavatory pan that could be flushed with water usually from a tank but sometimes from a water pipe.[77] Water-closets were considerably less drafty and somewhat less smelly than outdoor privies.

Cleaning up the yards within the Bank's walls and the footpaths in the exterior of the buildings was also part of the porters' early-morning roles. The concern for the exterior presentation of the institution reflects the changing streetscapes of Britain's towns and cities. Cruikshank and Burton note the dramatic changes in the way London's streets looked and were experienced over the Georgian period and attribute much of the change to two pioneering Acts of Parliament: the City of London Lighting

72. Quoted in Acres, *Bank of England from Within*, 1:145.
73. Cruikshank and Burton, *Georgian City*, p. 94.
74. Cockayne, *Hubbub*, p. 143.
75. Ibid.
76. Cruikshank and Burton, *Georgian City*, p. 96.
77. Ibid.

Act, 1736, and the Westminster Paving Act, 1762.[78] The latter took responsibility for the upkeep of pavements from the individual householder or property owner and placed it in the hands of local authorities with the power to tax residents.[79] The Act specified stone kerbs, raised pavements and kerbside gutters, which improved safety. The changes also eased the process of cleaning the streets, making it easier for scavengers and crossing sweepers to remove waste and, in the summer, allowing cleaning to be carried out using carts carrying barrels with holes punched into them from which water flowed to wash the streets.[80] Although the scavengers would have removed dirt from the highway, the resident was obliged to clean the steps and pavement in front of their house. For the Bank's porters, this meant the courtyards and, by the latter part of the eighteenth century, quite considerable expanses of pavement.

In undertaking these duties, however, the Bank contributed to developments that made the City a cleaner and more pleasant place to live by the latter part of the eighteenth century. It also responded to the bustle of the streets, the busyness of the area around Threadneedle Street, which daily was full of carts, coaches and pedestrians, and the accumulation of dirt that must have occurred. Cleaning around the Bank helped to preserve space for its polite and often wealthy patrons to distance themselves from the tumult of the streets. But it arguably also had meaning beyond the maintenance of order. Miles Ogborn has linked the improvement of the streets of London to the desire to 'create the appropriate urban geography for a commercial and civilised nation'.[81] In this respect the mundane routines of cleanliness link directly to the messages of integrity, security and politeness conveyed by the Bank's buildings.

Opening the Bank

Attempts to impose order and direction on the hustle and bustle of business were also obvious within the Bank. The management of daytime security began early since, at the time of the Inspection, once the gates were unlocked in the morning, they were set open and thus anybody could enter. This included both the front gate and the gate to the cartway, which led to the Bullion Office. As noted by the Inspectors, 'as soon as the Gates are opened in a morning any person is at liberty to come into the house &

78. Ibid., p. 13. See also George, *London Life*, p. 17.
79. Cruikshank and Burton, *Georgian City*, p. 13.
80. Ibid., p. 15.
81. Ogborn, *Spaces of Modernity*, p. 115.

go where he pleases, without any other restraint than what may probably arise from his or the porter's seeing him & questioning him upon his business'.[82] The porters charged with this responsibility were of two types: gate porters, of which there were two in the Bank, and house porters, of which there were five. There was also a door-keeper, Matthias Alcock, and a messenger, Samuel Cooper.[83] The door-keeper and gate porters were usually on duty at the Bank's exterior perimeter and were under the supervision of the chief accountant. The house porters staffed several of the offices and were under the supervision of the chief cashier.

The Inspectors took account of the porters' activity, as they did every other function of the Bank, and, as we shall see, in a number of other areas related to security, they found procedures wanting. Following their investigations, they required that instead of the gates being unlocked and set open early in the morning, they remain shut until half past eight with a porter attending to provide admittance to clerks as necessary. Inspectors particularly noted the importance of having a porter in constant attendance at the Threadneedle Street gate, as 'he might be of considerable use, for the purposes of keeping order, of having an eye on such persons as go in or out, of directing those who enquire the way to the several Offices'.[84] The Inspectors also asked that the gate porter appear properly attired at all times, with 'his Gown & Staff', and noted the need for the appointment of a deputy given that Mr Watkins could not be expected to be in constant attendance at the gate.[85] It is important to note here the concern for the 'public' that is implied in the Inspectors' comments. As might be expected in the febrile atmosphere of the early 1780s when criticism of the financial system was intense, one of the factors that guided the Inspectors' deliberations was the Bank's service to the public. Thus, they noted both regular complaints and the convenience of the public, in terms of ease of negotiation of the Bank's spaces and services and also with regard to the timeliness of delivery of those services.

The porters took up their positions around the Bank before 9:00 A.M. In addition to the man at the front gate, there were two porters in the Rotunda. Their role was to 'take charge of the Gate in Bartholomew Lane, to keep the avenues leading to the stock offices clear, [and] to direct the Public in their Enquiries'.[86] This was perhaps the most challenging of

82. BEA, M5/212, fol. 189.
83. See appendix 1.
84. BEA, M5/212, fol. 201.
85. Ibid.
86. BEA, M5/607, fol. 2.

the porters' jobs. The Rotunda was an open public place and attracted not just people with business there but also street sellers who saw the opportunity to offer their wares to the crowds. Thus, the porters were charged with preventing 'Persons from coming in to offer any article for sale or Exhibition. To suppress all disorderly behaviour among the Persons who daily attend in the Rotunda, and to preserve peaceable conduct as much as possible'.[87] The Bullion Office was also attended during its 9:00 A.M. to 3:00 P.M. working hours by porters who were, in addition, charged with attending the Bank's vaults and treasury. Their role was 'to assist in weighing money in the Hall & put Tickets on the Bags [and] To carry in and out of the strong room the Trucks of Books belonging to the Hall Department'.[88] The house porters were also charged with more general roles and expected to direct customers and visitors, keep everything clean and tidy, 'keep the Books in their proper places, and suffer no articles to remain about the office not belonging to it'.[89]

While the porters were cleaning offices and setting up for the day, the out-tellers were collecting their packages of notes and bills and heading out into the City. They were the first clerks to start work each day. Their role was described in the Minutes of the Committee of Inspection as to 'receive Money for bills of exchange & notes of hand at the houses of the persons to whom they are address'd'.[90] Out-tellers, who would come to be known as bank messengers, performed an important job which required honesty and encompassed not a little risk, as they would carry paper worth large amounts about in the City. It is a job about which very little has been written and one that became obsolete from the late 1980s as electronic transfers of money became the norm. Prior to the late twentieth century, however, bank messengers would have been a common sight on the streets of all major cities, and their activities were part of the rhythms of financial life and essential to the smoothing of the payments system.[91]

There were between ten and fourteen out-tellers at the Bank who worked each day, Monday to Saturday, and, according to the Inspectors'

87. Ibid., fol. 3. See also BEA, M5/213, fol. 166.
88. BEA, M5/607, fol. 5.
89. Ibid., fol. 6.
90. BEA, M5/212, fol. 2.
91. There are very few acknowledgements of the important role played by bank messengers, but there are some exceptions. Bank of Montreal, 'The Bank Messenger Had a Great Deal of Responsibility', accessed 2 May 2020, https://history.bmo.com/bank-messenger -great-deal-responsibility/; BNP Paribas, 'A Bygone Job—The Bank Messenger', accessed 2 May 2020, https://history.bnpparibas/dossier/a-bygone-job-the-collection-man/.

reports, covered between ten and twelve set 'walks' around the City.[92] Chief Cashier Abraham Newland noted to the Inspectors that the number of out-tellers was 'uncertain'.[93] There is no clarification of this point, but in the staff list for 1783 only twelve out-tellers are listed. Thus, it seems likely that other men in the Bank would be enlisted from time to time to do the job if needed.

At the Bank, the process of out-telling began the day before as clerks working in the Bill Office sorted through the bills which were to fall due the following day. A clerk then sorted the bills into 'walks' and stored them overnight in an iron chest.[94] That clerk then had to return early the next morning to deliver the parcels of bills to the out-tellers. Once the out-teller collected and signed for the bills, he was effectively committed to delivering the amount of the bills back to the Bank.[95] Indeed, it is quite clear from the Bank's record that at this point the process transferred responsibility from the institution to the individual, and the clerk giving his testimony to the Committee of Inspection noted that an out-teller's first task was 'at his peril to compare the bills he actually receives with the list of them in the Entry book'.[96]

It is impossible to reconstruct the out-tellers' walks, but they were allocated several hours for the task, leaving the Bank before 9:00 A.M. and not being expected to return until midday. Much of their time, however, might have been spent waiting for a customer to produce payment for a bill. Payment could be accepted in 'Money, Bank Notes, Bank Warrants or drafts on the Bank', and the payers should have been well aware of the due dates so prepared, in most cases, to make payment. Out-tellers could also accept payments via drafts on other bankers, but in that case, 'they must procure payment of them' before returning to the Bank to make up their accounts.[97] Thus, an additional stop would have been added to their walk.

The out-tellers had to be very mindful of security. Once they left the Bank they were beyond its protection and in danger from assault and theft. As a precaution, they were instructed to immediately cancel all banknotes they received, except those notes that were more than a year old and thus would not have been redeemable.[98] The out-teller was also to cancel the

92. BEA, M5/212, fol. 6.
93. Ibid.
94. Ibid., fols. 12–13.
95. Ibid.
96. Ibid., fol. 13.
97. Ibid., fol. 6.
98. Ibid.

clerk's name on every bank warrant and write his own name against it (for the purpose of creating an audit trail), to check all notes against a list of 'stopped notes' and to record in a notebook the details of all notes received and from whom they were received. The Inspectors were advised, however, that the 'multiplicity of business generally prevents these last directions being executed'.[99]

Out-tellers needed to have a detailed knowledge of the common forms of means of exchange and an understanding of how to distinguish genuine from counterfeit notes. This was clearly no easy task. Bank Governor Samuel Beachcroft's diary records a reprimand to 'Parker the out teller for negligence in not taking proper notice of a Bank note, which he told a clerk at Wickendens was a good one, when it was forged'.[100] Parker should perhaps have been forgiven for his error. Some forgeries were extremely good imitations, and the multiplicity of paper means of exchange in eighteenth-century Britain meant there was much to learn.[101] The amount of training available to an out-teller is not clear from the record, but the Inspectors noted that a senior out-teller, Thomas Fugion, received a gratuity for instructing the others.[102] Fugion also testified that he saw it as his job to 'enquire into the conduct of the junior out tellers & . . . see to their good behaviour & to report upon it to Mr Church [chief clerk in the Bill Office] whenever he heard anything against them'.[103] Undoubtedly potential personal liability for losses also kept the out-tellers vigilant. Each clerk at the Bank was expected to provide personal security against losses backed by an independent bond guarantor.[104] For less serious offences or occasions when the Bank incurred financial losses through negligence, clerks also could find their wages stopped in order to compensate the institution.

Two more of the Bank's processes required clerks to attend early to collect papers and equipment and then depart the institution for other premises: the printing of notes and the maintenance of the Bank's relationship with the Exchequer. With regard to the former, the Bank's notes were printed off-site at the house of Mr Cole, a process which required both the paper

99. Ibid.

100. BEA, M5/451, Governor's Diary—Samuel Beachcroft, 1775–1777, fol. 10.

101. Jack Mockford, "They Are Exactly as Bank Notes Are": Perceptions and Technologies of Bank Note Forgery during the Bank Restriction Period, 1797–1821' (unpublished PhD thesis, University of Hertfordshire, 2014); Hannah Barker and Sarah Green, 'Taking Money from Strangers: Traders' Responses to Banknotes and the Risks of Forgery in Late Georgian London', *Journal of British Studies*, 60 (2021), pp. 585–608.

102. BEA, M5/212, fol. 27.

103. Ibid., fol. 45.

104. For details, see BEA, M5/700, Clerks and their securities.

and the printing plates to be conveyed out of the Bank and beyond its control. This arrangement speaks to the complexities of the processes that the Bank controlled and the ways in which lack of space constrained some aspects of the institution's business. It is also another example of a process that the Inspectors identified as in need of rapid change in the interests of security and integrity. In their report they condemned the practice of printing notes off-site, acknowledging the danger to which both the paper and the plates were subjected all the time they were outside of the Bank's control.[105] Changing the process was not so easy, though, and the printing process was not brought on-site until 1791.[106]

In 1783 Mr Barber, the clerk who oversaw the printing process, attended the Bank early each morning to collect the printing plates required for that day from the Bank's Treasury and take them to Mr Cole's. The paper for the process was delivered separately by Mr Thompson, the second cashier. This was done at the start of each month, and it was Thompson's decision as to how much paper should be made available and what denomination notes were required.[107] Both men traveled more than a mile from the Bank to the printer's and followed a route that took them past Field Lane, a notoriously dangerous area.[108] Yet, they seem to have made this journey each working day with no additional oversight or accompanying security. The printer, Mr Cole, employed three men to do this work, which took place in a room in his house. Mr Barber's role for the rest of the day was to watch this process and not let the plates out of his sight until the printers were done, which was usually around three in the afternoon. At this point Mr Barber returned the plates to the Bank.

Additional security was no more in evidence for the men who worked at the Exchequer. Three Bank clerks went there each day 'to pay & receive Monies issued or brought in there for the use of the Government'.[109] One aim of this book is to understand the interconnections between the Bank, the state and the public at the level of day-to-day processes and not just at the level of politics and high-stakes lending. The work at the Exchequer was one element of this. It shows the Bank as manager of the state's finances in the most mundane of ways, essentially providing cashier services and means of payment to ensure that the business of government

105. BEA, M5/212, fol. 167.

106. A. D. Mackenzie, *The Bank of England Note: A History of Its Printing* (Cambridge, 1953), p. 38.

107. BEA, M5/212, fol. 128.

108. Mackenzie, *Bank of England Note*, p. 38.

109. BEA, M5/212, fol. 139.

could continue. Mundane though this work was, the sums involved were significant. One of the three clerks who attended the Exchequer went early to the Bank each day to withdraw sums in notes ranging 'from 50 to £100,000', in Exchequer bills usually between £500,000 and £2 million and the rather more paltry sum of £1,000 to £2,000 in ready money.[110] After the clerk signed for all this, notes, bills and cash were put into a 'small Tin Chest to which there is a padlock' and conveyed through the streets to the Exchequer.[111] Once at the Exchequer, the Bank clerks operated alongside government-appointed clerks to support the business of revenue collection and government payments to contractors and suppliers.

As those men were leaving the Bank, others were arriving to take up their places in the various offices. Their punctuality was required and lateness was noted. Matthias Alcock, the principal door-keeper, told the Inspectors that he kept an 'Appearance Book' in which he drew a line at ten minutes after nine every morning to indicate those clerks who did not arrive on time.[112] Alcock also made a note of any clerks who were sick or absent for other reasons but was reliant on the clerks themselves for this information.[113] The first task for the men arriving before 9:00 A.M. would have been to locate the relevant keys. Some had been taken home in men's pockets, but others were stored at the Bank. The key to the iron chest, and for which there was no duplicate, had to be collected from the lodging of the chief accountant, 'who returns it to whichever Clerk attends earliest the next morning, for him to deliver the Bills to the Bill Office'.[114] In order to be ready to receive customers in the banking hall and other customer-facing areas of the Bank, the clerks and porters then needed to retrieve ledgers and notes from where they had been stored overnight. They might also have collected stationery as well as 'paper, pens, Ink, packthread, little books, wax & wafers'.[115] The clerk who issued the stores took 'signatures in a book (for pens only) of such Clerks as come for them'.[116] The pens and ink made available for the use of customers in the banking hall would also have been replenished.

The in-tellers who worked in the Pay Hall were obliged to collect 'every morning from the warehouse such a number of Bank Notes as it is expected may be called for, these, together with their bags, deposited in

110. Ibid., fol. 140.
111. Ibid., fols. 140–141.
112. BEA, M5/213, fol. 165.
113. Ibid.
114. BEA, M5/212, fol. 52.
115. Ibid., fol. 57.
116. Ibid., fol. 58.

the warehouse the night before'.[117] The nature of their business, and the fact that they had to be ready for the arrival of customers at 9:00 A.M., meant that their supervisor Mr Campe was in the office regularly by 8:30 A.M.[118] Campe was probably one of the first senior men to arrive at the Bank each morning. Account books and ledgers were brought out from the safes and cupboards in which they had been lodged overnight. The chest which contained the discounted bills was unlocked so as to be ready for use at 9:00 A.M.[119] In the Transfer Offices, the ledgers were so large and unwieldy that they were taken out of the strong room by the watchmen before they finished their shifts and placed in the relevant offices around six or seven in the morning.[120]

As a precaution against fire, overnight duplicates of the stock and debt transfers made each day were sent out of the Bank every evening and taken to the house of Edward Payne, one of the directors. It was the job of the porters to retrieve them each day and return them to the relevant offices.[121] The primary ledgers in which the Bank's work was recorded were also returned from the overnight storage in the strong room. The General Ledger, the Treasury book and the Exchequer book (the book in which the delivery of Exchequer bills was recorded) were taken out by the watchmen and then sat exposed in the Accountants Office until Mr Edwards, the deputy accountant, arrived to take charge of them.[122]

Edwards's time of arrival in the office is not recorded, but, being one of the senior men, he likely was not in the office before 9:00 A.M. and probably often after. It was predominantly the junior men who prepared the Bank for the day. The rhythms and routines by which this process occurred were undoubtedly so familiar to the clerks as to require very little thought. The risks of those routines, the lapses in security, the ledgers left in unoccupied offices for much of the early morning and a lack of oversight by the senior men were clearly little considered before the Inspection. The Inspectors, however, were quick to recognise where procedures might be improved, and, as we shall see in the following chapters, the question of what responsibilities the senior men should take was returned to a number of times.[123]

117. Ibid., fol. 33.
118. Ibid., fol. 37.
119. Ibid., fol. 43.
120. BEA, M5/213, fol. 18.
121. Ibid., fol. 38.
122. Ibid., fol. 18.
123. See appendix 6, which reproduces the Inspectors' report on the conduct and behaviour of the clerks.

By 9:00 A.M., the area around the Bank and the institution itself would have been a hive of activity. London would have been filling with people with business to attend to, and the Bank sat at the heart of its commercial district. Within the Bank's walls, clerks would have been occupying their designated spaces in the offices ready to start work for the day and customers would have been starting to arrive in the banking hall. The early-morning routines set up the business of the Bank on a mundane and practical level. It has been shown how much needed to be prepared before the institution opened for the day. But those routines also set the scene for engagement in orderly and polite commercial exchange. The following chapters will show that the performance of virtuous banking was just as important as practical routines of the Bank's business.

CHAPTER TWO

Polite Banking

THE DAILY SCHEDULES of many of London's merchants, financiers and businessowners began early, and the busiest part of their day was the morning, which might be spent 'scrutinizing accounts and giving orders to their clerks, book-keepers and other staff' before 'embark[ing] on a per-ambulation of the key sites within the City'.[1] For merchants, in particular, the substantial business of the day needed to be done prior to attendance at the Royal Exchange and dining, thereafter, in the mid to late afternoon.[2] Of course, habits varied by individual, but a professional standing required 'a certain amount of public routine'.[3] Thus, the practicalities of exchange and the gathering of intelligence through face-to-face interactions, combined with the need for visibility and sociability in the conduct of business, made for a regular, and common, structure to the day.

For many, the morning routine would have encompassed a visit to the Bank of England's banking hall, the place where all 'Money Matters, Notes, Bills, Drafts &c. are transacted', as well as being one of the sites where the temperature of the wider economy might be taken.[4] Visitors would have entered the Bank through the Threadneedle Street entrance. After walking through the courtyard and passing under the statue of Britannia, they would have found themselves in the hall, a space described by Henry Fielding in 1776 as seventy-nine feet long and forty feet wide with

1. Perry Gauci, *Emporium of the World: The Merchants of London, 1660–1800* (London, 2007), p. 60.

2. Cruickshank and Burton, *Georgian City*, pp. 25–27.

3. Gauci, *Emporium of the World*, p. 61.

4. A Gentleman of the Bank, *The Bank of England's Vade Mecum; or sure guide; extremely proper and useful for all persons who have any money matters to transact in the hall of the Bank* (London, 1782), p. 3; Gauci, *Emporium of the World*, p. 72.

an eight-foot-high wainscot and fine fretwork ceiling.[5] It was a space designed to be elegant and to impress. The symbols of the Bank's connection to the state that we observed in the Bank's exterior view were echoed here. At the far end of the hall stood Henry Cheere's statue of William III, depicted as a Roman emperor and on a pedestal inscribed as follows:

> For restoring Efficacy to the Laws,
> Authority to the Courts of Justice,
> Dignity to the Parliament,
> To all his Subjects their Religion and Liberties
> And ascertaining them to Posterity,
> By the Accession of the illustrious Race of Hanover
> To the British Empire;
> To that most excellent Prince, William the Third,
> The Royal Founder of the Bank.[6]

Around the hall were desks for the cashiers and tellers and points of access for the various other offices that, with the banking hall, formed the Cashiers Department. The spaces would have quickly filled with people. It would have been noisy and confusing for those who had not had cause to use the Bank before and, because of the numbers of customers, sometimes frustratingly slow for those who had business there on a regular basis. London citizens were regarded as 'equally uncapable both of attention and patience'.[7]

The business conducted in the banking hall and its adjacent offices—the issuance of notes, the taking of deposits and payments and the making of loans in various forms—played a central role in the British economy. By the late eighteenth century, the Bank operated as the anchor for a monetary system that helped to lower transaction costs, increased the capacity for exchange of goods and services and eased the process of revenue raising for the state.[8] The Bank held the majority of the country's gold reserve, its notes circulated widely and dominated the London markets and business environment, and it was Britain's principal agency discounting

5. Fielding, *Brief Description*, p. 2.

6. Ibid., p. 3.

7. T. Brown, *Amusements Serious and Comical* (London, 1700), quoted in Gauci, *Emporium of the World*, p. 58.

8. Iain S. Black, 'The London Agency System in English Banking, 1780–1825', *London Journal*, 21 (1996), pp. 112–130; Forrest Capie, 'Money and Economic Development in Eighteenth-Century England', in Leandro Prados de la Escosura, ed., *Exceptionalism and Industrialisation: Britain and Its European Rivals, 1688–1815* (Cambridge, 2004), p. 216.

bills of exchange.[9] Other London bankers, kept small and limited in scope by the Bank's monopoly, relied on the Bank's notes, held accounts at the institution and used it for clearing balances. The country banks, which by the 1780s had grown in number but not in power, did not keep reserves at the Bank but nonetheless continued to be dependent on the London money market, especially when credit was scarce.[10]

The work of the Cashiers Department intertwined the private and public markets for money. The Bank's notes were not just a medium of exchange. Scholars have argued that we should think of Bank of England notes as a form of public credit 'advanced by the institution on behalf of the government' and endorsed by that government when it accepted notes against tax obligations and spent notes in payment to its suppliers.[11] Moreover, in addition to holding significant numbers of accounts for businesses and other institutions, such as the East India Company, the Bank controlled some of the payments systems for the state. This included government loans and lotteries, navy bills and management of the assets deposited with the Court of Chancery.[12] Government departments, other public authorities and many tax-receivers also held accounts with the Bank.[13] Thus, we must recognise the management of money and the maintenance of the credibility of the Bank's notes as part of the British financial revolution.[14]

The purpose of this chapter is to understand the routines in the banking hall and surrounding offices, spaces that were at their busiest in the morning and in service of London's business community. The Inspectors spent several months in their investigation of the Cashiers Department, and their findings and reports extend to nearly 40,000 words. What follows, therefore, must necessarily be selective in its coverage. An overview of the cashiers at work will be presented, firstly through the eyes of the Inspectors and then with a particular focus on the processes for discounting promissory notes and bills of exchange. These processes illustrate the

9. D. M. Joslin, 'London Private Bankers, 1720–1785', *Economic History Review*, 7 (1954), pp. 170, 175.

10. Desan, *Making Money*, p. 397. See also L. S. Pressnell, *Country Banking in the Industrial Revolution* (Oxford, 1956), pp. 75–76.

11. Desan, *Making Money*, p. 386. See also arguments in Carl Wennerlind, *Casualties of Credit: The English Financial Revolution, 1620–1720* (Cambridge, MA, 2011).

12. Since 1725, property belonging to the suitors in the Court of Chancery had been lodged at the Bank. Joseph Parkes, *A History of the Court of Chancery* (London, 1828), p. 318.

13. Clapham, *Bank of England*, 1:174–175.

14. Desan, *Making Money*, p. 386.

nature of the work undertaken by the clerks and its connections with the wider economy. Discussion will then turn to the experiences of those who used the Bank. It will be argued that the banking hall was a site of polite sociability, albeit one that was, at times, compromised by the press of business and the ways in which gifting and gratuities shaped the attention of the clerks. Finally, the chapter will consider the primary risks identified by the Inspection with regard to the issue of banknotes and will outline the steps taken to address those risks.[15]

The Inspectors in the Banking Hall

The Committee of Inspection began its investigation in March 1783 by interviewing the man responsible for work in the banking hall and its surrounding offices, the chief cashier, Abraham Newland. Newland, the son of a Southwark miller and baker, had joined the Bank in 1748, at the age of 18.[16] He was appointed chief cashier in January 1782, so he had been in that post a little over a year when called to appear before the Committee to explain the workings of his department. With 122 employees, the Cashiers Department was the smaller of the two great departments of the Bank. The larger was the Accountants Department, which, according to the employee list presented to the Court of Directors in March 1783, had a workforce of 195.[17] We will consider the accountants in later chapters.

Although commanding the smaller department, Newland, as chief cashier, was probably the most prominent employee in the Bank since his role connected directly with work for the public and for the state. However, he does not appear to have courted attention. Indeed, a biographer writing soon after Newland's death in 1807 found that his 'habits of retirement' meant that there were very few interesting anecdotes to relate.[18] His life was instead marked by 'enduring patience and plodding perseverance', but this was, perhaps, what made him an exemplary employee and safe pair of hands into which could be put control of the means of generating many millions of pounds.[19]

---

15. See appendices 2 and 3 for the Inspectors' recommendations for changes in these areas.

16. John Dyer Collier, *The Life of Abraham Newland Esq. Late Principal Cashier at the Bank of England* (London, 1808), pp. 4–7.

17. See appendix 1.

18. Collier, *Life of Abraham Newland*, p. iv.

19. Acres, *Bank of England from Within*, 1:257.

When Newland was interviewed, his first action was to present to the Committee of Inspection a list of the offices under his control. The list read as follows:

1. The InTellers who receive and pay Money.
2. The OutTellers who receive Money for bills of exchange and notes of hand at the houses of the persons to whom they are address'd.
3. The Clerks in the Drawing Office where the Accounts are kept of those persons who keep cash at the Bank.
4. The Clerks in the Bill Office where the Accounts are kept of the bills and notes left by those persons who keep cash at the Bank to be received when due and placed to their accounts. And the Clearers who receive of the OutTellers the money collected daily by them for payment of bills.
5. The Clerks at the Cash Books where the Bank Notes & Bank Post Bills are made out & entered when issued and when paid.
6. The Clerks in the Discount Office.
7. The Clerks in the Bullion Office.
8. The Clerks who receive the public money on account of loans.
9. The Clerks who attend the Receipt of his Majesty's Exchequer on the Bank's Account.
10. The Care of the Treasure in the Vaults under the inspection of the Cashiers.
11. The Clerks who pay the Interest to the Proprietors of Bank Stock & of such part of the national Debt as is transacted there.
12. The Clerks who check the same or the Warrant Office.
13. The Clerks who receive and pay money on account of the Suitors in the Court of Chancery.
14. The Clerks at the General Cash Book.[20]

The size and complexity of the Cashiers Department, as well as the variety of means of exchange handled by the Bank, is obvious from Newland's list. But the functions of his department can be summarised as (a) the receipt of money in various forms, including bullion; (b) the issue of money in various forms; (c) the extension of credit; (d) the management of what we would now describe as current accounts; (e) the creation of records related to the foregoing functions; and (f) the management and safe storage of money in its various forms.

20. BEA, M5/212, fols. 2–3.

In subsequent interviews, the Committee of Inspection was presented with accounts of the daily activities of each of these offices, initially given by Newland or the chief clerk of an office and then corroborated by other workers. The Inspectors used these testimonies not just to understand the processes that supported this work but, in keeping with the investigations conducted by the Commission for Examining Public Accounts, to test efficiency and identify security risks and possible instances of, or opportunities for, corruption. In response, they made recommendations for improvements in the organisation and mode of work that, as we shall see, led to significant changes, especially in the management of note issue. They also sought to understand the nature of the employment offered and the commitment required by workers to complete necessary tasks. In contrast to the work of the Commission for Examining Public Accounts, the Bank's Inspectors found no obvious sinecures. Nor did Abraham Newland or his senior colleagues raise any serious complaints about the men under their charge. Indeed, Mr Clifford, head of the Drawing Office, told the Inspectors that the 'Gentlemen under his charge were very regular & well qualified for their business, which was very necessary, for matters of immense consequence passed through their hands'.[21] The Inspectors, too, found relatively little to complain of with regard to the men's behaviour, although Samuel Bosanquet recorded in a notebook that he kept throughout the Inspection a 'great want of subordination in the Hall throughout'.[22] Outwardly, therefore, the staffing of the Cashiers Department of the Bank would seem to be consistent with John Brewer's arguments relating to the emergence of a class of knowledgeable and efficient administrators working within precisely defined roles.[23] As we shall see below, this was not the case for all of their colleagues in the Accountants Department.

The Inspectors tested the descriptions given of the work in the Cashiers Department in several ways, including through personal observations of the men at work and through examination of both senior and more junior clerks. For example, an account of the work of the in-tellers was first delivered by Newland. He explained their role and detailed the various forms of money they were obliged to receive and the authorisations on which they were obliged to make payments. He further described the method of accounting used by the in-tellers and the end-of-day procedures for the

21. Ibid., fol. 85.

22. BEA, M5/471, Memorandum book of Samuel Bosanquet, 1783–1791, 26 March 1783, unpaginated.

23. Brewer, *Sinews of Power*, pp. 79–87.

management and storage of the cash under their control.[24] The work of the in-tellers was then returned to two weeks later when the Committee interviewed Mr Campe, senior teller in the banking hall, and Mr Smith, senior teller in the Pay Office.[25] Both Campe and Smith were asked to corroborate previous testimonies and to provide additional details on the hours of work and the behaviour of the clerks who reported to them. In this way the Inspectors formed a picture of the work done in each office.

The details recorded in the Minutes with regard to the tellers make clear the Inspectors' priorities. They received a basic overview of the work noting that there were ten in-tellers working in the banking hall and a further six to nine working in the Warrant Office.[26] It was their job to issue ready money and banknotes in payment or exchange for notes from other institutions and the various warrants that were prepared by other clerks in the banking hall and surrounding offices.[27] For these purposes they were issued a sum of money daily for which they had to sign and for which they were held accountable.[28] The tellers also were obliged to exchange notes and bills for ready money, and they received sums from the out-tellers when they returned from their walks, from people paying money into their accounts and on account of the Court of Chancery.[29] Thus, the tellers interacted with fellow clerks across the Cashiers Department and with the majority of customers using the banking hall.

The Inspectors were also interested in both efficiency and security. Thus, they established that the tellers' role represented an important separation between the authorisation for payment and the payment itself. This type of separation of activities was typical of many of the Bank's processes and created checks and balances which, although not always successful, were intended to serve as a means of identifying errors and preventing embezzlement. This, however, did not relieve clerks of personal liability for errors. Of the twenty-one long-standing rules relating to transactions in the banking hall, five made specific mention of clerks' individual responsibility for avoiding errors.[30] There were also reminders that some responsibility for ensuring protection against customers with criminal

24. BEA, M5/212, fols. 4–5.
25. Ibid., fols. 30–37, 38–41.
26. BEA, M5/212, fol. 3.
27. Ibid., fol. 4.
28. Ibid., fol. 3.
29. Ibid.
30. BEA, G4/5, fols. 229–232.

intent fell to the tellers themselves. Thus, they were required to keep their own lists of lost and stolen banknotes and were obliged to update that list daily from the master copy that hung in the cash office.[31]

Given the nature of the Bank's business, however, not all risks could be eliminated. Clerks took shortcuts that increased risks. Thus, for the sake of convenience, the tellers sometimes failed to store their cash in the lockers provided. Mr Campe noted that he had 'upon occasion seen a bag of money on the ground with the clerk holding his foot on it & has always taken notice of it as improper & ordered him to lock it up'.[32] Errors were easily made, especially in an environment where people were in a hurry and money came in many forms. Mr Clifford of the Drawing Office noted that when clerks were in a rush, cash paid in might be entered under an incorrect name, 'or that a mistake may be made in an entry in the Clearer's Books: if either of these can happen, the error goes through all the Books, & cannot be detected untill the Person who paid in the money shall send his Book to be settled'.[33] The Inspectors sought to put an additional check in place to eliminate such errors.[34]

Although each clerk who gave testimony spoke of their own experiences or the work of their office, their narratives reveal multiple interconnections between offices and tasks. The work of the Warrant Office is a good example. The Office was charged with keeping records of the warrants issued to authorise the payment of dividends on government and Bank stocks.[35] In order to know which warrants had been paid, the clerks were obliged to make daily collections from three sources: the Clearers, who would have processed warrants received by the out-tellers; the in-tellers in the Pay Office; and those in the Drawing Office.[36] The accounts of warrants paid were abstracted in order that the totals could be recorded by the cashiers as part of the General Balance. In addition, daily, monthly and annual abstracts of the sums paid on each government stock were presented to the chief cashier for the purpose of managing the Bank's account with the government.[37] Finally, the paid warrants had to be cancelled, 'punched, entered, & filed' and then stored until the following day, when a clerk from the Cheque Office in the Accountants Department took

31. Ibid.
32. BEA, M5/212, fol. 31.
33. Ibid., fol. 84.
34. Ibid., fols. 84–85.
35. Ibid., fol. 123.
36. Ibid.
37. Ibid., fols. 124–125.

them away to commence the process of entering the amounts in the individual accounts.[38]

The impression given from such descriptions is that the Bank was a busy space full of movement and interactions between individuals. Many interactions would have been regular and would have served to build relationships between clerks in different offices and between clerks and the public. Clerks were not just busy; they worked under pressure. The volume of work was emphasised in a number of interviews. It was asserted, for example, that the issue of 4 per cent annuities during the War of American Independence resulted in the need to open 19,500 new accounts in one day.[39] More than 65,000 dividend warrants were issued for payment on 5 January 1783 and nearly 59,000 in April 1783.[40] The clerks who kept the K cash book, in which were recorded notes in long lists for the Exchequer, other public offices and some bankers, estimated that they made up around 20,000 notes a month.[41] Mr Isaac Pilleau estimated that 137,000 bills of exchange had been discounted in the course of 1782. In order to manage these volumes, each clerk, cashier and teller working in the banking hall and surrounding offices operated in a specialised capacity. The tasks allotted to them would often have been mundane and were usually repetitive, but they required accuracy, diligence and concentration. It was work generally done by hand. Until the advent of the typewriter and the automated bookkeeping machine in the late nineteenth and early twentieth centuries—and, indeed, arguably until the advent of the computer—much of the Bank's work could not be replaced or even significantly aided by technology.

The Cashiers at Work

Much of the cashiers' work had a direct and obvious relationship to the business of the state insofar as it related to the management of stocks or the issue and exchange of notes, but by the late eighteenth century the Bank was also forming links to the wider economy, albeit somewhat more reluctantly. These connections are particularly illustrated by the business of discounting promissory notes and bills of exchange. These instruments were, in simple terms, 'a written acknowledgement of the existence of a debt', an order embodying the promise by one individual to pay another,

38. Ibid., fol. 124.
39. BEA, M5/213, fols. 43–44.
40. BEA, M5/212, fol. 126.
41. Ibid., fols. 91, 99.

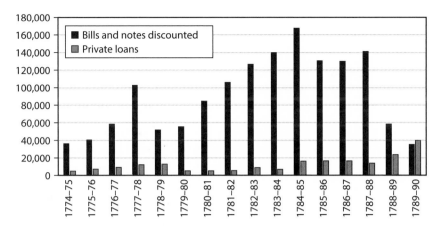

FIGURE 2.1. The bank's income from discounts and private loans.
Source: Clapham, *Bank of England*, 1:302.
Note: The year is calculated from 31 August to 31 August.

usually at a fixed time in the future.[42] Bills of exchange, in particular, were a flexible and secure form of payment and, for these reasons, had become one of the dominant means of both inland and international commercial exchange by the late eighteenth century. Some bills were payable on demand, but those that gave a promise to pay at a future time could be 'discounted' with an appropriate intermediary. This meant that a third party—in our case, the Bank—would lend money at a discounted rate against the bill. When the bill fell due, it would be redeemed by paying the full amount. The Bank's profit came from the difference between the discounted rate lent and the face value of the bill repaid. As shown in figure 2.1, it was a lucrative business and would have been a common reason for visiting the Bank.[43]

The Bank also made loans through the discount process.[44] Thus, those borrowing from the Bank would sign a bill of exchange, usually for three months, and receive a loan in notes. As with ordinary bills, they received a discounted amount and promised to repay in full when the bill was due.[45] This business was regular but not significant to the Bank over the course

42. W.T.C. King, *A History of the Discount Market*, with an Introduction by T. E. Gregory (Abingdon, UK, 2016), p. xv.

43. Eric Kerridge, *Trade and Banking in Early Modern England* (Manchester, UK, 1988).

44. Clapham, *Bank of England*, 1:122–123; Ranald C. Michie, *British Banking: Continuity and Change from 1694 to the Present* (Oxford, 2016), pp. 35–38.

45. Michie, *British Banking*, p. 35.

of the later eighteenth century. The institution's principal lending activities were always with the state rather than with the private market.[46]

The Bank was the country's dominant discounter from the later eighteenth century, and so there was a growing expectation that, through this business, the Bank would play a role in the regulation of the British economy. In particular, although it did not always choose to use it, the provision of credit on a large scale to the London business community gave the Bank the power to smooth financial crises through either the extension or withdrawal of credit at key points. It was a power that the state did not have at this time. It also arguably gave the Bank the power to act as a lender of last resort: an institution that could, and was willing to, lend to another financial entity for which no other avenues of credit might be open. There is some scholarly debate about the point at which the Bank started to act in this way.[47] Michael Lovell has argued that the Bank was behaving as a lender of last resort from as early as the 1760s. He found behaviour consistent with this function in response to the financial crisis of 1763 caused by the collapse of the De Neufville banking house in Amsterdam.[48] Equally, as Kosmetatos has shown, the more widely examined banking crisis of 1772 demonstrates similar behaviour on the part of the Bank. He also notes that this was not an isolated occurrence and that other peaks in the Bank's discounting activity corresponded with periods of financial and political crisis.[49] This suggests that the Bank's directors were willing to accept a role in the stabilisation of the economy, although offering no guarantee that they would act in this way in any given situation. Moreover, there is no doubt that the Bank's directors did not feel obliged to extend credit to all. As Clapham notes, there was a 'reluctance to do business with particular firms for precise reasons'.[50] Although it is not clear which firms or individuals might be excluded under these terms,

46. Clapham, *Bank of England*, 1:114.

47. For a detailed discussion of the development of the lender of last resort, see Forrest H. Capie and Geoffrey E. Wood, *The Lender of Last Resort* (London, 2007).

48. Mike Lovell, 'The Role of the Bank of England as Lender of Last Resort in the Crises of the Eighteenth Century', *Explorations in Entrepreneurial History*, 10 (1957), pp. 8–21. See also Isabel Schnabel and Hyon Song Shin, 'Liquidity and Contagion: The Crisis of 1763', *Journal of the European Economic Association*, 2 (2004), pp. 929–968; John A. James, 'Panics, Payments, Disruptions and the Bank of England before 1826', *Financial History Review*, 19 (2012), pp. 289–309.

49. Paul Kosmetatos, 'Last Resort Lending before Henry Thornton? The Bank of England's Role in Containing the 1763 and 1772–3 British Credit Crises', *European Review of Economic History*, 23 (2019), p. 302.

50. Clapham, 'Private Business', p. 82.

Kynaston asserts that anti-Semitism was part of the Bank's culture 'for its first two and a half centuries, and arguably even a little longer'.[51]

Bills of exchange came into the Bank from a variety of sources, including from individuals wanting to discount single or several bills and nascent bill brokers.[52] The Minutes of the Inspection particularly noted the country receivers, agents who corresponded with country bankers, and bills brought in from the Custom House.[53] The Bank's Discount Office was the first port of call for those wanting to discount. They were required to present the bills along with a written list of what they were presenting, and the receiving clerk's first task was to check the bills against the list. Once this was done, a decision had to be made about whether to discount the bills. This task did not lie with the clerks. They had to seek approval to proceed from the Committee in Waiting, a committee of directors, organised on a rota basis, to attend the Bank in order to superintend the day-to-day business.[54]

The basis for decision-making by the Committee was not recorded by the Inspectors since they were not concerned with the work of their fellow directors. Nonetheless, some assumptions can be made about the ways in which decision-making was facilitated. Personal relationships and knowledge remained an important part of the decision to discount. The Bank's policy was that discounters had to be resident in London and had to have the recommendation of a director.[55] Discounters also were obliged to hold an account at the Bank, and some customers would have been given a limit against which they could draw or discount.[56] There would have been an expectation that notes or bills were delivered in person or by 'known servants', again indicating a continuing reliance on personal connections.[57]

Yet, in a business grown large and encompassing a great number of individuals, understanding the current position of any one customer and taking any appropriate decision also had to be based on an analysis of current capacity to pay and previous credit history. The Bank's records were used to facilitate this analysis. Notably, drawing accounts were maintained in ways that allowed credit checking. As with a modern current account,

51. Kynaston, *Time's Last Sand*, p. 44.
52. King, *Discount Market*, pp. 5–8.
53. Joslin, 'London Private Bankers', p. 183.
54. Clapham, *Bank of England*, 1:109.
55. Ibid.,1:203.
56. Ibid., 1:122.
57. Ibid., 1:124.

customers could make deposits and hold money in the account, draw from it and, in some instances, were allowed to over-draw. A balance for each account was drawn up after every fourth transaction so that it was possible to see clearly how the account stood.[58] Drawing accounts also encompassed bills and notes discounted and the 'amount of bills in the Clearer's Cash book'—in other words, the bills that fell due that day and were, at the time, out with the out-tellers.[59] The account, therefore, offered an up-to-date statement of capacity to pay. Equally, it presented details regarding previous credit history. The records did not just facilitate a check on transactions that had proceeded. A 'black book' was kept in which details of rejected bills were recorded.[60]

The process for discounting promissory notes was similar except that they were brought in only once a week and had to pass through a two-stage approval process: they were examined by the Committee in Waiting on a Wednesday and by the Court of Directors the following day. Preparation for the presentation of promissory notes to the Court of Directors was undertaken by one of the senior men in the Discount Office. He was obliged to compile lists of those approved by the Committee in Waiting and those left 'dubious' and to check the lists against the Note Ledgers to ascertain the amount of notes running with, and upon, each individual. The lists were then sent to the Accountants Office so that the same process could be carried out with regard to bills against each individual. A further list was made of what notes would fall due in the next week for each customer.[61] The sheets were preserved as a record after the decisions of the Court were made known in a process that served the same purpose as recording rejected bills in the 'black book'.[62] The unknown in this process, however, is the nature of the information used by the Committee in Waiting at the first stage of decision-making. The approval of some discounts prior to the process of checking accounts would suggest that personal knowledge of some borrowers, gained perhaps through regular transactions and a history of prompt repayment, might suffice.

Once the decision to discount had been made, the process commenced of maintaining the complex records which served to both register the customer's liabilities and create the timeline for future steps in the transaction. The processes here are illustrative of those in other areas and again

58. BEA, M5/212, fol. 77.
59. Ibid., fol. 78.
60. Ibid., fol. 49.
61. Ibid., fol. 53.
62. Ibid., fol. 54.

show interaction between the different offices in the Bank. Thus, accepted bills were given to an entering clerk to make out a warrant for payment. The entering clerk was obliged to record 'the particulars of each bill and when it falls due; at which time he always computes it both as to sum and time and sees it is properly stamped'.[63] The warrant was then passed on to another clerk who computed the amount of the discount and wrote it on the warrant. In the meantime, one of the two senior men in the office took the bills and entered details of them in the 'waste book', gave each bill a number and did a separate calculation of the discount. The entering clerk then 'calls out to the person who has the warrant to check with him the amount of the discount & if they agree he signs the warrant'.[64] The warrant then went to the Drawing Office, where the amount was entered on the customer's account, thus entitling that customer to draw the money if that was their wish.[65]

The nature of the business had led to some efficiencies. For example, the waste book for recording bills was divided into two so that both of the senior clerks could work on it at the same time. Many processes, although necessary for the purpose of managing and accounting for the discounted bill, were, however, simply time-consuming and laborious. Thus, once the bills were recorded in the waste book, they were passed to three entering clerks for the completion of separate records, which would facilitate checking and ordering the bills in relation to their maturity.[66] Once processed in these ways, the bills were counted once again and then delivered to a clerk from yet another office, the Bill Office. At the Bill Office the bills were filed in drawers specially designed for the purpose of storing them in order by the date which they fell due.[67] This was apparently an efficient system since relatively few people came to repay early. Mr Holland, a senior clerk with seventeen years' experience in the Bill Office, estimated that it might happen two or three times a week.[68] When the bills fell due, they were generally managed by the out-tellers in processes described in the previous chapter.

The cycle of work undertaken by the clerks in the Discount Office demonstrates elements of complex decision-making in the eighteenth-century credit system. It shows that the Bank had a clear reliance on recorded data

63. Ibid., fol. 50.
64. Ibid.
65. Ibid.
66. Ibid., fols. 51–52.
67. Ibid., fol. 47.
68. Ibid.

relating to capacity to pay and previous repayment history. This confirms Muldrew's assumptions about the decision-making processes of businesses dealing with large numbers of 'relative strangers'.[69] He has argued that, for these enterprises, 'rationally determined future profitability and the accumulated physical or monetary capital of an enterprise' became as important as the determination of the character of the borrower.[70] Yet, although the Bank was operating on a larger scale than other lenders, there is no evidence that it was distinctive in its decision-making processes. Both Alexandra Shepard and Tawny Paul have shown that private lenders likewise often had an understanding of the physical wealth and existing obligations of individuals to whom they extended credit.[71] Further, while the Bank relied on records relating to personal wealth, this did not mean it eschewed the social determinants of creditworthiness of good character, appearance and reputation.[72] We have seen that there were shortcuts in the processes, which indicates the continuing importance of personal connections in the Bank's business. Institutions like the Bank of England, therefore, did not entirely depersonalise the late eighteenth-century credit market. Nor did the bringing together of record-keeping and quantitative analyses of assets and behaviour represent a decisive break with actions of an earlier period.

The Customer Experience

The customers using the Bank's services found its doors open six days a week, Monday to Saturday, chiefly between the hours of 9:00 A.M. and 5:00 P.M., although some offices closed in the mid-afternoon. The public clearly had an expectation of service from the Bank that went beyond what might have been common to other businesses. The institution observed around fifty public holidays a year by the later eighteenth century, and on those days it maintained a skeleton staff in the banking hall and the

69. Craig Muldrew, 'Interpreting the Market: The Ethics of Credit and Community Relations in Early Modern England', *Social History*, 18 (1993), pp. 163–183.

70. Ibid.

71. Alexandra Shepard, *Accounting for Oneself: Worth, Status and Social Order in Early Modern England* (Oxford, 2015); Tawny Paul, 'Credit and Social Relations amongst Artisans and Tradesmen in Edinburgh and Philadelphia, c. 1710–1770' (unpublished PhD thesis, University of Edinburgh, 2011), pp. 74–75.

72. Craig Muldrew, *The Economy of Obligation: The Culture of Credit and Social Relations in Early Modern England* (Basingstoke, UK, 1998); Margot Finn, *The Character of Credit: Personal Debt in English Culture, 1740–1914* (Cambridge, 2008).

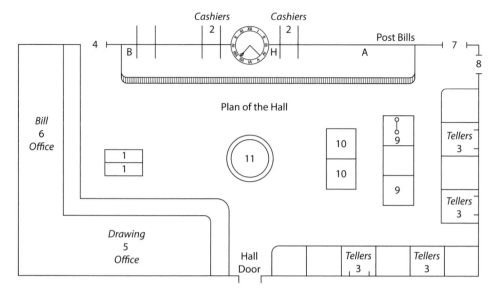

FIGURE 2.2. Plan of the Hall.
Source: Modified from Gentleman of the Bank, *The Bank of England's Vade Mecum*, unpaginated, BEA, M5/616. © Bank of England.
Key to the plan: 1. Writing desk for customers; 2. Cashiers; 3. Tellers; 4. Passage to Accountants Office and other offices; 5. Drawing Office; 6. Bill Office; 7. Passage to the Bullion Office; 8. Entrance to the Treasury; 9. Scales for weighing money; 10. Tables for counting and examining money; 11. Fireplace; A. Clerks who issue banknotes; B and H. Clerks who exchange large notes for small.

offices most concerned with serving the public.[73] Three more or less contemporary images can help us understand what the Bank's customers experienced when they visited the Cashiers Department: a plan of the hall as produced in the *Vade Mecum* (1782), a plan of the adjoining offices in the same publication and Thomas Rowlandson's *Great Hall of the Bank of England* (1808). As can be seen in these images, in the hall the public would have seen desks for the cashiers and the in-tellers. These individuals could be identified by signs high on the wall over their desks. Also in the hall were desks for the convenience of customers needing to write out their names and addresses on notes and to weigh, count and examine ready money (marked 1, 9 and 10 in figure 2.2). The top part of the scale is visible in figure 2.3. In the middle of the room was a large and ornate fireplace, which can also be seen in figure 2.3. Around the hall were points of access to the Bill Office and the Drawing Office, the former at point 6 on the plan

73. BEA, ADM30/12, General staff lists.

FIGURE 2.3. Thomas Rowlandson, *The Great Hall, Bank of England* (1808). *Source:* Metropolitan Museum of Art, The Elisha Whittelsey Collection, The Elisha Whittelsey Fund, 1959, CCO.

shown in figure 2.2 and the latter at point 5. At point 7 on figure 2.2 was the door to the Bullion Office, and in figure 2.3 a porter with a barrow can be seen heading in that direction.

If a customer exited the hall through the door marked 4 on figure 2.2, they would find themselves in a passage leading down to a number of other offices where regular customers may have had business. Figure 2.4 shows the entrances to the Accountant's Office (A), the Discount Office (K), the Chancery Office (I) and the Office of the Cashiers, which dealt with the instruments of the national debt (B). In this space were also access points to the Directors Room (C, D and G) and to the Coffee Room (E). There are no preserved sources on the Coffee Room, but it is likely to have been open to both staff and customers and was probably a space in which business was regularly done. At point L was a staircase to the Bank Note and Exchequer Offices and to the Secretary's Office, and at point M was the private entrance to the Accountant General's Office.

Plan of the Passage

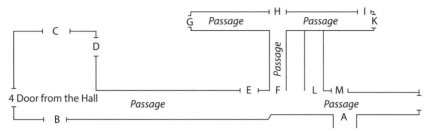

FIGURE 2.4. Plan of the Passage.
Source: Modified from Gentleman of the Bank, *The Bank of England's Vade Mecum*, unpaginated, BEA, M5/616. © Bank of England.
Key to the plan: A. Accountant's Office; B. Cashiers Office; C. Directors Room; D. Another door to the Directors Room; E. Coffee Room; F. Passage to the Back Passage; G. Private door to the Directors Room; H. A sham door; I. Chancery Office; K. Discount Office; L. Stairs to the Bank Note, Exchequer and Secretary's Offices; M. Private door to the Accountant General's Office.

The banking hall and surrounding offices were choreographed spaces, each desk catered to a particular type of business. But although counters were neatly divided and labelled, and way-finding was facilitated through signage over desks and doorways, the uninitiated may have struggled on their first visit to understand how to transact their business. They perhaps would have followed the example of other customers in the hope that the mysteries of the Bank would be revealed. They also could have asked one of the porters or clerks for assistance, but this might have entailed delay and inconvenience and the cost of a tip in recompense for the information. Others might have prepared for their visit by picking up a copy of *The Bank of England's Vade Mecum*, a guide produced in 1782 and intended to inform the public 'how to transact that Business with Ease, Safety, and Dispatch, and also to prevent the numerous Inconveniences which so daily happen'.[74] In addition to the plans in the *Vade Mecum*, the author provided instruction on how to find desks and offered ways of navigating the space, aside from signage. Readers were advised to use the 'great Window', the statue of William III or the clock to orient themselves.[75] Precise instructions were also offered on how to conduct business. Thus, those who wanted to exchange a note for ready money, for example, were told to ensure that they first wrote their name and address 'between the two

74. Gentleman of the Bank, *Vade Mecum*, p. 3.
75. Ibid., pp. 9–10.

dotted Lines at the Top, in the Front of your Note'.[76] The notes could then be presented to the cashiers 'through the little rails', an action clearly visible to the left of figure 2.3. The cashier signed the note as being approved for payment and the customer was then obliged to take it to the in-tellers, at the desk under the statue of William III, to collect the payment.[77]

There is a rich literature relating to eighteenth-century public spaces which emphasises the user's sensory and haptic experiences.[78] Financial historians have been less concerned with such matters, and I do not intend to argue that a financial transaction encompassed the same pleasures as shopping or a visit to the pleasure gardens. Nonetheless, a visit to the Bank was a sensory experience. It was noted above that the Bank was a grand space and visually impressive. It would have been noisy at times. Visitors might have been aware of a variety of languages being spoken. Commercial environments were noted for the diversity of their participants.[79] At busy times, and especially in the morning, there would have been many people in the hall and other offices. The mix of individuals would have produced a mix of smells. James Adair, writing in 1790, stated that in crowded public rooms an 'offensive impression' emanated from 'the blended effluvia from the fires, lights, and perfumes'.[80] There would have been a mingling of odours from customers, clerks and porters, and Tobias Smollett's description of the Bath assembly rooms might give us some idea of the mix of smells from perfumed bodies to 'putrid gums, imposthumated lungs, sour flatulencies, rank armpits, sweating feet, running sores and issues'.[81]

76. Ibid., p. 9.

77. Ibid.

78. See, for example, Helen Berry, 'Polite Consumption: Shopping in Eighteenth-Century England', *Transactions of the Royal Historical Society*, 12 (2002), pp. 375–394; Peter Borsay, 'Pleasure Gardens and Urban Culture in the Long-Eighteenth Century', in Jonathan Conlin, ed., *The Pleasure Garden, from Vauxhall to Coney Island* (Philadelphia, 2006), pp. 49–77; Hannah Grieg, '"All Together and All Distinct": Public Sociability and Social Exclusivity in London's Pleasure Gardens, ca. 1740–1800', *Journal of British Studies*, 51 (2012), pp. 50–75; Kate Smith, 'Sensing Design and Workmanship: The Haptic Skills of Shoppers in Eighteenth-Century London', *Journal of Design History*, 25 (2012), pp. 1–10; William Tullett, 'The Macaroni's "Ambrosial Essences": Perfume, Identity and Public Space in Eighteenth-Century England', *Journal for Eighteenth-Century Studies*, 38 (2015), pp. 163–180; Claire Walsh, 'Shop Design and the Display of Goods in Eighteenth-Century London', *Journal of Design History*, 8 (1995), pp. 157–176.

79. John Gallagher, *Learning Languages in Early Modern England* (Oxford, 2019), p. 3.

80. James Makittrick Adair, *Essays on Fashionable Diseases* (1790), quoted in William Tullet, *Smell in Eighteenth-Century England: A Social Sense* (Oxford, 2019), p. 187.

81. Tobias Smollett, *The Expedition of Humphrey Clinker* (1771), quoted in Tullet, *Smell*, p. 188.

The crowd and thus the need to wait to be served may have produced feelings of impatience. At several points in the Minutes the need to serve the public more quickly was noted. Thus, with regard to the production of banknotes, the Inspectors recorded that 'at present many persons refuse to wait at the Bank the time necessary to have their Notes changed & made out afresh, & go away to Bankers to have their business done with less delay'.[82] The crowd that gathered at the Bank might also have provoked anxiety. Thieves naturally found the Bank and its environs a good place to ply their trade, creating a risk to both customers and clerks and requiring active, and sometimes rather inventive, intervention by the Bank.

In 1765, for example, John Hazard, a clerk at the Bank, brought a prosecution for pickpocketing against Richard Bond, alias Clark, and John Smith. Hazard had apparently observed Clark loitering around the Bank yard and in Bow-China Passage for several weeks. Knowing him to have no business with the Bank, and as 'numbers of people had lost things' in the area, Hazard suspected Clark of being a pickpocket.[83] Hazard, therefore, set out to entrap Clark. As he informed the Court,

> I went out, and pulled my pocket-case out in the yard, as he might see it, and put it in again: I went out, and he followed me into Castle-alley; there was nobody with him then: I stopped at the lottery-office-window, in Castle-alley, and he came and stood by me, on that side the book was: then I came through the alley into Cornhill, and stood at Mr. Kentish's toy shop; he came and stood there by me; then I turned into Pope's-head-alley, and stood at Mr. Shepherd's toy-shop; he followed me there likewise: then I passed him a little way, and stood to make water; then I went on, into Lombard-street, into the shop of Messrs. Breffey Ive, and Co. bankers; he followed me to their door, and staid there, and took notice of what I was doing in the shop.[84]

This attempt ultimately failed, partly, it would seem, because the pocket-book selected by Hazard was too full to slip easily out of his pocket. A further attempt, with a slightly less well-stocked pocket-book, met with greater success. This time Clark was joined by an accomplice (Smith), who helped to distract Hazard while his property was being removed from his pocket. Both men were easily apprehended as Hazard was being watched

82. BEA, M5/212, fol. 117.

83. *Old Bailey Proceedings Online* (www.oldbaileyonline.org, version 8.0, 9 January 2022), September 1764, trial of Richard Bond, otherwise Clark John Smith (t17640912–33).

84. Ibid.

by another of the Bank's clerks.[85] Like the clerks, many customers also would have been aware of the danger from thieves. They might have been wary of strangers and would have weighed up each encounter in the banking hall, vigilant against distractions and close bodily contact and keeping their hands firmly on their pocket-books or purses.

Business in the banking hall was a haptic experience in less threatening ways too. In particular, ready money and notes needed to be examined to ascertain their value and integrity. Prominent in the banking hall were tables and scales to facilitate the weighing of coin and examination of the detail of notes. These actions combined the visual and the material, with users seeking to ascertain not only how a full-weight coin or genuine note looked but also how it felt.[86] Such examinations were second-nature to many of the Bank's customers. Because of the nature of the coinage, which was made of precious metal and, thus, vulnerable to wear, clipping and counterfeiting, vigilance was necessary. A compromised coin could not be passed easily on to someone else, and thus its acceptor would incur a loss. Banknotes were similarly vulnerable to counterfeiters. Moreover, the use of touch and close examination with regard to notes and specie was common to customers and clerks. Clerks who failed to be vigilant risked much. Thus, the diary of Governor Samuel Beachcroft records that he 'reprimanded Mr Fidoe before Mr Jewson, Mr Newland & Mr Greenway for taking in guineas under 5:6 & allso hammered guineas'.[87] At the same time three other clerks were reprimanded for taking clipped and light coin. They were told that, in the future, 'they must make it good to the Bank & if found guilty they must be discharged the service'.[88]

Although sometimes hurried, noisy and anxiety-inducing, doing business in the banking hall and its surrounding offices was, arguably, a polite experience, for some at least. It was noted above that the directors created an aesthetic appropriate for polite commercial exchange and an affluent and influential clientele. We should also think of the Bank of England as a regulated space, one in which many types of people might mix, but one from which those who obviously had no business there were supposed to be excluded, assuming, of course, the vigilance of the Bank's gate-keeper and porters. Paul Langford has argued for the 'polishing effect' that such spaces had on the manners of the middling sorts and, in particular, has shown that the 'professions that serviced propertied society were naturally

85. Ibid.
86. Mockford, 'Exactly as Banknotes Are', chapter 2.
87. BEA, M5/451, fol. 58.
88. Ibid.

influenced by changing fashions and values' and adopted polite behaviour to make themselves amenable and to smooth the distinctions between persons of different ranks.[89]

The Inspectors paid attention to such matters and had a clear expectation of service to the public. Judgements were made about the ways in which clerks interacted with each other and with customers. Thus, Mr Campe was regarded as 'a good hand [and] intelligent' and his counterpart Mr Smith equally competent, although 'not over fond of being under Campe'.[90] Not all clerks lived up to expectations. Mr Bridges, the supervisor in the Dividend Office, was described as 'a chattering fellow' and 'not fit to be placed in any more conspicuous light'.[91] Mr Gardner was apparently 'a poor hand, obstinate and prejudiced to the old mode', as well he may have been after serving thirty-nine years in the Bank.[92] Change was also imposed in order to ease customers' interactions with the Bank. For example, the Inspectors noted the need for an additional gate porter to accommodate 'the Publick by any little services . . . the want of which has frequently been complained of'.[93] The clerks likewise frequently demonstrated an outward attention to the needs of the public in their interviews with the Inspectors. Changes that might result in greater expedition and convenience for customers were frequently suggested and sometimes approved.

If the Bank as a polite space shaped the behaviour of some of the clerks, it was also likely to have shaped the behaviour of customers. Referring to shopping, Helen Berry emphasises the 'unwritten social rules of encounter' which guided polite behaviour and necessitated awareness of deportment, gesture, language and polite exchange and 'a ritualised pattern of behaviour as the customer engaged with the shopkeeper'.[94] The *Vade Mecum*, with its careful delineation of space within the Bank and its attempt to impose order on the business of managing money, indicates that certain modes of behaviour were preferred. Likewise, the very existence of the *Vade Mecum* locates the Bank within the sphere of polite commerciality. It was certainly one of the 'very useful manuals' identified by

89. Paul Langford, 'The Use of Eighteenth-Century Politeness', *Transactions of the Royal Historical Society*, 12 (2002), pp. 318–321. See also Benjamin Heller, 'The "Mene Peuple" and the Polite Spectator: The Individual in the Crowd at Eighteenth-Century London Fairs', *Past and Present*, 208 (2010), pp. 131–157.

90. BEA, M5/471.

91. Ibid.

92. Ibid.

93. BEA, M5/212, fol. 201.

94. Berry, 'Polite Consumption', p. 377.

Lawrence Klein as 'offering people what they needed to pursue a given occupation or assume or reinforce a certain social personality'.[95] The *Vade Mecum* provided a means of navigating the space at the Bank, offered instruction in the correct manner and order in which to complete a transaction and provided a guide to the vocabulary that had to be employed in order for one's business to be understood. In doing so, the author not only instructed customers how to transact their business but also gave them the key to appearing comfortable in a complex and commercially important space.

Much was at stake for those who violated the expected codes of behaviour at the Bank. Governor Samuel Beachcroft's capacity for censure did not stop at the Bank's own clerks, and in his diary was noted a reprimand of Mr Smith, partner in the company of Smith, Wright & Gray, for 'sending bad silver, & giving other hindrances to our clarks'. Smith apparently 'promised in future to alter their method & behave better'.[96] The governor's ability to sanction other City businesses would have operated at two levels. The first would have been to potentially deny them access to important support and clearing facilities, and the second would have been to undermine their reputation. We have seen that, despite the use of the Bank's records in credit checks, personal knowledge and observation of character and behaviour remained a key determinant of creditworthiness. Moreover, in the close-knit financial and business environments of the City, reputation lost in one arena would have compromised the ability to act in another. These potential threats would have operated as a powerful reinforcement of polite behaviour.

Nonetheless, the notion that the behaviour of clerks and customers within the Bank was rooted entirely in accepted modes of politeness can be challenged. The orderly social mingling characteristic of polite spaces could be compromised in crowded and hurried environments.[97] Further, the exchange between clerk and customer was clearly determined by considerations other than what Helen Berry has described as a 'polite regard for the person'.[98] Obtaining excellent service in the banking hall and, as we shall see, other areas of the Bank remained dependent on a system of

95. Lawrence E. Klein, 'Politeness for Plebes: Consumption and Social Identity in Early Eighteenth-Century England', in Ann Bermingham and John Brewer, eds., *The Consumption of Culture, 1600–1800: Image, Object, Text* (London, 1995), p. 367.

96. BEA, M5/451, fol. 5.

97. For discussion of how distinction was managed in social spaces, see, for example, Grieg, '"All Together and All Distinct"'; Heller, '"Mene Peuple" and the Polite Spectator'.

98. Berry, 'Polite Consumption', p. 394.

gifting and gratuities. Thus, as in other eighteenth-century contexts, the taint of corruption challenged the ideals of politeness.[99] This was a particular problem in the public-facing roles played by clerks in the banking hall and its adjacent offices.

Mr Rogers, head of the Discount Office, told the Committee that although nothing was ever asked for, customers made gifts at Christmas in the amount of '3 or £400 in one year, in other years it has not exceeded £200'. Mr Rogers received all monies and distributed it at his discretion according to the time of service of the clerks working in the office.[100] Mr Clifford of the Drawing Office told a similar story of presents being given and the senior clerks overseeing division of the funds by seniority of the clerks, as did Mr Etheridge of the Bullion Office.[101] Corporate customers also gave presents to the Bank's clerks. Thus, the Bank of Scotland sent £60 per year, which, after the chief cashier took 20 guineas, was distributed to the clerks in the Drawing Office, the Bill Office and the Chief Cashier's office.[102] Mr Collins of the G cash book stated that Mr Steers, the Chancery broker, gave a guinea to each of the three clerks who worked the book.[103]

Mr Rogers's assertion that 'nothing was ever asked for' is an interesting one, and the Committee of Inspection's consistent and detailed concern with the type and amount of presents given to clerks by customers suggests that the Inspectors were sceptical about the nature of the transactions. Such concerns were heightened by the fear that favourable treatment was offered to customers who were known to make presents to the clerks. One particular incident, reported to the Committee of Inspection, concerned a draft of £5,500 that had been refused because it would have left the account over-drawn to the sum of £38.[104] It seems it was typical under such circumstances to allow payment, and on this occasion it was deemed that, at best, the refusal to grant the overdraft was an error. Yet, the Committee of Inspection carefully questioned clerks as to whether the customer in question gave any Christmas boxes at the Bank. No direct accusations appear to have been made when they discovered that he did not, but it is clear that there was at least a suspicion that the customer had been poorly treated because of his lack of generosity to the clerks.[105]

99. Jenny Davidson, *Hypocrisy and the Politics of Politeness: Manners and Morals from Locke to Austen* (Cambridge, 2004), p. 2.

100. BEA, M5/212, fols. 59–60.

101. Ibid., fols. 85, 132.

102. Ibid., fol. 147.

103. Ibid., fol. 108.

104. Ibid., fol. 216.

105. Ibid., fols. 216–217.

The Inspectors do not appear to have pursued this case further, but throughout their investigations they remained interested in the ways that systems of gifting influenced the behaviour of the clerks. Despite assertions about the integrity of the Bank, however, their responses to these issues were not always shaped by concerns to prevent, or to be seen to be preventing, corruption. Indeed, they found gifting practices so embedded in the business of the Bank that they were torn between 'abolishing the practice altogether [or regulating it] by excluding the Chiefs from any participation, & ordering equal distributions amongst the inferior Clerks'.[106] This may seem odd given the remit of the Committee and its connections to economical reform. Nonetheless, the approach taken acknowledged that such gifting practices were an accepted part of eighteenth-century commerce and thus a point of 'genuine moral ambiguity' about the nature and meaning of their use.[107] It also marked an acceptance that gratuities provided a necessary uplift in the remuneration of clerks who, especially early in their careers, were not well paid. Undoubtedly, controlled acceptance of gifts and gratuities was preferable to men falling into the temptation to top up their salaries through embezzlement.

Identifying Risks and Enacting Change

The Inspectors had cause to be concerned about the possibility of embezzlement. In the year before the Inspection, the crimes of the Bank clerk Charles Clutterbuck were revealed, clearly indicating the vulnerabilities of the Cashiers Department. Clutterbuck had developed a gambling habit and lost a considerable amount of money at the EO tables.[108] In order to fund his habit, he had, over a period of time, used his position as a clerk on one of the Bank's cash books to counterfeit notes to the value of £5,930. He had been able to cash some of the notes and had passed on others.[109] It was a prominent case, reported in many of the newspapers, and highlighted because, at the time, London was in the grip of a

106. BEA, M5/213, fols. 158–159.

107. Mark Knights, 'Anticorruption in Seventeenth- and Eighteenth-Century Britain', in Ronald Kroeze, André Vitória and G. Geltner, eds., *Anticorruption in History: From Antiquity to the Modern Era* (Oxford, 2018), p. 189.

108. EO (Even, Odd) was an early form of roulette. Players could bet against the owner of the table and against each other. Donna T. Andrew, "'How Frail Are *Lovers Vows*, and *Dicers Oaths*": Gaming, Governing and Moral Panic in Britain, 1781–1782', in David Lemmings and Claire Walker, eds., *Moral Panics, the Media and the Law in Early Modern England* (London, 2009), p. 177.

109. Acres, *Bank of England from Within*, 1:234.

moral panic about gambling, especially at EO.[110] Clutterbuck absconded to France when his crimes were discovered. His freedom was, however, short-lived. While the French authorities refused to extradite him, they were willing to prosecute, and in September 1785 he was sentenced to life in the king of France's galleys.[111]

Dealing with notes took up the majority of the *Vade Mecum*, indicating that it was this business that brought in customers most in need of guidance. The author described not only the process for exchanging notes for ready money but also how to obtain new notes, how to break a large denomination note into smaller notes, how to make an exchange which combined notes and ready money, and how to stop payments.[112] The author further dealt with processes for managing Bank post bills, which were promissory notes payable at seven days' sight, and cashing drafts.[113] Bank of England notes were by no means ubiquitous at the time of the Inspection since the institution only issued notes in denominations of £10 and over until 1797. Nonetheless, they would have been encountered regularly by the middling sorts and those of higher socio-economic status.

Moreover, Bank of England notes had a 'unique stature' in the monetary landscape because of the relationship between the Bank and the state enshrined by the 1708 Bank of England Act.[114] The Act primarily restricted joint stock companies of more than six people from issuing 'notes that would represent immediate value, or compet[ing] with the currency constituted by the Bank's issue'.[115] This ensured the dominance of the Bank's notes, and their integrity was further underpinned by several factors. Firstly, the 1708 Act imposed a limit on the number of notes that could be issued. Although this was regularly breached by the Bank, it remained constrained by the personal liability of its shareholders and by its guarantee to cash all notes issued.[116] Secondly, an Act of Parliament in 1696 made the counterfeiting of any Bank of England note a felony and thus punishable by death. As Carl Wennerlind asserts, this linked Bank and state in the deterrence against the undermining of the Bank's notes.[117]

110. Andrew, "'How Frail Are *Lovers Vows*'", p. 186.
111. Acres, *Bank of England from Within*, 1:234.
112. Gentleman of the Bank, *Vade Mecum*, pp. 11–14, 19.
113. Ibid., pp. 14–18.
114. Desan, *Making Money*, pp. 311, 316; 7 Ann c30.
115. Desan, *Making Money*, p. 316.
116. Ibid.
117. Wennerlind, *Casualties of Credit*, p. 147. See also Randall McGowen, 'The Bank of England and the Policing of Forgery, 1797–1821', *Past and Present*, 186 (2005), pp. 81–116.

Lastly, and perhaps most importantly, the value of the Bank's notes was supported directly by the action of the state because it was willing not only to issue those notes in payment of its debts but also to accept the notes in taxes.[118]

Nonetheless, the value of Bank of England notes could not be taken for granted. The notes did not yet have the status of legal tender, and thus they were potentially vulnerable to any loss of public trust.[119] The Inspectors recognised this and acknowledged that note issuance was central to the 'two great & principal Objects [of their work]; the Security of the Bank; & the Accommodation of the Publick'.[120] Their investigation, however, revealed problems with 'the whole process concerning Bank Notes from their formation for currency to their final discharge'.[121] Moreover, they expressed their concern that crimes like those committed by Clutterbuck had the potential to 'still occur every day'.[122]

The Inspectors first decried the paper manufacture and printing processes, which took place entirely off-site. The paper was manufactured at Mr Portal's paper mill, near Whitchurch in Hampshire, and, as we have seen, the notes were printed by a Mr Cole in Kirby Street, near Hatton Garden. The latter, in particular, was, in the view of the Inspectors, a significant security risk. They noted the following:

> From the mode of conducting business described by [Mr Barber] we conclude that the Blank Notes must necessarily be exposed to considerable hazard but without his information we should certainly condemn the practice of suffering plates to be ever taken out of the Bank, if there were a possibility of printing off the Blank Notes within it. We need not particularise the danger that both the Paper & plates must be subject to, from the moment they leave the Bank to that of their return, & we apprehend that it will be perfectly easy to avoid all future risk by causing the Notes to be printed within the House.[123]

However, because of the constraints of space, it was not possible to act on these concerns. Ultimately, the Committee's recommendations were not taken up until 1791, when the Bank's architect John Soane was instructed

---

118. Desan, *Making Money*, pp. 312–318.
119. Bank of England notes became legal tender in 1833.
120. BEA, M5/212, fol. 164.
121. Ibid., fol. 157.
122. Ibid., fols. 159–160. The Committee's second report is reproduced in full in appendix 3.
123. BEA, M5/212, fol. 167.

to design an apartment for the purpose of bringing the engraving and printing of the notes within the Bank's premises.[124]

Further problems were identified with practices at the Bank.[125] At the time of the Inspection, notes were printed without an issue number, date, payee or cashier's signature. These details were completed by hand by one of the clerks at the Bank's six cash books, labelled A, B, C, H, K and O. Each book had a particular purpose. The clerks who managed book A made out and entered all notes related to money tickets issued by other offices in the Bank. The clerks handling the B book were charged with splitting large notes into smaller denominations. The C book clerks managed the work of the Drawing Office and thus were situated adjoining that office. The H book clerks supported their colleagues at the B book, especially during the busier times of the day. The A, B and H books were situated in the banking hall under the clock.[126] The O book was kept in the Chancery Office, and the clerk made out all notes drawn on that office. The K book was for the production of notes on a large scale, notably for 'Mr Newland for the Pay Office; to Mr Cowper for the Exchequer; & to the Public Offices; or Bankers wanting long Lists'.[127] The clerks at the K book were always extremely busy and were also short-staffed at the time of the Inspection, having only four clerks where there should have been six.[128]

An additional complication for the K book was that no cashier sat near the clerks, and so once the notes were made out, they had to be sent to the hall for signing. The notes were sometimes taken by one of the clerks, but this might also be done by the person to whom the notes belonged, thus creating a risk of alteration between issuance and signature.[129] A further risk in the process was that there were no checks by the cashiers who signed the notes. As Mr Boult described, 'Whenever any Notes are given or sent from a Cash book to a Cashier to be signed, he always signs them without any other voucher than the name of the entering Clerk who has countersigned them; & without any knowledge of the effects brought in; nor does he keep any account of them'.[130] Noting the length of time taken for this process, Mr Lander, one of the cashiers, said he could sign

---

124. That apartment was completed in 1794. Acres, *Bank of England from Within*, 1:253.

125. For an alternative discussion of these changes, see D. Batt, 'The 1783 Proposal for a Readymade Note at the Bank of England', *Financial History Review*, 29 (2022), pp. 72–97.

126. BEA, M5/212, fols. 90–91.

127. Ibid., fol. 91.

128. Ibid., fol. 99.

129. Ibid.

130. Ibid., fol. 110.

'100 Notes in 20 Minutes if not interrupted'.[131] At around twelve seconds per note, Lander's estimate confirms the process left little time for detailed inspection.

Lack of scrutiny opened up opportunities for fraud, which was exacerbated at certain times of the day. During the period when clerks would take their dinner—from one to three in the afternoon, for example—there was usually only one clerk at each of the books, thus removing such checks and balances as were in place. The situation was the same on the public holidays when the Bank remained open with a skeleton staff. Further, there appeared to be no effectual check on the clerks at the cash book until the following day, when the books were examined in the Accountant's Office.[132] The problem was compounded because the cash book clerks were generally junior to the cashiers, and it was, the Inspectors asserted, rather the case that the chief responsibility should lie with the senior men:

> For surely the Trust (& great indeed it is) was intended to be placed in the Cashiers, Men who from their Age, their length of service, & other circumstances that have probably raised them to such a station of confidence, may be supposed to deserve it: whereas in the present practice, the sole reliance is on the honesty & vigilance of the entering Clerks, each separately entrusted, not barely with a sum of money, but with the power of creating it to allmost any amount.[133]

The Inspectors were nonetheless keen to assert that they did not wish to 'impute negligence to the Cashiers', acknowledging that, as the work was currently organised, it was impossible for them to do otherwise than 'depend on the fidelity & exactness of the entering Clerks'.[134]

The Inspectors also identified risks in the storage of notes at the various stages of the issue cycle. Blank notes could be taken from the warehouse by clerks at will and without independent checks.[135] Following collection from the warehouse, notes sat on the cash book clerks' desks in either a box or a drawer, compartmentalised for the blank notes of different values. This was a 'circumstance of danger, as many Persons totally unconnected with the business of making out Bank Notes have frequent access to them by intruding where they have no right to come: an abuse often complained of by the Cashiers & Clerks who nevertheless

131. Ibid., fol. 117.
132. Ibid., fol. 159.
133. Ibid.
134. Ibid.
135. Ibid., fol. 40.

find it impossible to prevent it'.[136] Although the Inspectors were not specific, this might imply more prominent customers as well as other Bank
employees. Equally, the processes for withdrawing and returning bundles
of notes from the warehouse were not attended with sufficient checks.
The Inspectors found that, in this respect, procedures were such that 'it
would be difficult to ascertain whether [any shortfalls in the notes] arose
from the Negligence of the Cashier who signed the Notes; of him who
collected them to deposit in the Warehouse; or from a Fraud committed
afterwards'.[137] Additionally, given that the stores of notes were usually in
the range of £100,000–£300,000, the Inspectors felt this was too large a
sum 'ever to be entrusted to a single Person, unless obliged to account for
the balance in his hands every evening'.[138]

In order to mitigate the risk of another Clutterbuck, the Inspectors
devised a plan which they presented to the Committee of Treasury to issue
ready-made notes instead of relying on the completion of blank notes by
request. Ready-made notes were already being used in the Dividend Office
and at the Exchequer, so there was precedent for the change. The Inspectors proposed to create a constant store of notes made up in the names of
either of the two chief cashiers. This allowed them to remove many of the
cash book processes and reduce the risks of keeping blank notes and making out notes in the banking hall. The number of clerks dealing with delivering notes to customers could also be reduced to '3 of the Clerks of the
Bank, whose abilities, conduct, & discretion have been tried & approved . . .
with such additional Salaries as may be thought equal to the trust reposed
in them, & the close attendance required. And that 3 inferior Clerks be
appointed as their Assistants'.[139] The sum of notes to be kept was '500,000
Pounds Stg, a sum which from the information of the two Chief Cashiers
we think we are well founded in asserting need never be exceeded'.[140] The
Inspectors argued that the Committee of Treasury should not be concerned with the increase in the amount of notes kept in the store, because
this risk was to be mitigated by giving more attention to the types of men
who would have access to that store.[141]

The Inspectors gave equal attention to the processes by which the new
system of issuing banknotes would be managed. In particular, they argued

136. Ibid., fol. 161.
137. Ibid., fol. 163.
138. Ibid., fol. 164.
139. Ibid., fol. 170.
140. Ibid., fol. 165.
141. Ibid.

for the creation of a new office space to accommodate the pay clerks, one that would be 'properly inclosed with only one Entrance into it'.[142] To ensure greater security for the notes used in the banking hall, they proposed the manufacture of special drawers that would lock into place at the clerk's desk when in use but could be removed entirely to be stored in the warehouse each evening.[143] They also restricted access to the store of notes and introduced more effective checks and balances to ensure the accountability of those with access to the notes.[144]

Typically for the Inspectors, they had previously consulted extensively on the plan, showing a trust in the knowledge and experience of the men who served the Bank and performed the roles that were being reviewed. Indeed, they asserted in their report on the matter that they would not have presumed to suggest such a change if, 'notwithstanding the conviction of our own Judgement, our opinion had not been corroborated by those of Mr Newland, Mr Thompson, & most of the other Cashiers'.[145] They also noted an additional advantage of their scheme: 'that the Publick will be accommodated on demand without the delay they are now subject to, a consideration not to be overlooked as it may have a tendency to increase the Circulation of Bank Notes'.[146] It is interesting to note the Inspectors' concern with the circulation of banknotes, although it may be assumed that this related to the position of the Bank itself rather than a concern for the economy more generally.

The Inspectors' concerns about the production and issue of banknotes illustrate several of the main purposes of the Inspection: managing the potential for corruption and criminal activity, ensuring the integrity of processes that were under the public view and ensuring that the Bank's service to the public was without question. The Inspectors' resolution was one that put the security of the Bank and service to the public to the fore. Their approach to the problems of banknote issuance illustrates the diligence and perceptiveness with which they pursued their work, but it also raises the question of why procedures were not identified as risky and amended prior to the Inspection. This question is particularly pertinent given the risks that had been exposed the year before the Inspection by the Clutterbuck case. The answer is not clear but is likely to lie in the difficulties of expecting change to be driven by senior men who clearly did

142. Ibid., fol. 170.
143. Ibid.
144. Ibid., fol. 165.
145. Ibid., fol. 164.
146. Ibid., fol. 166.

not feel empowered to take action in their areas and, given the significant increases in business the bank experienced over the late eighteenth century, a lack of time and opportunity to reflect on processes.

The early hours of the business day at the Bank were dominated by the work of the Cashiers Department. The cashiers delivered a set of services that were essential to the economy of London and to the state. Indeed, this chapter has shown the extent to which the business of managing the state's money, and a nascent responsibility for providing support for the economy, was contracted out to the Bank. This work was organisationally complex. Most clerks were responsible for a discrete set of activities, and thus processes, such as note issue or discounting bills, could only be accomplished with the contribution of a number of individuals working together. The clerks were under a great deal of pressure, and many of them held a high level of responsibility. They often had at their disposal the means of creating paper of significant value. Most warranted the trust placed in them, but men like Charles Clutterbuck could easily use the Bank's complex and dispersed processes for deceitful purposes. One of the key outcomes of the Inspection was the implementation of change which improved security and reduced opportunities for mendacious behaviour by the clerks.

The Inspection also made changes which showed the extent to which service to the public guided the Bank's work. Indeed, much of the work done by the cashiers was in the service of public credit. The public would have experienced the banking hall as a site of commercial sociability, in many ways clear and supported by way-finding, porters and perhaps recourse to the *Vade Mecum*. It was an outward politeness that spoke of service to the public but which also reinforced connections to the state and the business community and to the growing economy. Nonetheless, relationships were mediated, and personal interactions remained important. From the unfortunate whose requests might be turned down because they neglected the clerks' Christmas boxes to the individuals who, being known to the Committee in Waiting, were clearly not subject to such stringent checks, personal connections made a difference.

CHAPTER THREE

Making the Market

AT AROUND 11:00 A.M. there arrived at the Bank 'a vast crowd of Stock-brokers, Stock-jobbers, and other persons having business in the Funds'.[1] They gathered in the Rotunda to trade in government stocks and Bank shares and to meet with counterparties and register their trades, as they were required to do, all such business being conducted in person by the owners of the stock or their attorneys. When their business was done—and certainly from 1:00 P.M., when the transfer desks closed—the brokers and jobbers drifted away to the other spaces occupied by the market: East India and South Sea houses, Exchange Alley, the various coffee houses in the vicinity and the newly established Stock Exchange.[2] While they were at the Bank, they brought noise, disruption and an intense period of work for the transfer office clerks. Thomas Mortimer, who wrote the only comprehensive eighteenth-century guide to the financial market, advised those entering the Rotunda of 'the wild uproar, and confused noise which will at first strike your astonished senses'.[3] The Bank's own records also note the crowds, the cacophonous noise and, indeed, the potential dangers. The Inspectors were informed of the activities of a pickpocket who had recently robbed a woman of 30 guineas.[4] And Mr Vickery of the Three Per Cent Consols Office recommended the attendance of a number of Bank porters to 'keep an eye upon persons loitering about'.[5]

1. Quoted in Abramson, *Building the Bank*, p. 70.

2. BEA, M5/213, fol. 57; S. R. Cope, 'The Stock-Brokers Find a Home: How the Stock Exchange Came to Be Established in Sweetings Alley in 1773', *Guildhall Studies in London History*, 2 (1977), p. 217. The Stock Exchange was opened in 1773.

3. Thomas Mortimer, *Every man his own broker: Or a guide to Exchange-Alley* (London, 1762), p. 133.

4. BEA, M5/213, fol. 120.

5. Ibid.

FIGURE 3.1. Thomas Rowlandson, *The Bank* (London, 1792).
Source: Metropolitan Museum of Art, The Elisha Whittelsey Collection, The Elisha Whittelsey Fund, 1959, CC0.

If the Rotunda and surrounding offices were places where someone might be as likely to lose their pocket-book as make a fortune speculating in the stocks, it was nonetheless an exciting and intriguing environment. Indeed, to borrow a phrase from historians studying leisure spaces, it was a place of 'social theatre', a place where brokers, jobbers, speculators and investors 'performed' their roles and could be observed doing so.[6] This point is underlined by the architecture of the Rotunda, which, as can be seen in Thomas Rowlandson's 1792 image in figure 3.1, echoed places of commercialised leisure such as Ranelagh Gardens, the music room at Vauxhall Gardens and the domed ballroom at Oxford Street Pantheon.[7] Thus, it was unusual as a market space. In being circular rather than rectangular, it left participants free to occupy the space as they wished rather than taking up fixed positions as they did in other market environments. It also 'maximised visibility and intensified opportunities for contact among the professional brokers and jobbers'.[8] Its position as a place for observation

6. P. Borsay, 'A Room with a View: Visualising the Seaside, c. 1750–1914', *Transactions of the Royal Historical Society*, 23 (2013), p. 181.

7. Abramson, *Building the Bank*, p. 70.

8. Ibid.

as well as action was reinforced by the fact that the Bank, along with other financial and commercial buildings, was a popular tourist destination. Visitors came to experience one of London's landmarks and view the workings of the financial market. An early nineteenth-century guidebook advised visitors to the Bank that they would see 'a crowd of eager money-dealers assemble, and avidity of gain displays itself in variety of shapes, truly ludicrous to the disinterested observer'.[9]

Implied in this 'performance' was not just the administration of public credit but also the connections the Bank facilitated between the state and its creditors. Indeed, as Natalie Roxburgh asserts in her persuasive work on the representations of public credit, the Bank, and its continuing management of the national debt, formed part of an inferred 'contract' between the public creditors and the state.[10] It was a contract that implied 'an economy of mutual benefit' and through which the state could be held to account to keep the promises that underpinned the national debt.[11] The performing of credit at the Bank of England demonstrated to public creditors that their savings were in safe hands, but it does raise a question about how necessary and meaningful this display was in maintaining confidence.

North and Weingast's arguments, in particular, have been powerful in asserting the easy acceptance of public indebtedness, the importance of allocated tax funds in creating 'credible commitment' and the embeddedness of property rights in the eighteenth-century state.[12] This is misleading. A more careful reading of the relevant sources shows that the creditworthiness of the state continued to be contested throughout the eighteenth century. Each successive conflict raised the debate about the nature of the national debt and the likelihood of imminent state bankruptcy.[13] Tax funds that were supposed to support the debt were often underpaid, even towards the end of the eighteenth century. In the midst of the War of American Independence, the tax funds allocated to pay the debts incurred stood in arrears to the tune of more than £2 million. Outstanding Exchequer bills, issued in anticipation of tax revenues, stood at £4.5 million, while the taxes budgeted to cover were only supposed to yield £2.5 million; and it

9. Quoted in ibid., p. 74.

10. Natalie Roxburgh, *Representing Public Credit: Credible Commitment, Fiction and the Rise of the Fictional Subject* (London, 2016), p. 41.

11. Ibid.

12. North and Weingast, 'Constitutions and Commitment'.

13. Takuo Dome, *The Political Economy of Public Finance in Britain, 1767–1873* (Abingdon, UK, 2004).

was known that those funds, the land and the malt tax, usually fell short.[14] Property rights were violated in numerous ways, although sometimes with the best of intentions. Henry Pelham's conversion of the outstanding debt in 1749, which created the 3 per cent consolidated annuities, was a case in point. At that time the interest paid to the public creditors was forcibly lowered and the terms of their loans renegotiated.[15] The resolution of the South Sea Scheme had required similar sacrifices.[16] Moreover, Julian Hoppit has uncovered a number of cases throughout the eighteenth century in which the property rights of British subjects were undermined, noting that 'to them there was precious little "credible commitment"'.[17]

The integrity of the public funds, therefore, was at risk and did need to be demonstrated. Thus, the Bank's role and the transparency, regularity and efficiency of its management of the debt were very necessary. That the Inspectors recognised this is clear from the closing words of their final report, in which, as we have seen, they wrote of the Bank as the 'grand Palladium of Public Credit'.[18] Yet, as this chapter will demonstrate, despite the stated, and justified, confidence in the Bank as the protector of the nation's debt, there were failings in the Bank's service to the public creditors. In particular, the Inspectors quickly discovered that many of the transfer and dividend clerks were taking advantage of their proximity to the market and trading in securities, in addition to either directing business to favoured brokers or taking advantage of a captive clientele by acting as brokers themselves. We must consider the extent to which this compromised the Bank's self-proclaimed guardianship of the interests of the public creditors.

The Market in the State's Debt

The state contracted the Bank of England to manage both initial offerings of its debt and the majority of transfers made in the secondary market. The former processes were formal and operated by tender rather than by open subscription. Contracts generally went to 'some favoured consortium of big jobbers, businessmen and their political allies'.[19] The favoured

14. Reitan, *Politics, Finance, and the People*, p. 134.

15. Dickson, *Financial Revolution*, pp. 228–241.

16. Ibid., pp. 157–198.

17. Hoppit, 'Compulsion, Compensation and Property Rights', p. 125.

18. BEA, M5/213, fol. 178.

19. Henry Roseveare, *The Treasury, 1660–1870: The Foundations of Control* (London, 1973), pp. 112–113. O'Brien also questions whether an open system would have been effective. O'Brien, 'Mercantilist Institutions," pp. 24–25.

individuals would undertake to purchase the debt at initial offering either by their own means, sometimes with the aid of advances from the Bank, or through their own consortia of contacts.[20] They would then sell their allocations in the open market and generally for a significant profit. It was a system that was based on patronage, but it had proved effective and indeed an attempt to issue debt through an open subscription in 1757 failed.[21] The system was nonetheless expensive and became much discredited during the War of American Independence. A £12 million loan raised in 1781, for example, represented a cost of £21 million at initial offering and yielded profits to the subscribers of between 7 and 11 per cent.[22] It was certainly an attractive proposition for subscribers but hardly a cost-effective fund-raising solution for the state.

At the Bank the process of initial offering was handled by the cashiers, who opened accounts for new customers, accepted monies paid in against subscriptions and cleared balances with the Exchequer. The Bank also kept registers of ownership of the debt and recorded when it was bought and sold. The secondary market in the debt was, however, informal.[23] It operated outside of the state's or the Bank's control and generally was not subject to significant regulation.[24] Yet, it was an essential element of the financial revolution since it facilitated the liquidation of holdings at will and thus allowed individuals with diverse motivations to participate in the ownership of state debt. Had the ability to transfer with ease not been available, it is unlikely that the state's debt would have been viewed as such an attractive investment opportunity.[25] The emergence of such a market, however, required not

20. Clapham, *Bank of England*, 1:174.

21. Roseveare, *Treasury*, p. 113.

22. Ibid.

23. For more on the development of early modern financial markets, see William N. Goetzmann and K. Geert Rouwenhorst, eds., *The Origins of Value: The Financial Innovations That Created Modern Capital Markets* (Oxford, 2005); A. M. Carlos and Larry Neal, 'Amsterdam and London as Financial Centres in the Eighteenth Century', *Financial History Review*, 18 (2001), pp. 21–46; P. Mirowski, 'The Rise (and Retreat) of a Market: English Joint Stock Shares in the Eighteenth Century', *Journal of Economic History*, 41 (1981), pp. 559–577.

24. Stuart Banner, *Anglo-American Securities Regulation: Cultural and Political Roots, 1690–1860* (Cambridge, 1998); Anne L. Murphy, 'Financial Markets: The Limits of Economic Regulation in Early Modern England', in Carl Wennerlind and Philip J. Stern, eds., *Mercantilism Reimagined: Political Economy in Early Modern Britain and Its Empire* (Oxford, 2013), pp. 263–281.

25. Dickson, *Financial Revolution*, p. 457; Ann M. Carlos, Karen Maguire and Larry Neal, 'Financial Acumen, Women Speculators and the Royal African Company during the South Sea Bubble', *Accounting, Business and Financial History*, 16 (2006), pp. 219–243.

only a broad range of participants but also accessible spaces and the capacity to transfer holdings with minimal costs. The beginnings of this market emerged during the 1690s but developed over a longer period of time.[26]

Moreover, it took much of the first half of the eighteenth century for the state to establish a reputation for financial probity and to nurture the relationships and techniques that allowed it to manage its debt effectively.[27] The early financial revolution was characterised by experiments with expensive and inefficient fund-raising instruments.[28] During the late seventeenth and early eighteenth centuries, the needs of the private individuals who devised those experiments took precedence over the needs of the state.[29] The early financial revolution was also punctuated by shocks, such as the loss of the City in 1710 and the South Sea Bubble of 1720.[30] By the late 1740s, however, the state was able to take advantage of a strengthening reputation to rationalise what had become an over-complex and expensive system. Thus, in 1749 Henry Pelham, first lord of the Treasury, proposed a scheme that would consolidate much of the outstanding debt and reduce interest rates on those funds from 4 to 3 per cent. This was no simple task. 'Pelham's conversion', as it became known, was the subject of significant resistance from both financiers and ordinary investors, but Pelham eventually secured a voluntary conversion of 88 per cent of all the various 4 per cent stocks.[31] This resulted in the creation of the Consolidated Fund and from it emerged the three per cent consols, a single instrument held by many investors and the mainstay of many late eighteenth-century and Victorian investment portfolios. The widespread acceptance and use of

26. Anne L. Murphy, *The Origins of English Financial Markets: Investment and Speculation before the South Sea Bubble* (Cambridge, 2009).

27. Sussman and Yafeh, 'Institutional Reforms'.

28. Dickson, *Financial Revolution*, pp. 39–156; Murphy, *Origins of English Financial Markets*, pp. 39–65.

29. Murphy, *Origins of English Financial Markets*, pp. 39–65; Koji Yamamoto, *Taming Capitalism before Its Triumph: Public Service, Distrust, and 'Projecting' in Early Modern England* (Oxford, 2018). Graham also offers a detailed and nuanced account of the intersections between public service and private interests in the management of aspects of the state's finances. Aaron Graham, *Corruption, Party and Government in Britain, 1702–1713* (Oxford, 2015).

30. Hill, '"Loss of the City"'; James Macdonald, 'The Importance of Not Defaulting: The Significance of the Election of 1710', in D'Maris Coffman, Adrian Leonard and Larry Neal, eds., *Questioning Credible Commitment: Perspectives on the Rise of Financial Capitalism* (Cambridge, 2013), pp. 125–146; Richard Dale, *The First Crash: Lessons from the South Sea Bubble* (Princeton, NJ, 2004); Paul, *South Sea Bubble*.

31. Dickson, *Financial Revolution*, pp. 228–241. See also C. Chamley, 'Interest Reductions in the Politico-Financial Nexus of Eighteenth-Century England', *Journal of Economic History*, 71 (2011), pp. 555–589.

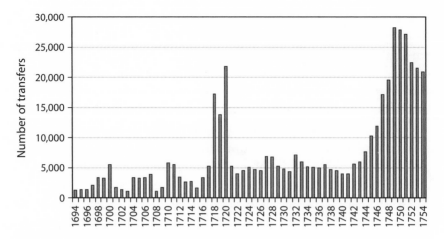

FIGURE 3.2. Annual numbers of transfers of stock, 1694–1754.
Source: Dickson, *Financial Revolution*, pp. 529–532.

consols served to further support the growth of the secondary market. Indeed, the ease with which the new consols could be exchanged is amply demonstrated in the consequent rise in number of transactions from the late 1740s (see figure 3.2).

Although a liquid instrument was now available, other aspects of the market, including the process of price discovery and the location of a counterparty with whom to trade, remained challenging. There was certainly an abundance of price information available to the investor. Thomas Mortimer tells us that brokers published printed lists of the prices of traded stocks and that these were available daily at around one o'clock in the afternoon in and around the Exchange and both within coffee houses and 'stuck up at the windows'.[32] Prices were also printed in newspapers and periodicals.[33] Studies indicate that information flow between professional market actors was sufficient to ensure that arbitrage opportunities did not remain for long.[34] Yet, it is necessary to acknowledge the continuing barri-

32. Mortimer, *Every man his own broker*, p. 5.

33. S. R. Cope, 'The Stock Exchange Revisited: A New Look at the Market in Securities in London in the Eighteenth Century', *Economica*, 45 (1978), p. 19.

34. On the flow of information between financial centres, see G. Dempster, J. Wells and D. Wills, 'A Common-Features Analysis of Amsterdam and London Financial Markets during the Eighteenth Century', *Economic Inquiry*, 38 (2000), pp. 19–33; L. Neal, 'The Integration and Efficiency of the London and Amsterdam Stock Markets in the Eighteenth Century', *Journal of Economic History*, 47 (1987), pp. 97–115; A. R. Bell, C. Brooks and N. Taylor, 'Time-Varying Price Discovery in the Eighteenth Century: Empirical Evidence from the London and Amsterdam Stock Markets', *Cliometrica*, 10 (2016), pp. 5–30.

ers for ordinary investors that resulted from slow communication around a market which remained quite widely dispersed.[35]

Furthermore, published price information was not the sole determinant of a decision to invest in the state's debt. It had to be supplemented by verbal networks of information that would have provided context, advice and a guide to the location of a counterparty.[36] Thus, direct conversations with bankers, brokers and jobbers but also friends, family and acquaintances probably formed the basis of decision-making and action for many. Observation of the market at work was also important. Unlike today's electronic markets, earlier markets were intensely visual and aural. The noise of the market and the body language of its participants, as experienced dealers in the stocks would have known, were central to a good understanding of the market's volatility and trajectory. Indeed, even Thomas Mortimer advised his readers to go to the market themselves and first to 'Advance . . . and attend a few minutes to the confused cries that resound from all quarters'.[37] All these factors point to a necessary presence in the market, especially for brokers and jobbers. This, of course, required a place in which to meet, but during the eighteenth century this was complicated by the peripatetic nature of the market.

As noted above, the market was located in a variety of places throughout the day, including the coffee houses of Exchange Alley (especially Jonathan's), the offices of the main monied companies and the Stock Exchange. A lack of sources makes it impossible to be certain, but it appears as though each of these spaces served different functions. The offices of the monied companies, including the Bank, were open outcry markets for ready money and immediate settlement.[38] They dominated trading in the mornings through to the early afternoon, when their transfer books were open, and because the

35. Michie is more sceptical about the speed and accessibility of financial information. Ranald C. Michie, 'Friend or Foe? Information Technology and the London Stock Exchange since 1700', *Journal of Historical Geography*, 23 (1997), pp. 304–326.

36. Murphy, *Origins of English Financial Markets*, chapter 5; A. Preda, 'In the Enchanted Grove: Financial Conversations and the Marketplace in England and France in the 18th Century', *Journal of Historical Sociology*, 14 (2001), pp. 276–307.

37. Mortimer, *Every man his own broker*, p. 133.

38. Abramson, *Building the Bank*, p. 70. An open outcry market is one in which intention and price are signalled by verbal means or through hand signals. Open outcry markets have a long history but are now being replaced by electronic means of trading. Jerry W. Markham and Daniel J. Harty, 'For Whom the Bell Tolls: The Demise of Exchange Trading Floors and the Growth of ECNs', *Journal of Corporation Law*, 33 (2007–2008), pp. 865–939.

Bank managed the majority of the public debt, its Rotunda continued to provide the most important daily opportunity for brokers, jobbers and public creditors to meet and arrange their transactions.[39] Trading at Jonathan's coffee house, which picked up after midday, seemed to encompass the main market for trading and settling time bargains, and it appeared that most business there was conducted through brokers.[40] This implies an active market for time bargains among regular market participants, but it should be noted that the options market, while a feature of trading during the late seventeenth and early eighteenth centuries, had been severely curtailed by the regulation introduced by Barnard's Act in 1734.[41] Both the offices of the monied companies and the coffee houses were open spaces. The new Stock Exchange, on the other hand, was an attempt to create an exclusive market space. Although providing a venue for brokers and jobbers to meet, it 'failed to capture the market' and appeared to make little difference to the nature of trading in London before the early nineteenth century.[42]

Although the market was essential to the functioning of the national debt, it was not valued by all. Critics argued that the creation of a secondary market encouraged speculation and over-reaction to external shocks.[43] They accused the market of creating opportunities for profiting from the nation's exigencies and especially the needs of war.[44] The character of stockjobbers was particularly maligned. As the author of *The Art of Stock-jobbing* suggested, many believed that jobbers were incapable of telling the truth:

A Painter's Fancy will his Flights pursue,

And dares draw any thing at the first View:

Your Jobbers too with these claim equal Share,

39. Clapham, *Bank of England*, 1:103.

40. Cope, 'Stock Exchange Revisited', pp. 5, 17. Cope emphasises the informal and varied nature of settlement arrangements during the eighteenth century.

41. 7 and 8 Geo. II, c. 8, 'An Act to prevent the infamous practice of stock-jobbing'. Cope, 'Stock Exchange Revisited', p. 8; Dickson, *Financial Revolution*, p. 508. Other historians have questioned the effectiveness of the Act. See E. V. Morgan and W. A. Thomas, *The Stock Exchange: Its History and Functions* (London, 1969). Since such transactions by their nature were not registered, there is no means of testing the veracity of these claims, but there is certainly little mention of options trading in the contemporary literature. Moreover, the clerks questioned by the Inspectors mentioned trading for time a number of times but did not mention options trading. BEA, M5/213, passim.

42. Michie, *Global Securities Market*, pp. 45–46.

43. Dickson, *Financial Revolution*, pp. 15–38. For alternative treatments of criticism of and satire on the financial markets, see Colin Nicholson, *Writing and the Rise of Finance: Capital Satires of the Early Eighteenth Century* (Cambridge, 1994); Patrick Brantlinger, *Fictions of State: Culture and Credit in Britain, 1694–1994* (Ithaca, NY, 1996).

44. For a summary of these arguments, see Dickson, *Financial Revolution*, chapter 2.

And any thing that's plausible may swear:
For we may prove Stockjobbers from our Youth,
Provided that we seldom speak the Truth;
For Truth with them as incoherent seems,
As Honesty with crafty Courtiers Schemes.[45]

As both Dickson and Paul show, distaste for stockjobbing was reinforced by racial and religious prejudice, with anti-Semitism being particularly prominent in the contemporary literature.[46] Thomas Mortimer's *Every man his own broker* clung to such tropes throughout the mid- to late eighteenth century. Mortimer dismissed jobbers as rumour-mongering 'foreigners', 'our own gentry, merchants and tradesmen' addicted to gaming and neglectful of their other duties and those from the lower sorts who 'transact more business in the several government securities in one hour, without having a shilling of property in any one of them, than the real proprietors of thousands transact in several years'.[47] In another publication Mortimer warned his readers that, in order to gain advantage, these 'pests of human society' would use 'every mean artifice, every scandalous forgery or false reports, however detrimental to their country and their fellow subjects'.[48]

Mortimer's volume went through fourteen editions and sold as many as 50,000 copies, and thus his views were widely disseminated.[49] It is possible to find corroborating evidence for such claims. Bowen, for example, cites the case of 'scaremongering' accounts in newspapers in 1768. These reports detailed East India Company losses in Madras and alleged that the French were amassing troops at Pondicherry. These false accounts led to a market crash in 1769, and contemporaries were convinced that it was the work of 'the schemes and designs of speculators'.[50] Yet, other scholars have cast doubt on the capacity of such individuals to influence prices in significant ways.[51] Moreover, if accounts of the constant duplicity of participants are to be accepted without question, the idea of a credible market in which the

---

45. Anon., *The Art of Stock-Jobbing: A poem in imitation of Horace's Art of Poetry, by a Gideonite* (London, 1746), p. 14.

46. Dickson, *Financial Revolution*, p. 34; Paul, *South Sea Bubble*, pp. 94–95.

47. Mortimer, *Every man his own broker*, pp. 33–35, 41–49.

48. Thomas Mortimer, *The Elements of Commerce, Politics and Finance in Three Treatises* (London, 1780), quoted in H. V. Bowen, '"The Pests of Human Society": Stockbrokers, Jobbers and Speculators in Mid-eighteenth-century Britain', *History*, 78 (1993), p. 42.

49. Cope, 'Stock Exchange Revisited', p. 4.

50. Bowen, '"Pests of Human Society"', p. 43.

51. Murphy, *Origins of English Financial Markets*, p. xx; O'Brien, 'Mercantilist Institutions', pp. 17–18.

ordinary investor could repose trust would be nonsensical. To explain the persistence of an active secondary market that was able to attract a broad range of participants, we have to consider a different interpretation of the dominant actions of brokers and jobbers.

There is little consistent evidence, outside of contemporary comment, that all brokers and jobbers deserved their reputation as 'the pests of human society'.[52] Certainly, they made their living from the fluctuations of the market and the price differentials they could achieve by selling high and buying low, and these goals probably operated to the detriment of many less experienced or more naïve participants. Yet, the face-to-face nature of transactions and the fact that they most often took place in front of witnesses meant that, as Muldrew asserts of other markets, the discourse of self-interest, so emphasised by many contemporary commentators, was countered by one which stressed 'credit relations, trust, obligation and contracts'.[53]

Brokers, in particular, would have been both reliant on word-of-mouth recommendations from satisfied clients and concerned with attracting repeat business. Their incentive to deceive their clients was, therefore, low. Those who were licensed also operated within a regulatory framework provided by the City's Court of Mayor and Alderman. These regulations imposed an admission fee and an annual subscription, thus creating a barrier to entry, and they required each broker to keep a record of their transactions. They also provided for fines to be imposed on those acting without a license.[54] Mortimer made much of the fact that many brokers operated outside of the regulation.[55] Yet, Jackson Tait's analysis shows that the judiciary were reluctant to support prosecution of these individuals and that this inaction was regarded as being positive for the development of the market. Moreover, an attempted prosecution of unlicensed brokers in 1767 saw the acquittal of the defendants as a victory for public credit in allowing individuals to employ their friends to act for them in the market.[56] This suggests that unlicensed brokers were not always unwelcome or untrustworthy.

52. Mortimer, *Elements of Commerce*, quoted in Bowen, '"Pests of Human Society"', p. 42.

53. Muldrew, 'Interpreting the Market', p. 163.

54. Cope, 'Stock Exchange Revisited', pp. 2–3.

55. Mortimer, *Every man his own broker*, p. 116.

56. Jackson Tait, 'Speculation and the English Common Law Courts, 1697–1845', *Libertarian Papers*, 10 (2018), pp. 9–10.

Brokers acted primarily as the intermediaries between counterparties, whereas jobbers provided the basis for exchange because they were usually prepared to make a market by offering a price to either buy or sell, as required. Thus, jobbers became an invaluable mechanism for the market. But they were few in number and therefore prominent, which would have operated as a check on overtly duplicitous behaviour.[57] Equally, because of the relatively low daily trading volumes in the market during most of the eighteenth century, brokers and jobbers tended to have dual occupations. Acquiring a reputation for dishonesty in one aspect of a working life would have had a detrimental impact on other business dealings and, thus, would have been avoided.[58] Indeed, there can be no question about the extent to which, in essentially small and local markets—an appropriate description for stock markets until the end of the eighteenth century—the need to know participants, and be known, acted as a control over undesirable behaviour.

The participants in the market also acted to impose restraints on each other. As Adam Smith acknowledged, 'Persons who game must keep their credit, else no body will deal with them. It is quite the same in stockjobbing. They who do not keep their credit will soon be turned out, and in the language of Change Alley be called a lame duck'.[59] Indeed, transgressors of the market's rules were punished through public embarrassment and sometimes expulsion from the spaces in which the market existed. Notably, the names of those with poor credit were written on a 'public blackboard' for all to see.[60] The market was, therefore, sufficiently public to facilitate regular scrutiny of actions, increasingly self-regulated and willing to recognise and punish poor behaviour amongst participants. It was not quite the den of iniquity painted in Mortimer's work.

The Crowd in the Rotunda

What of the ordinary public creditors who visited the Bank? Rowlandson's depiction of the Rotunda (figure 3.1) shows a lively environment and various interactions among men and women seemingly primarily of the middling sort. There is a crowd of excited bidders on the right of the image and more measured conversations happening elsewhere. Individuals

57. Dickson, *Financial Revolution*, p. 511.

58. Murphy, *Origins of English Financial Markets*, p. 164.

59. Adam Smith, *Letters on Jurisprudence* (1766), quoted in Tait, 'Speculation and the English Common Law', p. 1.

60. Tait, 'Speculation and the English Common Law', p. 14.

obviously in search of someone with whom to trade are pictured on the left, and we can also see those who have already been approached by a broker. The records preserved in the Bank's archive can help us add more detail to this image. What follows draws on a sample of 2,989 transactions in the three per cent consols recorded in the Bank's transfer books during 1784.[61] The Bank's transfer books recorded the names, socio-economic status and locations of both buyer and seller. Also recorded were the amount and date of the transaction and whether the transaction was being conducted by an attorney.

The transfer books can be assumed to offer an accurate picture of the market. They formed the only legally binding record of ownership of the debt, and thus the clerks aspired to, and appear to have attained, a high level of accuracy. When examining holdings in the public debt, we need not be particularly concerned that ownership might be concealed by nominee holdings and other such devices.[62] Such actions appear to have related chiefly to splitting stock holdings for the purpose of creating voting rights in the main monied companies. This was not a concern with government debt, and thus ownership records were unlikely to have been significantly affected.[63]

Nonetheless, while an examination of participation in the market is possible using the socio-economic descriptors registered in the transfer books, these must be used cautiously. Notably, occupations, especially those concerned with production and distribution, were not always specialised in this period, making sectoral divisions of the economy somewhat arbitrary. Equally, there is no consistent method of determining the size or value of business commanded by public creditors. Thus, some occupation groups may disguise large variations in wealth and rank.[64] Most importantly for our purposes, there is no clear way to identify a rentier class from the

---

61. The sample constitutes around 5 per cent of the total ready money transactions registered at the Bank that year in the most actively traded stocks. There was no obligation to register time bargains, and thus it is impossible to establish the extent of this market. The year 1784 was selected as a peace time year. The War of American Independence continued throughout most of 1783.

62. Dickson, *Financial Revolution*, p. 251; S. E. Whyman, *Sociability and Power in Late-Stuart England: The Cultural Worlds of the Verneys, 1660–1720* (Oxford, 2002), p. 76.

63. Dickson, *Financial Revolution*, p. 253; J. F. Wright, 'The Contribution of Overseas Savings to the Funded National Debt of Great Britain, 1750–1815', *Economic History Review*, 50 (1997), pp. 661–662.

64. For a further discussion of these issues, see W. A. Armstrong, 'The Use of Information about Occupation', in E. A. Wrigley, ed., *Nineteenth Century Society: Essays in the Use of Quantitative Methods for the Study of Social Data* (Cambridge, 1972), pp. 191–253; P. J. Corfield, 'Class by Name and Number in Eighteenth-Century Britain', *History*, 72

socio-economic descriptions given. The description 'gentleman' was frequently used by market participants, but by the late eighteenth century it no longer implied gentle birth and freedom from paid employment.[65] Indeed, it is clear from the institutional addresses given by many of the 'gentlemen' in the sample that they were regular jobbers, brokers and financiers. Other occupations may also have been concealed by the descriptions used, especially in the case of female participants, who were usually described as either wife, widow or spinster. Female 'servants' were identified in the transfer books, but it is likely that many other female public creditors would have been engaged in paid employment or would have been contributing to the paid work being undertaken by their households.[66]

Table 3.1 shows the socio-economic status of buyers and sellers of each transaction in the sample. Individuals may have traded, and often did trade, more than once during the period. The sectoral breakdown of the economy follows that used by the Cambridge Group for the History of Population and Social Structure. However, in presentation, less detail has been given for the primary and secondary sectors, which were not strongly represented among public creditors. Greater detail is offered for the tertiary sector, and an additional category has been added for women and those who described themselves by social status rather than occupation.[67]

Table 3.1 shows that contemporary commentators were certainly correct to assert that the Rotunda was dominated by brokers and jobbers. More than half of the sales and over a quarter of the purchases were conducted by financial professionals. Within this group, relatively few individuals dominated. Just six men conducted 21 per cent of the total sales in the sample. Moreover, these figures are certainly an under-estimation. For the most part, these individuals have been identified not by their socio-economic status but by their address, given either as the 'Stock Exchange' or 'Exchange

---

(1987), pp. 38–61; H. Horwitz, 'The Mess of the Middle Class' Revisited: The Case of the 'Big Bourgeoisie' of Augustan London', *Continuity and Change*, 2 (1987), pp. 263–296.

65. Corfield, 'Class by Name', p. 43.

66. For a discussion of female occupations and contributions to the household economy, see Amy Louise Erickson, 'Married Women's Occupations in Eighteenth-Century London', *Continuity and Change*, 23 (2008), pp. 267–307; Jane Whittle, 'Enterprising Widows and Active Wives: Women's Unpaid Work in the Household Economy of Early Modern England', *The History of the Family*, 19 (2014), pp. 283–300; Nicola Phillips, *Women in Business, 1700–1850* (Woodbridge, UK, 2006); Hannah Barker, *The Business of Women: Female Enterprise and Urban Development in Northern England, 1760–1830* (Oxford, 2006).

67. For an overview of the occupational structure used, see Leigh Shaw-Taylor and E. A. Wrigley, 'Occupational Structure and Population Change', in Roderick Floud, Jane Humphries and Paul Johnson, eds., *The Cambridge Economic History of Modern Britain*, vol. 1, *1700–1870* (Cambridge, 2014), pp. 53–88.

Table 3.1. Socio-economic status of sellers and buyers of three per cent consols, 1784.

	Number of individual sellers	Seller (%)	Number of individual buyers	Buyer (%)
Primary Sector	14	0.46	47	1.44
Secondary Sector	143	4.65	230	7.07
Tertiary Sector				
Dealers and sellers	255	8.30	355	10.91
Transport	22	0.72	39	1.20
Clergy	18	0.59	59	1.81
Military	33	1.07	42	1.29
Legal	18	0.59	40	1.23
Medical	20	0.65	63	1.94
Finance	1,578	51.37	930	28.59
Servant	15	0.49	47	1.44
Other services and professions	22	0.72	27	0.83
Others				
Women	158	5.14	424	13.03
Titled aristocrats	12	0.39	24	0.74
Gentlemen	454	14.78	514	15.80
Esquire	224	7.29	300	9.22
Institutions	3	0.10	12	0.37
Unknown	83	2.70	100	3.07

Source: BEA, Transfer books, passim.

Alley'. Most of these men used the designation 'gentleman' to describe themselves. Where it was not possible to positively identify an individual using their address, those transactions have been allocated to the category 'gentleman', but it is likely that many of those assigned to this category were engaged with work that connected them to finance.

The use of the designation 'gentleman' is an interesting one as it indicates those individuals who sought to locate themselves within a polite commerciality. A gentleman was one 'who merits this denomination: the man elevated above the vulgar'.[68] By the late eighteenth century it

68. David Hancock, *Citizens of the World: London Merchants and the Integration of the British Atlantic Community, 1735–1785* (Cambridge, 1995), p. 280.

included those who had distinguished themselves by 'superior accomplishments' and not just by birth.[69] This offers further evidence to challenge the characterisation of the financial market as dominated by duplicitous and manipulative actors. Nor, outwardly, do the activities of these individuals seem to have been directed towards the speculative or manipulative. As asserted above, their prominence in the market would have created some checks on behaviour. It is also likely that many would have been seeking primarily to turn a profit from a regular turnover of sales to, and purchases from, other participants.

One such individual was William Kilbinton, who primarily traded with his fellow financiers and most often at reasonably high values.[70] Peter Duthoit's customer base was much more varied. He certainly traded with bankers and other jobbers but also with a coachman, an engraver, a victualler, a stationer and with female public creditors. The amounts in which Duthoit traded ranged from £25 to £1,350.[71] William Gillbee was one of the most prolific jobbers in the sample, and his activity was diverse. Although his average transaction amount was £1,042, trades ranged from £5 to £9,000.[72] His customer base spread across all sectors of the economy but was concentrated within the professional sector with nearly 50 per cent of his transactions being with counterparties describing themselves as gentlemen, esquires or individuals employed in the clerical or legal professions. Around 15 per cent of Gillbee's counterparties were women, which is consistent with their presence in the wider market.[73] None of his activity, or the activity of any of the other individuals identified here, suggests a deliberate targeting of a naïve or vulnerable customer base.

It is less straight-forward to use the transfer books to explore the extent of broker involvement in the market. The role of intermediary was not recorded, and thus we only see brokers acting on their own accounts. Just thirteen individuals who self-identified as brokers appear in the sample. In the majority of cases, their transactions were with other market professionals. Thus, of the eighteen transactions to which the broker Thomas Fry was counterparty, only five were not with an identifiable financial or legal professional. Three of the remaining five were conducted through the same attorney, Thomas Corbyn, suggesting the dominant relationship was with the attorney. Of the other two transactions, both

69. Ibid.
70. BEA, Transfer books, passim.
71. Ibid.
72. Ibid.
73. Ibid.

saw Fry purchasing stock, in the first case from a harpsichord maker, and in the second from an individual whose occupation was unrecorded. Cope suggested that this type of transaction might be the consequence of a broker enacting orders in the only way available to them if they could not find an alternative counterparty.[74]

While financial professionals would have dominated the Rotunda by the regularity of their presence and frequency of their transactions, the majority of the crowd would have been ordinary public creditors making either single or a small number of purchases. These were people like Mary Lager, a servant living on Thames Street in London, who bought £175 in the three per cent consols in December 1784; Emanuel Jacomi, a seaman from Old Gravel Lane, who sold £375 in the same stock and confirmed the sale by making his mark; and Robert Rickards, a vicar from Glamorganshire in Wales, who purchased £75 in the consols.[75] The analysis presented in table 3.1 shows that these people were occupied mostly in the tertiary, or service, sector of the economy and that women were an important minority in the market.

Although the transfer books give a picture of the market rather than an overview of debt holdings, the findings are not inconsistent with analyses of ownership. Dickson's study found that the public debt was chiefly held by individuals from the church, the army, the civil service and the professions.[76] Merchants were also significant public creditors, and, at the lower end of the ownership scale, artisans, tradesmen and craftsmen dominated.[77] It is notable that titled individuals were not significantly involved in the market during the 1780s, which is also consistent with Dickson's analysis of the holders of the national debt during the mid-eighteenth century.[78]

Public creditors were not just individuals. Although not a significant presence in the market, the funds were being used by a range of institutional, corporate or quasi-corporate investors.[79] The Court of Chancery was one of the most prominent of these. The office of the Account-General of Chancery had been created in 1726 with the power to control suitors' funds, and the office was, by the mid-eighteenth century, one of the

74. Cope, 'Stock Exchange Revisited', p. 3.

75. BEA, AC28/4275; BEA, AC28/4273; BEA, AC28/4276.

76. Dickson, *Financial Revolution*, p. 260.

77. Ibid., pp. 301–302, 282.

78. Ibid., p. 295.

79. Carole Shammas, 'Tracking the Growth of Government Securities Investing in Early Modern England and Wales', *Financial History Review*, 27 (2020), pp. 95–114.

Table 3.2. Stated addresses of sellers and buyers of three per cent consols, 1784.

	Seller (number of transactions)	Seller (%)	Buyer (number of transactions)	Buyer (%)
Exchange Alley/Stock Exchange	1,419	47.47	846	28.30
Institutional address, London	70	2.34	95	3.18
London	1,153	38.57	1,298	43.43
South East	152	5.09	313	10.47
South West	55	1.84	137	4.58
East Anglia	18	0.60	34	1.14
Midlands	18	0.60	53	1.77
North of England	28	0.94	67	2.24
Wales	4	0.13	11	0.37
Scotland	2	0.07	4	0.13
Ireland	7	0.23	5	0.17
Netherlands	17	0.57	17	0.57
Foreign (other)	10	0.33	54	1.81
Unknown	36	1.20	55	1.84

Source: BEA, Transfer books, passim.

prominent holders of government stock.[80] The Electorate of Hanover invested in the name of the Regency and also for the support of various funds, including 'Benefit of Widows of Electoral Military Officers' and 'Hanoverian Hospitals of Invalids and the Military Pension Chest'.[81] Gonville and Caius College in Cambridge purchased £1,600 in the three per cent consols in December 1784.[82]

Also consistent with Dickson's findings is that, as shown in table 3.2, the market remained dominated by individuals who claimed a place of residence in London or the South East of England. Activity among provincial investors remained very low, although the number of individuals who might have been resident in the provinces but using a London address for the purpose of investment cannot be known. Perhaps surprisingly, there were very few transactions conducted by investors domiciled outside of Britain in the sample. This, however, was not representative of overall

80. Dickson, *Financial Revolution*, pp. 292–293.
81. BEA, Transfer books, passim.
82. Ibid.

ownership of the debt. J. F. Wright's careful analysis has shown that, with regard to the three per cent consols, in 1776 around 11 per cent of investors in this stock were domiciled overseas and they held around 20 per cent of the stock.[83] Nonetheless, foreign investment, and Dutch investment particularly, had declined during and after the War of American Independence.

Although Mortimer sought to depict the market as a mix of the duplicitous and the naïve, among the public creditors, there would have been a range of experience of trading and appetites for risk. The national debt served speculative aims, the holding of capital in anticipation of the emergence of other, more lucrative, opportunities or the diversification of a portfolio of investment and business activities. Thus, the merchant John Newman Coussmaker, who appears five times in the sample, purchased a total of £9,000 in the three per cent consols and at various points in the year.[84] For the more cautious investor, the funds might have been used for the building of a nest-egg against an anticipated retirement from paid work, the creation of an investment yielding a regular income or the provision to facilitate smooth inter-generational transfers. John Johnston, an illiterate lighterman, made a purchase of £14 5 shillings 8 pence in the three per cent consols in September 1784, which may have been for a similar purpose.[85] A great deal of the activity in the sample was substantial, and the average transaction amount was £759. The smallest amount traded was 4 shillings 6 pence between two gentlemen of the Stock Exchange and thus was probably a transaction relating to the adjustment of balances between the two individuals.[86] The largest amount transacted was £26,000, which related to the settlement of the estate of the deceased Charles Boddam.[87]

For many individuals their transactions would have been a matter of individual consideration and decision-making based on information available to them through printed media and conversations with market professionals. Others would have been influenced by conversations within families or households. As can be seen in table 3.3, around 6 per cent of buyers operated in groups. This was sometimes for the purpose of managing an estate or trust, but in other cases it might have been a way of

83. Wright, 'Overseas Savings', p. 666.

84. BEA, Transfer books, passim.

85. BEA, Transfer books, AC28/4268, 9 September 1784.

86. Between Thomas Fielder and Arthur Pratt. BEA Transfer books, AC28/4269, 8 December 1784.

87. BEA, Transfer books, AC28/4284, 7 December 1784.

Table 3.3. Gender of sellers and buyers of three per cent consols, 1784.

	Number of transactions	Buyer (%)	Number of transactions	Seller (%)
Male	2,422	81.03	2,762	92.41
Female	375	12.55	146	4.88
Company	12	0.40	11	0.37
Group—male	138	4.62	58	1.94
Group—female	6	0.20	0	0.00
Group—combined	36	1.20	12	0.40
Unknown	0	0.00	0	0.00

Source: BEA, Transfer books, passim.

pooling resources. Individuals also made their own purchases at the same time as others in their family or circles of acquaintance, indicating shared decision-making. In June 1784 three servants in the household of Sir Samson Gideon visited the Bank together to make purchases. Jonathan Partridge and Patrick Winter purchased £25 each and Ann Boardman purchased £50.[88] Also in June of that year Mary Garland and Elizabeth Garland visited the Bank at the same time. Both were servants but in different households. Mary made a purchase of £50 and Elizabeth bought £25 in the three per cent consols.[89]

Although the Rotunda was an overwhelmingly male space, as we can see in table 3.3 and in Rowlandson's depiction, there was also a significant minority of female investors who came to the Bank and were able to act on their own behalf. Mortimer characterised female investors as particularly vulnerable and advised that their male relatives act on their behalf. Rowlandson's depiction seems to suggest that some women were indeed accompanied by male connections. Nonetheless, modern scholarship has revealed women to have been capable of independent and assertive action.[90] As Amy Froide has shown, women used the public debt because of the 'decent rates of interest, their relative security, their reliability of payment, and for their easy liquidity'.[91] In the sample, the average female purchase was £437. The lowest amount was purchased by Elizabeth Rew, spinster and servant to Mr Sutton, who bought £12

88. BEA, Transfer books, AC28/2453, 8 June 1784.

89. Ibid.

90. Carlos, Maguire and Neal, 'Financial Acumen', pp. 219–243.

91. Amy Froide, *Silent Partners: Women as Public Investors during Britain's Financial Revolution, 1690–1750* (Oxford, 2017), p. 206.

Table 3.4. Occupation/social status of female sellers and buyers of three per cent consols, 1784.

	Seller	Seller (%)	Buyer	Buyer (%)
Unknown	6	4.11	12	3.14
Titled	1	0.68	1	0.26
Occupation	3	2.05	25	6.54
Spinster	54	36.99	186	48.69
Widow	54	36.99	137	35.86
Wife	28	19.18	21	5.50
Total	146		382	

Source: BEA, Transfer books, passim.

in the three per cent consols in September 1784.[92] The largest amount was purchased by Ann Allen, a spinster from Pembrokeshire. She bought £12,000 in the three per cent consols in March 1784.[93] As can be seen in table 3.4, the majority of female investors self-identified using their marital status, but there was also a group of women who gave their occupations. Of those, all but one were servants. Elizabeth Sinclair was a slopseller and purchased £600 in the three per cent consols in June 1784.[94]

The crowd in the Rotunda formed an open outcry market which helped lay the necessary foundation for the credibility of the state's financial promises. Indeed, as one anonymous pamphleteer writing in the mid-eighteenth century argued, public credit required an open market where people could complete their transactions with 'ease, readiness and dispatch'.[95] Another argued that investors appreciated the market because 'they can change their Property without Difficulty, and at a Small Expense'.[96] Whatever Mortimer would have had his audience believe, there is little consistent evidence to show that the ordinary public creditor was at risk in this market or was being manipulated by devious jobbers and brokers. Each element of the market was rather

92. BEA, Transfer books, AC28/4269, 9 September 1784.

93. BEA, Transfer books, AC28/4251, 6 March 1784.

94. BEA, Transfer books, AC28/4269, 8 June 1784.

95. Anon., *Reasons Humbly Offered to the Members of the Honourable House of Commons* (London, 1756?), quoted in Banner, *Anglo-American Securities Regulation*, p. 97.

96. Anon., *Some Considerations on Public Credit and the Nature of its Circulation* (London, 1733), quoted in Banner, *Anglo-American Securities Regulation*, p. 103.

essential to its smooth functioning, and different individuals with differing motivations came together to provide a reasonable level of efficiency and liquidity.

Managing the Market

The Rotunda was an impressive and intriguing place, but it was far more crowded and far less regimented and orderly than the banking hall. It was noisy and disruptive, with business on busy days spilling out into the transfer halls and disrupting the work of the clerks. It served a variety of purposes aside from the exchange of stock. It was a space where street sellers might have sought to ply their trades, had they been able to slip past the porters' sometimes watchful eyes. It was a place where tourists came to gawp at the jobbers and brokers at work. It was a place where certain types of businessowners, merchants and financiers came to be seen and to connect with others. As noted, it was a place where the performance of public credit could be observed. And it was a space where discussions encompassed the 'state of the world', national and international commerce, news and politics.[97] The changing prices of the debt being exchanged reflected this news and, in turn, the market participants' confidence in the state. The Rotunda was, therefore, a key site for the formation and communication of public opinion, an opinion which a state, ever concerned with its capacity for financial stability, ignored at its peril. The Bank, therefore, had cause to be concerned about its accommodation of the market and how that might have compromised, or been perceived to compromise, its connections with government and its position as the guardian of public credit.

One way in which the risks to the Bank could be managed was in the separation of the business of managing the debt from the other work of the institution. Thus, in Robert Taylor's 1760s extensions to the Bank, the Rotunda and transfer offices were made accessible only through the courtyard or through a separate entrance in Bartholomew Lane. In this way the relatively refined space of the banking hall was to be kept separate from the chaos of the market. Another way in which the Bank sought to demonstrate its separation from the chaos of the market was in the carefully managed operation of the processes which supported the transfer of the debt.

97. Preda, 'Enchanted Grove', p. 294.

The Inspectors spent a great deal of time in the transfer offices, thus allowing us to reconstruct this business in some detail.[98] In his testimony to the Inspectors, Mr Payne, the chief accountant, listed the transfer offices as follows:

1. The Office of the Bank Stock and Consolidated Long Annuities, under the supervision of Thomas Millington;
2. The Office of the Consolidated Reduced Annuities, under the supervision of Daniel Turner;
3. The Consolidated Three Per Cent Annuities (the Consols), under the supervision of Bowler Miller and Abraham Vickery. Their areas of control were divided alphabetically with Miller controlling transactions by public creditors with surnames starting A to K and Vickery L to Z;
4. The Office of the Consolidated Four Per Cent Annuities, supervised by Joseph Poole;
5. The Office of the Three Per Cent Annuities 1726 and the Consolidated Annuities for 28 years. This was located in the same office as the Three Per Cent Consols and was under the supervision of Nathan Dell.[99]

The largest of those offices was the Three Per Cent Consols Office. It employed fifty-four clerks, who worked under the supervision of Bowler Miller and Abraham Vickery. Vickery was quite a character. When he was first called in front of the Inspectors, he informed them 'that as soon as he heard this Committee was appointed, he informed all the Clerks under him that, when called before the Committee, he should openly & candidly declare all he knew concerning their conduct'.[100] Vickery was the only senior man who directly criticised his subordinates during the Inspection. His candour appears to have been primarily a cover for his own shortcomings. As such, he is a historian's delight, and we will return to his revelations. Clearly, however, he was one of those colleagues we all do our best to avoid.

Miller informed the Committee of Inspection that twenty-two ledgers, the records of individual accounts; twenty-two alphabets (or indexes); twenty-four dividend books; and forty-eight transfer books, in which

98. BEA, M5/213, passim. Mortimer also explains the process. Mortimer, *Every man his own broker*, pp. 137–145.

99. BEA, M5/212, fol. 205.

100. BEA, M5/213, fol. 63.

individual transactions were recorded, were in use in the office.[101] Supervising the work were three principal clerks: Miller, Vickery and an assistant in case of absence. Three men were charged with registering wills, and three with making out powers of attorney. The remaining men were divided into '4 subdivisions, A to E, F to K, L to R, & S to Z, but of this number are generally 8 to 10 absentees from illness or other causes'.[102] The men working in these subdivisions had the task of registering the transfers. They were divided into two groups: 'lookers' and 'enterers'. Lookers checked that the seller's account had sufficient funds, and enterers completed the transfer. In order to expedite the work of the lookers, a specially prepared abstract was made of the main jobbers' accounts since it was assumed that they would be at the Bank regularly and it was deemed more efficient to have their details to hand. These abstracts were also used as a running balance during the day. Following completion of the transaction, and usually the following day, the stock ledgers in which records of each public creditor's account were kept were updated.

There was an interesting contrast in the management approaches of Vickery and Miller. Vickery told the Inspectors that he had a

> place for himself inclosed, but he seldom attends there, as he is always about the Office; & avoids as much as possible applying himself to any particular business, conceiving the general inspection of the Office to be more immediately required of him. That Mr Miller is more employed in writing at his own desk, of which he does as much as any Clerk in the Office, but this prevents his giving so much attention to the other Clerks.[103]

Mr Turner of the Three Per Cent Reduced Office described a similar structure. In that office there were twenty-nine men—the chief clerk, two whose job it was to register wills, two who made out powers of attorney and three individuals for each alphabetised division. In each case there was one looker and two enterers.[104] Mr Turner told the Inspectors that 'the first 5 mentioned sit in an enclosed space at one end of the Office, where they are much crowded for want of room, which is a complaint throughout the Office'.[105] In the much smaller office, which dealt with the Consolidated 28 Year Annuities and the 1726 Annuities, there were only five staff, and the head of the office,

101. Ibid., fol. 60.
102. Ibid.
103. Ibid., fol. 63.
104. Ibid., fols. 42–43.
105. Ibid., fol. 42.

Nathan Dell, claimed 'the greatest harmony subsists in the Office, & without attaching themselves to any particular part of the business, each one applies himself to transact what is requisite to be done'.[106]

For the public creditors, the actual process of transferring government debt was straight-forward. The clerks operated what was known as the inscribed stock system, which simply meant that the transfer of any holding out of a stock-holder's name was achieved only when it was recorded in the Bank's books and that, likewise, the stock-holder's title was evidenced only by records kept at the Bank. Thus, no stock certificate was issued, and although the stock-holder received a receipt of the transaction, this served only as a memorandum. It was not legally binding.[107] Because of the way the system worked, personal attendance was required by the seller or their appointed attorneys.

The counterparties were required to inform the transfer clerks of their intention to make a transfer. They did this by writing out the names, titles and addresses of each party, along with the details of the fund and the amount. The example offered by Thomas Mortimer read as follows:[108]

John Jolly, Esq. of Southampton Street,
In the Parish of St. Paul, Covent-Garden,
100l. Three per Cent consolidated Bank Annuities.
To
James Goodman, Coal-Merchant, on Snow-Hill,
In the Parish of St. Sepulchre.

The form was then submitted to the appropriate transfer clerk. Mortimer advised public creditors to stay close to the desks so that they would hear their names when called, because 'if you are out of the way, the clerk will not wait for you, but proceed to other business'.[109]

---

106. Ibid., fol. 99.

107. BEA, AC4/5, An outline of the history and working of the inscribed stock system, fol. 2. See also BEA, AC4/1, A short history of the development of the system of transfer of British government stocks by instrument in writing.

108. Mortimer, *Every man his own broker*, p. 136.

109. Ibid., p. 131.

The buyer was also supposed to attend to sign his acceptance of the stock in the transfer book, but in practice, although it remained part of the constitution of the Bank, the requirement seems to have been dropped from around the 1760s onwards. The sample of transactions examined seems to confirm this practice. Using a signature in the transfer books as a proxy for attendance at the transfer office, only 6.42 per cent of sellers were not in attendance themselves, whereas 63.6 per cent of buyers did not sign the book to register their attendance for the completion of the transaction.[110] This does not indicate that they were not present for any negotiations conducted in the Rotunda or that they did not remain at the Bank to see the conclusion of the transaction. They would have wanted to receive their receipt, which was signed only after completion.

It was the role of the looker to establish the seller's capacity to transfer the stock. This involved making sure that the account had sufficient stock and that the seller had the right to act on their own behalf. In this respect, a book compiled in 1758 detailed a set of rules and opinions of counsel to be considered in the transfer of debt and the collection of dividends. They cover a multitude of circumstances, including actions to be taken in respect to the ownership of stocks by married women and minors. The former could not act without the consent of their husbands, and, at marriage, accounts standing in their unmarried name would be frozen. Nor would a newly married woman be able to manage her account without the permission of her husband.[111] Minors could accept stock but not dispose of it, and dividends were typically paid to their executors.[112] The book also records that a minor who came of age and then died did have the right of disposal of their stock, presumably through a will, even though they had never formally taken possession of that stock.[113] Someone either '(restored or) recover'd from his Lunacy' was allowed to act for themselves, providing they could produce a Revocation of the Commission of Lunacy'.[114]

Once the transaction was completed, a receipt was signed by the clerks. This was made up at the time of the transfer by the transferring parties using pre-printed forms that were made available for the public's use.

110. BEA, Transfer books, passim.

111. BEA, AC7/1, Rules necessary to be well understood for the true transacting of business, fol. 29.

112. Ibid., fol. 33.

113. Ibid.

114. Ibid., fol. 37.

Again, Mortimer reproduced the form; the elements required to be completed are in italics.

Consolidated *3l. per Cent Annuities, at 57 5/8*

Received this 10th Day of May, 1784, of *James Goodman, Coal-Merchant on Snow Hill*, the Sum of *Fifty-seven Pounds Twelve Shillings and Six Pence*, being the Consideration for *One Hundred Pounds* Interest or Share in the Joint Stock of Three-per Cent. Annuities, erected by an Act of Parliament of the Twenty-fifth Year of the Reign of King George II. intitled, An Act for converting the several Annuities therein mentioned into several Joint Stocks of Annuities, transferable at the Bank of England, to be charged on the Sinking Fund, together with the proportionable Annuity at 3l. per Cent. per Annum attending the same, by me this Day transferred to the said *James Goodman.*
    Witness my Hand,
Witness,   *John Jolly.*
[Here the Clerks sign]

Mortimer advised that the receipt be kept until such time as the first dividend had been received, which served to confirm the stock was registered in the correct name. Following this, the receipt should be destroyed, 'for by people's keeping them in families (at their death) they sometimes cause a great deal of confusion, especially among the lower sort of people; and prove great disappointments to many who think, in finding them, they have found a treasure'.[115]

The Inspectors judged the service provided as generally secure. They observed that 'so many checks [were] established as to render it scarcely possible that an error should be overlooked'.[116] They also noted the measures taken to protect the records of ownership of the public debt. Thus, each day an abstract of all transfers made was taken and put into the mail to be removed from the Bank overnight as a precaution against the loss of the records due to fire or some other accident. Records that had to remain in the Bank overnight were stored in wheeled trucks that could be easily rolled out of the Bank in an emergency. The Bank's processes were also subjected to, and stood up to, scrutiny. Much of the Bank's public-facing

115. Mortimer, *Every man his own broker*, p. 132.
116. Ibid., fol. 23.

business took place in open plan offices, which allowed the process of maintaining and recording ownership of the public debt to be observed.[117] The ledgers could be called upon and inspected either by individual public creditors or by those acting on their behalf.

The Bank's processes also generally complied with the requirements of the Acts of Parliament which established the funds. The Acts stipulated that the transfer books be kept open at all reasonable times so that the legal owners of the stocks, or their appointed attorneys, could transfer their holdings when they desired. Equally, they prohibited the taking of fees, rewards or gratuities 'for receiving or paying the said contribution moneys . . . or for any transfer of any sum, great or small, to be made in pursuance of this act'. A fine of £20 was to be levied against transgressors.[118] The buying, selling and transfer of government debt, therefore, was intended to be 'as free for a servant, who has only ten pounds to lay out, as for a merchant with twenty thousand'.[119]

The supposed equality of the public creditors was echoed in the testimony given to the Inspectors. Clerks in the Three Per Cent Consols Office claimed there was 'a constant rule in this Office to make no distinctions of persons, but to dispatch every one in the order he comes, as far as they are able to judge'.[120] Clerks also were on hand to assist those customers who were unsure of the process. Mr Drinkwater of the Three Per Cent Reduced Office told the Inspectors that 'sometimes a Stranger coming to make a Transfer will employ one of the Clerks to make out the ticket'. He also noted that, although it was not required, a two shillings and sixpence gratuity might be offered in exchange for this service.[121] Presumably, because the gratuity was voluntary, it did not violate the requirements of the Acts of Parliament. Although not usually specifically related to buying and selling stocks, a number of other functions in the Transfer Offices attracted gratuities. According to Mr Miller, these included registration of wills, 'private transfers' and making out powers of attorney. Gifts were also given by merchants who had long lists of dividends.[122] The sums that could accumulate through these arrangements seem to have been

117. I am indebted to Natalie Roxburgh for ideas about the transparency of the functions of the Bank of England, especially bookkeeping, and their value in demonstrating the integrity of public credit. Roxburgh, *Representing Public Credit*.

118. Mortimer, *Every man his own broker*, p. 149.

119. Ibid., p. 150.

120. BEA, M5/213, fol. 61.

121. Ibid., fol. 51.

122. Ibid., fol. 62. Unfortunately, the Minutes do not record what constituted a 'private transfer'.

considerable. The men in the Three Per Cent Reduced Office noted that they each received around £25 a year in gratuities.[123] The men in the Three Per Cent Consols Office gave a similar account, with Mr Crockford, one of the supervisors, noting that his share for the previous year had amounted to '£37 or £38'.[124] This system of exacting payment for enhanced service to the public once again went unchallenged by the Inspectors. Neither they nor the clerks wrote of those payments in any way that suggested the practice was regarded as corrupt.

There is no record that the public objected to the fees charged, but some were far from satisfied with other aspects of the service they received. In their testimonies to the Committee of Inspection, the clerks in the transfer and dividend offices repeatedly mentioned the stresses of working under pressure, the need to provide timely service to the public, and the number of customer complaints when that could not be achieved. In their fourth report, the Inspectors noted in particular the 'very frequent complaints, in regard to delays and inconveniences experienc'd by the Publick in receiving their Dividends'.[125] The problem was that transfers were often not completed before the Bank-imposed deadline of one o'clock, which then delayed the payment of dividends, which was not supposed to start until all transfers had been completed. The problem was exacerbated by the jobbers all putting their tickets in at around quarter to one and by the confined space in the offices, which often necessitated piling books on top of each other. The issue was common to all the transfer offices but particularly bad in the Three Per Cent Consols Office. In this office that meant that while the transfers were supposed to be completed by 1.00 P.M., the work invariably dragged on until 2.00 P.M. or later, thus delaying those who were waiting to collect their dividends.[126]

It is a measure of the importance of the service offered to the public creditors that the Committee spent 'a good deal of our time [ascertaining] how far the very frequent complaints, in regard of the delays & inconveniences experienc'd by the Publick in receiving their Dividends, are well founded, from what causes they arise, & to what degree they may be remedied'.[127] They concluded that the problem stemmed from conducting two types of business—transfers and the payment of dividends—in the same office. This

123. Ibid., fols. 49–53.
124. Ibid., fols. 82–85.
125. Ibid., fol. 136. See appendix 5 for complete text of the Inspectors' Fourth Report.
126. Ibid., fol. 68.
127. Ibid., fol. 136.

occasioned 'interruptions' and 'confusion'.[128] As was by now typical of their methods of working, the Inspectors consulted with key staff, including the chief accountant and the deputy accountant, the heads of the various offices and the most experienced clerks. Due consideration was given not only to the needs of the public but also to the requirements of the brokers and job-bers. They thus proposed separating the two elements by moving the issu-ing of dividends into its own office. To facilitate this, they suggested moving various offices and increasing the number of clerks to seven. This would allow, the Inspectors argued, changes 'extremely useful to the Publick & conducive to the honour of the Bank'.[129]

Managing the Clerks

Yet, while issues relating to the timeliness of service were addressed, the Inspectors found that the line the Bank had tried to create between its own functions and the market was blurred in a number of respects. The rela-tively open offices that helped to demonstrate the accountability of the Bank's processes also allowed persons who were familiar with the system to go behind the desks and peruse the ledgers whenever they pleased. The clerks protested, but as Mr Vickery noted, 'There are 2 or 3 Gentlemen of the first consideration in Trade who persist in doing so, notwithstanding his remonstrances against it'.[130] The market spilled out into the transfer offices on busy days, disrupting work and making the space difficult to manage. Most problematic, though, was the blurring of the lines between the Bank and the market that flowed from the Bank itself as the clerks who worked in the transfer offices supplemented their incomes by trading in the stocks and by acting as brokers and jobbers.

Paid involvement in the financial market was banned by the Bank since, in the view of the directors, such activity distracted the clerks, led to problems with the jobbers and brokers, and was incompatible with the Bank's attempts to assert its integrity as mediator between the state and its creditors. As the Inspectors noted, clerks who did indulge were in danger of having their minds seduced 'from regular employment in an easy service, & attaching them to objects inviting though dangerous'.[131] Nonetheless, it seems that the rules were commonly flouted. Hence, when the Inspectors took testimony from the clerks, they found numerous men

128. Ibid., fol. 141.
129. Ibid., fol. 142.
130. Ibid., fol. 64.
131. Ibid., fols. 173, 154.

acting in some capacity in the market. A total of sixty testimonies were recorded in the Minutes, and, of those, only twenty-four men stated they engaged in no activity in the secondary market. The types of activities mentioned included personal trading through brokers and jobbers who were regularly at the Bank. Thus, Mr Bibbins of the Bank Stock Office thought most of his colleagues were on

> such good terms with the Brokers that they rarely, if ever, charge them any brokerage, & he farther said, that if the business is to be transacted in the Stock of their Office they can allways do it without the intervention of a Broker, by speaking to one of the Jobbers, who will as readily deal with them as any other.[132]

Clerks were also clearly able to gain pecuniary advantage from those connections by buying and selling 'for their friends through the means of a Broker who generally allows them 2/3rds, & sometimes a larger proportion of the Commission'.[133] Some, however, were keen to distance themselves from the market in time bargains. Mr Carpenter of the Three Per Cent Consols Office acknowledged that he acted 'as a Broker in ready money transactions, but never deals for time'.[134]

Some clerks owned up to jobbing in the stocks. Mr Richardson of the Three Per Cent Reduced Office told the Inspectors that he did job in the reduced stock but only for immediate settlement and 'in partnership with a Person, not in the service of the Bank, who undertakes the whole management of it, & therefore it does not interfere with his [Mr Richardson's] business in this House'.[135] Mr Pearce of the Four Per Cent Consols Office similarly confessed that 'he jobs with some Stock of his own, which he has standing in his name, for which he employs a person who is allways in the Market, & that he never leaves the business of the Office to transact the jobbing by himself'.[136] Notable here is Richardson's and Pearce's claims that their jobbing did not interfere with their work. Mr Windsor said he had acted as a broker, and although he had not jobbed recently, 'he has now & then sold & bought a little stock which he has held for his friends'. Mr Crockford allowed that 'he had made Bargains in Stock for time, both on his own account & on that of his Principals'.[137]

132. Ibid., fol. 36.
133. Ibid., fol. 27.
134. Ibid., fol. 86.
135. Ibid., fol. 57.
136. Ibid., fol. 111.
137. Ibid., fols. 67, 84, 85.

A number of men attempted to claim that they did not know of any order against activity in the markets or relationships with brokers and job-bers.[138] This seems disingenuous at best. Governor Samuel Beachcroft's diary, which covered the period from 1775 to 1777, contained a number of references to anonymous informers against clerks acting as jobbers and brokers, suggesting that this kind of activity was brought to the Bank's attention on a regular basis. Moreover, Beachcroft's disapproval was passed on to the clerks. He recorded the following in his diary:

> Mr Pearce & Mr Pemberton were call'd in & reprimanded for dealing in Stocks by the Brokers transferring stock into their names & retrans-ferring said stock by way of cloak to the brokers name, upon their promising never to act again in the same manner they were forgiven . . . Mr Stonehouse & Mr Jewson were call'd in & order'd to acquaint every clerk in each of their departments that if they were found acting as brokers in future they would certainly be discharged.[139]

Beachcroft's admonishments seem to have made little impact. Both Pearce and Pemberton were still employed by the Bank in 1783 when the Com-mittee of Inspection convened, and both confessed to still being involved in the financial markets.[140] One possible explanation for why men contin-ued to act in the markets despite the Bank having rules to the contrary was offered by Mr Martin of the Three Per Cent Consols Office. He claimed that when he started work in the office 'he found it was customary for the Clerks to act as Brokers, & that it is well known that a great number do so constantly, & he therefore thought he might do like the rest'.[141]

Transfer office clerks, therefore, did have opportunities for taking advantage of their positions to generate additional earnings. Indeed, from the evidence of the Committee of Inspection, it appears that stock-jobbing and broking were practiced with worrying regularity by clerks who were, of course, in the right place at the right time. It is impossible to know how much these activities yielded. Some men undoubtedly dabbled occasion-ally in the markets, making a few pounds here and there. Others, especially those operating in partnerships with brokers, might have made significant profits. But it should also be acknowledged that such activities encom-passed some risk for the clerk. Mr Kingdon of the Three Per Cent Reduced Consols Office informed the Committee that while he did not regularly act

138. Ibid., fol. 96.
139. BEA, M5/451, fol. 76.
140. BEA, M5/213, fols. 111, 109.
141. Ibid., fol. 72.

as a jobber or broker, he had in the past purchased £2,000 stock on time for a friend who had later refused to accept the deal, leaving Mr Kingdon with a £150 debt.[142] Mr Shudall of the Three Per Cent Consols Office also confessed to having 'done business for time, & in one instance lost differences to the amount of £340, which his Principal left on his hands & he found means to settle'.[143]

Although the full story did not emerge at the time of the Committee of Inspection's report, one of the most interesting violators of the Bank's rules was Abraham Vickery of the Three Per Cent Consols Office. As noted above, he was the only one of the office heads to criticise his staff openly to the Inspectors, and he made a myriad of off-the-record complaints which were recorded in the private notebook kept by Samuel Bosanquet.[144] Many of those complaints touched on clerks operating in the markets. But also in the pages of Bosanquet's notebook we find other clerks' criticisms of Vickery. It seems that a number of clerks had poor relations with Vickery, that 'bad words' had been exchanged in a number of instances and that there was 'cause for discontent in the Consols Office against Mr Vickery'.[145] Moreover, Mr Nesbitt reported that Mr Vickery had many enemies in the Stock Exchange because he was viewed to have too close a connection with one of the brokers. Elsewhere in Bosanquet's notes it was recorded that it was not uncommon for Mr Vickery to 'desire a ticket to be put forward'—in other words, to ask for a transfer to be made ahead of its turn.[146] Nesbitt further noted that Vickery 'acts improperly & over rough with the clerks' and that he sometimes came late to work. Nesbitt himself was perceived by Bosanquet to have been intelligent, gentlemanlike and respectable, so his testimony might be judged as being reliable.[147] Other clerks too spoke of Mr Vickery as being a partner in a broking firm and privileging his own customers over those of the Bank. It is not possible for us to know precisely the rights and wrongs of the squabbles in the Consols Office, but one thing clearly emerges: the supposed separation between Bank and market was thoroughly compromised in the case of Abraham Vickery. Indeed, in the 1790s the Bank discovered that Vickery was still in a formal partnership with a stockbroker named Salmon. Having been required by the directors to dissolve the partnership, Vickery initially tried to bypass this by putting

142. Ibid., fol. 56.
143. Ibid., fols. 96–97.
144. BEA, M5/471, passim.
145. Ibid.
146. Ibid.
147. Ibid.

his share in his daughter's name. This was not sufficient for the directors, and Vickery was asked to dissolve the partnership. The connection, or its rewards, could not be given up so easily, though. A few years later Vickery was found to still be indulging in the stock-broking business, at which point he was forced into retirement from the Bank.[148]

It was noted above, and in the previous chapter, that when the Inspectors had been called upon to make a ruling about the issue of gaining additional earnings through gratuities, they proved themselves reluctant to ban the practice. They were much more determined on the issue of banning the clerks from broking or jobbing. In their fifth report they stated the following:

> As we are decidedly of opinion that the practice of the Clerks acting as Brokers or Jobbers is not only inconvenient & pernicious in itself, but that it may eventually lead to even fatal consequences by the powerful temptations it holds out to Men, not in affluent circumstances; we think the Court cannot too soon interpose its Authority, in order to put a stop to an evil of such magnitude.[149]

They asked for the order to be strictly enforced and transgression punished, including by dismissal if necessary. Wishing also to remove the possibility of future pleas of ignorance of the rules, they also ordered that there should be painted on the walls of the Rotunda and all transfer offices 'By order of the Court of Directors, the Clerks of the Bank are not permitted to act as Brokers or Jobbers in the Publick Funds'.[150]

By the middle of the eighteenth century, the Bank of England found itself in a most peculiar position. It was commissioned by the state to manage its debt and had used this to secure its position as the country's dominant financial institution. It was also the self-styled guardian of public credit, an institution which stood aloof as mediator between the state and its creditors. Yet, at the same time, it was the location of a market that was often criticised for its exploitation of the naïve public creditor and its supposed attempts to undermine the stability of the state by taking financial advantage of the exigencies of war. The Bank dealt with this by attempting to create both physical and business separation between the management of public credit and trading in government's debt.

---

148. Acres, *Bank of England from Within*, 1:244–245.
149. BEA, M5/213, fol. 155. See appendix 6.
150. Ibid., fol. 156.

The Inspectors found that, in this, the Bank was largely unsuccessful. The market encroached on the office spaces. The chief jobbers and brokers took advantage of their access to the Bank's inner spaces by going behind the desks to check ledgers, and dividend and transfer clerks were often tempted into jobbing and broking. Although they had declined to take action against the supplementing of salaries through gratuities, when it came to broking and jobbing, the Inspectors were forceful. They called upon the directors to strictly enforce the rules and set an expectation of the dismissal of clerks who violated those rules. The evidence provided by Vickery's subsequent career at the Bank would seem to indicate that clerks, nonetheless, continued to find ways to play the market. The Bank, in other words, failed to maintain the separation from the market that, to judge from its administrative and architectural arrangements, it deemed necessary to demonstrate its careful management of the state's debt.

We might argue that this fatally compromised the institution's claims to be the grand palladium of public credit or, at least, raised questions about its efficiency as a state contractor. The reality, however, is more complex. The location of the market within the Bank's walls served several useful purposes. It made the market easy to locate and accessible, if not always easy to negotiate. It allowed the visitor to the Bank to observe all the processes of providing public credit. Indeed, the Bank was undeniably a space in which public credit was put on display and the financial integrity of the state was demonstrated. From its grand architecture to the open-plan arrangement of the offices to the Rotunda where the brokers and jobbers gathered, visitors were invited to witness public credit at work.

Arguably, then, despite all the potential disadvantages of locating the market within the Bank, some wider and more important purposes were realised: those of exposing the functioning of the market in the state's debt to scrutiny and demonstrating the credibility of public credit. This tells us something about the nature of credible commitment. Rather than residing in state institutions that might have seemed rather nebulous in the eyes of most public creditors, perhaps by the mid-eighteenth century 'credible commitment' could be found and observed at the Bank of England. There, credibility lay in the provision of liquidity and a one-stop-shop in which all business relating to the public debt could indeed be done with 'readiness, ease and dispatch'.[151]

---

151. Anon., *Reasons Humbly Offered*, quoted in Banner, *Anglo-American Securities Regulation*, p. 97.

CHAPTER FOUR

Management and Neglect

AS THE CLERKS at the transfer desks were mopping up trailing business and closing their ledgers, the work of issuing dividend warrants commenced. This business was variable. There would have been days when few people were waiting to collect dividends and the clerks would have busied themselves with other work. The busiest times were those immediately following the dividend issue dates. Dividend payment was complicated in some offices by the need to confirm ownership of stock. This meant that all transfers were supposed to be completed before the collection of dividends. It was a rule rigidly adhered to in some offices, but Mr Poole of the Four Per Cent Consols told the Inspectors that they never delayed payment of dividends 'allways dividing their Hands in such a manner, that [it] may go on at the same time with the entry of Transfers'.[1] Such flexibility reflected lower volumes of business in the Four Per Cent Office but also a desire to meet the demands of the public creditors. It was a recognition that dividend payment was a key service and those public creditors who were kept waiting were unlikely to hold back their complaints.

Although dealing with impatient customers was clearly challenging, the process of issuing dividends was straight-forward since much of the preparation had been done when the books were closed. Once drawn up, the warrants were alphabetised and stored in sliding drawers to await collection. The preparation period was intensive. Mr Walsh of the Three Per Cent Consols Office noted that, at the previous 'shutting', the time allotted to the clerks for making up the warrants had been curtailed and 'they were obliged to work the whole Sunday preceding the payment, & the Clerks in general made exertions that to him were surprising, & without which, the

1. BEA, M5/213, fols. 107–108.

Dividend could not have been paid at the time appointed'.[2] The work done at that time, however, ensured a relatively smooth process of collection for public creditors. To further expedite the process, some of the systems of checks, including requiring a transfer to have been formally 'accepted' by the purchaser prior to dividend issue, had been waived. As Mr Vickery of the Three Per Cent Consols Office explained,

> If the non-acceptances were to be mark'd on the Warrants, & the Public required to accept all their Stock before they receive a Dividend, it would occasion an intolerable delay, besides a great confusion: for the Dividend payer would be obliged to go all over the Office to search for & procure the Transfer books wanted, while the number of persons coming for their Dividends would be constantly increasing, & making complaints that there was no Clerk stationed at the Book to deliver their Warrants to them.[3]

Although a nineteenth-century depiction, George Elgar Hicks's *Dividend Day at the Bank* (figure 4.1) offers a sense of the people who gathered and demanded the attention of the clerks. The image suggests a diverse crowd of public creditors but a change of pace from the frenetic work of the market and the press of brokers and jobbers seeking to register their transfers. Hicks's work shows the range of social classes collecting their dividends, the clearly affluent mixing with those lower down the social order. Women are prominent in the crowd, and there are depictions of those who were obviously past the working phase of their lives. Some of these individuals were dependent upon dividends as their sole or primary source of income. Thus, many public creditors would have collected their dividends as soon as they were issued. Nonetheless, collection could take place at any time of the customer's choosing, and warrants were retained against that eventuality. Mr Browning of the Bank Stock Office made mention of retaining the warrants for four years in his office, and, thereafter, they were stored in the Cheque Office until they were called for.[4]

There was always a risk that fraudulent attempts might be made to claim dividends, and thus public creditors were expected to sign for their warrants. The extent to which this provided a guarantee against fraud is questionable, but in 1787 a signature was the means of apprehending Francis Parr in his attempt to claim the dividend of Isaac Hart. Parr was

2. Ibid., fol. 103.
3. Ibid., fols. 119–120.
4. Ibid., fol. 24.

FIGURE 4.1. George Elgar Hicks, *Dividend Day at the Bank* (1859).
Source: Bank of England Museum accession 0187. © Bank of England.

a clerk to a broker and, therefore, had a good understanding of the Bank's
processes. This was sufficient to allow him initially to convince the issuing clerk of his claim. The suspicions of the clerk, Edward George, were
aroused because Parr 'had wrote a long J. in the name Isaac, and he put
his finger over it to make a short I'.[5] George then checked Parr's signature
against the signature in the previous dividend book and saw that they differed. He acted immediately on his suspicions, and Parr was apprehended
prior to his leaving the Bank. Although this type of fraud does not appear
to have been common, it clearly was a concern for the clerks and thus
Mr Ward recommended to the Inspectors that the ledgers 'be bound up
with a blotting paper between each leaf, which would prevent any person,
signing the Dividend book, from looking over more names than those contained on the page which his name stands on'.[6]

While work in transfer offices continued, elsewhere in the Bank footfall
was slowing. Regular customers would have known that midday was a

5. *Old Bailey Proceedings Online* (www.oldbaileyonline.org, version 8.0, 4 September 2021), January 1787, trial of Francis Parr (t17870115-1).
6. BEA, M5/213, fol. 93.

cut-off point in the banking hall for the management of bills and drafts.[7] As we have seen, the out-tellers' business began in the early morning and ended at midday, and although one of their number was commissioned to go out on a second walk at midday, for the remaining out-tellers their working day, at the Bank at least, had ended. The banking hall must have been far less busy at this time than it had been earlier in the morning. The focus of London financial and mercantile life was shifting to the other side of Threadneedle Street, to the Royal Exchange and the coffee houses of Exchange Alley. For merchants in particular, attendance at the Royal Exchange for the early-afternoon 'high' session was required.[8] Negotiations at the Exchange would have occupied them until three o'clock, and thereafter many would have dined. The brokers and jobbers switched their location to the coffee houses of Exchange Alley, where the afternoon activity in time bargains was concentrated, or to the new Stock Exchange to connect with their fellow market professionals and consolidate their positions.

The Bank's clerks took the opportunity afforded by the reduced numbers of customers to take a break from work. Because cover at the various desks had to be maintained, dining times reported to the Inspectors show an ordered and coordinated pattern of absences and demonstrate the importance of the clock in regulating the work of the various offices.[9] The clerks' return to work following dinner ushered in a new phase of the day. A number of offices, including the Bullion Office, the Cheque Office and the Office of the Secretary of the Bank, closed their doors. At this time of the day, many of the senior men considered their work to be complete and they left the Bank to spend the late afternoon at leisure. Some clerks at the lower end of the pay scale finished work in the mid-afternoon but could not afford the luxury of leisure time. Instead, they prepared to take up second jobs, either at the Bank or elsewhere.

This chapter will explore the rhythms of the mid-afternoon and what they can tell us about the clerks' habits outside of the office and the ways in which the work of the Bank and the work of the City were interconnected. However, given the early departure of the senior men, the primary focus of the chapter will be the management of the Bank. What follows will note the managerial hierarchy, taking account of the fitness for management of the senior men and the qualifications of their juniors on whom much of

7. BEA, M5/212, fols. 22–23.

8. Gauci, *Emporium of the World*, p. 61.

9. Anne L. Murphy, 'Clockwatching: Work and Working Time at the Late-Eighteenth-Century Bank of England', *Past and Present*, 236 (2017), pp. 99–132.

the burden of managing the end-of-day procedures would fall. Finally, the rewards and punishments that kept men loyal to the Bank and working in its interests, even in the absence of direct supervision, will be explored.

Dining Out

Dinner, taken in the mid- to late afternoon, was the main meal during the late eighteenth century. The Bank's clerks were, for the most part, permitted to take ninety minutes for dinner, sufficient time to walk to an eating-house and dine at relative leisure. In order to ensure that all clerks had the opportunity for a break while maintaining sufficient cover in the various offices, dinner times were regulated. Thus, Mr Collins, the keeper of the G cash book, noted that there were three clerks working in his section and 'one of them goes to dinner at 1 & returns at 3, another goes off at 2 & returns at ½ past 3, & the third goes off at 3' and, if business was quiet, sometimes did not return.[10] Among the tellers in the banking hall, four or five went to dinner at 1:00 P.M. and returned at 2:30 P.M.; the remainder then went to dinner and returned at 4:00 P.M.

Not all offices allowed a break for dinner. Under some circumstances clerks may have eaten at their desks. Samuel Beachcroft's diary notes that 'the weighers of light guineas' were to be allowed some bread, cheese and porter every day at one o'clock but 'by no means [was their supervisor] to suffer any ale house boy to attend'.[11] Other offices did not allow a break, because they closed early. In the Drawing Office, which closed at 3:00 P.M., there was an expectation that men would dine after work. Only the clerk whose job it was to close the office for the day and who was expected to stay until 5:00 P.M. was 'allow'd an absence of 2 hours for dinner, from 1 to 3, the rest never go out to dinner, but if the business is very heavy a dinner is allow'd them in the Office'.[12] Other offices operated a mixed model. Mr Campe, the senior in-teller, reported that on quiet days he would make the decision to leave early and would allow some men under him to do the same, but in that case they were not allowed to have a dinner break.[13]

Although there was no suggestion that men should forgo dinner, there was acknowledgement of the problems created by absences in sparsely staffed departments. Hence, the keeper of the H cash book commented, 'That this Book is generally left with only one Clerk, during the hours of

10. BEA, M5/212, fol. 108.
11. BEA, M5/451, fol. 60.
12. BEA, M5/212, fol. 59.
13. Ibid., fol. 36.

Dinner; a circumstance very disagreeable to the Clerks themselves, as it is attended with much Risque'.[14] Mr Jones of the Drawing Office pointed to the problems of cover during public holidays, when only half the usual number of clerks were in the office and generally only one senior man. This meant that during one of the two scheduled dinner breaks, there would be no supervisor in attendance.[15]

Cruikshank and Burton suggest that the dining hour was not fixed during the eighteenth century; however, the clerks who dined at one o'clock probably were eating a little earlier than their counterparts.[16] Other City-dwellers noted three o'clock, after the closing of the Exchange, as dinner time.[17] For the clerks who ate out, there were plenty of 'comfortable, convenient . . . commodious' and affordable cook-shops, eating-houses, taverns and coffee houses.[18] Cook-houses served broth, meat and bread, sometimes for as little as a few pence. The more affluent clerks might have dined at a chop-house, as depicted in Rowlandson's image (figure 4.2). There they would have found,

> Generally four spits, one over another, carry round each five or six pieces of Butcher's meat (never anything else; if you would have a fowl or a pidgeon you must bespeak it). Beef, Mutton or Veal, Pork and Lamb; you have what quantity you please cut off, fat, lean, much or little done; with this, a little salt, and mustard upon the side of a plate, a Bottle of beer, and a roll.[19]

There is no indication of the clerks' dining habits in the Minutes but no reason to doubt that dinner was an opportunity for them to socialise with each other. It is likely that friendships formed within and across offices. There were business connections between men who might have been brokers or jobbers on behalf of their fellow clerks and that might have prompted men to dine together. Dinner may also have allowed men to connect with family members working at the Bank. There were numerous family connections amongst the staff, especially fathers and sons as well as siblings. Direct evidence of collegial working relationships is offered by an incident in June 1782 when a group of seven Consol Office clerks failed to return to work after dining together in Lime Street, about a ten-minute

14. Ibid., fol. 98.
15. Ibid., fol. 87.
16. Cruikshank and Burton, *Georgian City*, p. 29.
17. Ibid.
18. Ibid., pp. 32–33.
19. Ibid., p. 32.

FIGURE 4.2. Thomas Rowlandson, *An Eating House* (c. 1815).
Source: Metropolitan Museum of Art, The Elisha Whittelsey Collection, The Elisha Whittelsey Fund, 1959, CCO.

walk from the Bank.[20] Their excuse was that it had started to rain and thus they stayed where they were. Given that these men would have walked to and from work in all kinds of weather, it seems a poor excuse, and we may speculate that the conversation was perhaps so distracting, or the beer so free-flowing, that the office was quite forgotten.

Closing Early

By three o'clock most of the clerks would have returned from dinner. Only the tardy might have remained finishing their meal or taking a leisurely walk back to the office. There was plenty to divert them in the vicinity of the Bank. They may have stopped to read the news or study stock market prices from the notices posted on the pillars at the Royal Exchange or in the windows of the coffee houses. Given the importance of men as consumers during the eighteenth century, they may have dawdled past shops looking in the windows at displays or shopping for themselves or their families.[21] Visitors to London marvelled at the array of shops, 'fashion

20. Ibid., p. 234.
21. Margot Finn, 'Men's Things: Masculine Possession in the Consumer Revolution', *Social History*, 25 (2000), pp. 133–155.

articles or silver or brass shops—boots, guns, glasses—the confectioner's goodies, the pewterer's wares' and the tempting displays 'and in such abundance of choice as almost to make one greedy'.[22]

Business at the Bank wound down by three in the afternoon. Mr Barber observed that his shift with the banknote printer finished around that time and he returned to the Bank and deposited the printing plates safely back in the warehouse.[23] Mr Holmes of the Drawing Office told the Inspectors that business there 'on a common day is over about 2, or before 3 o'clock'.[24] The transfer offices were also closed by three o'clock, as was the Secretary's Office. Aside from attending the Bank's Court to take the minutes of meetings, the secretary's role was primarily to draw and validate legal documents in relation to transactions. Thus, he dealt with all letters of attorney and drew up 'Bonds & Covenants for lost Notes, & the Servants Security Bonds, [and] the forms of Affidavits'. He also attended to 'the stopping of the Notes, & [kept] Copies of all Instruments passing the Court'.[25] The bulk of his business, therefore, had to be carried out when the Bank was at its most active.

These closures are a further indication of the extent to which the Bank followed the rhythms of the City. Access to accounts did not need to be maintained after three in the afternoon, when the majority of the business community were occupied at the Exchange or were dining. For the same reason, the Bullion Office closed its doors at that time.[26] This office managed the purchase of bullion on the Bank's own account. Indeed, under the Bank's Charter it had the right to trade in gold and silver, and it did so throughout the eighteenth century, most prominently through the firm of Mocatta and Goldsmid.[27] Once again, however, the Bullion Office was most obviously aligned with the needs of other businesses and financiers in the City. One of its roles was 'to receive & deliver the Bullion which comes from abroad on Merchants Accounts'.[28] Thus, the Office managed

22. Sophie von La Roche, *Sophie in London—1786, Being the Diary of Sophie v. la Roche*, trans. Clare Williams (London, 1933), quoted in Alison F. O'Byrne, 'Walking, Rambling and Promenading in Eighteenth-Century London: A Literary and Cultural History' (unpublished PhD thesis, University of York, 2003), pp. 213–214.

23. BEA, M5/212, fol. 127.

24. BEA, M5/213, fol. 13.

25. Ibid., fol. 148.

26. BEA, M5/212, fol. 132.

27. Giuseppi, *Bank of England*, pp. 47–48; see also Paul H. Emden, 'The Brothers Goldsmid and the Financing of the Napoleonic Wars', *Transactions (Jewish Historical Society of England)*, 14 (1935–1939), pp. 225–246.

28. BEA, M5/212, fol. 130.

the transport and storage of bullion on behalf of its owners. If bullion was sold, the Office's role was to 'turn out, examine & weigh it, & to deliver it to the Buyer'.[29] Although this business was also managed by independent gold brokers, by the mid-eighteenth century, according to evidence given to the House of Commons by the goldsmith George Masterman, 'all Captains of Men of War make it a rule to go to the Bank', whereas merchantmen would sometimes sell initially to a gold broker or goldsmith, who would keep what he needed and then carry the remainder to the Bank.[30]

Closures at, or by, three o'clock also reflected the internal rhythms of the Bank. The business of the Cheque Office was 'on a common day . . . over about 2 o'clock'.[31] This office was directly connected to the work of the transfer offices and dividend payments. It kept a 'duplicate of the Dividend books in the several Annuity Offices'.[32] Using these records, the clerks were able to check the paid dividend warrants against the dividend books and thus could not undertake this work while the books were in use. With the winding down of business in the banking hall and its surrounding offices, the Chief Cashier's office was also 'shut up' at three in the afternoon, at which point Mr Newland and his deputy left the Bank.[33]

Indeed, although it was not the case in every office,[34] it was revealed to the Inspectors that the majority of the senior men left the Bank at this time. Thus, Mr Church, the chief clerk in the Bill Office, left the Bank at about three o'clock every day.[35] Mr Rawlins, acting principal of the K cash book, stated that by 'custom' the senior man only stayed until three o'clock.[36] Mr Campe, chief in-teller, generally left the Bank by three o'clock.[37] It is not clear how these men would have occupied themselves during what remained of the day, and doubtless some might have been tending to other work in the late afternoons. Yet, it also seems reasonable to assume that once clerks had attained the highest office available to them within the Bank, they chose to take additional leisure time. This certainly seems to have been the case for Abraham Newland, who, according to a biography produced after his death in 1807, spent his afternoons and evenings at

29. Ibid.

30. L. Stuart Sutherland, 'The Accounts of an Eighteenth-Century Merchant: The Portuguese Ventures of William Braund', *Economic History Review*, 3 (1932), p. 371.

31. BEA, M5/212, fol. 6.

32. Ibid., fol. 205.

33. Ibid., fol. 146.

34. See, for example, the Drawing Office, BEA, M5/212, fol. 85.

35. BEA, M5/212, fol. 18.

36. Ibid., fol. 99.

37. Ibid., fol. 36.

his house in Highbury, drinking tea, playing cards and engaging in 'free, unreserved communication with a few intimates'.[38]

Although almost certainly a long-standing custom by the time of the Inspection, the early departure of the senior men was something at which the Inspectors claimed surprise. They stated in their final report that they regarded it as

> impossible that [the practice] ever could have received the deliberate approbation of a Court of Directors; & however Time may have sancti-fied the custom, the reverse of it would have appeared a much more natural regulation: for surely if in any situation of Trust a compleat superintendence is desireable, it must be more immediately necessary where the Trust is of such infinite importance.[39]

The Inspectors went on to recommend to the Court of Directors that ways be found to ensure that the chief accountant and the chief cashier or their deputies remain in the Bank 'to exercise a general superintending care' until it closed and was made secure.[40]

It was not just senior men who left the Bank in the mid-afternoon. Junior clerks working in the offices that closed early also would have left around three o'clock. Others were permitted to leave at that time as staffing was reduced in some offices. Thus, of the eight cashiers in the hall, four took a break for dinner, and on their return the other four were allowed to leave the office.[41] Mr Windsor of the Three Per Cent Consols Office observed that 'whenever the business will allow, some few of the Clerks are permitted to quit the Bank at ¼ or ½ an hour before 3 o'clock'.[42] The financial circum-stances of the more junior men, however, were unlikely to have afforded them the opportunity to spend the rest of the afternoon at leisure.

Other Sources of Income

Overall, the pay and promotion profile at the Bank placed its senior clerks firmly in the ranks of the middling sorts. However, their more junior colleagues remained financially vulnerable, with some, in all likelihood, just clinging to respectability. The starting wage of £50 per annum had not changed since the Bank's establishment in 1694, and this was barely

---

38. Collier, *Life of Abraham Newland*, p. 101.
39. BEA, M5/213, fol. 174. See appendix 7.
40. BEA, M5/212, fol. 174.
41. Ibid., M5/213, fol. 117.
42. BEA, M5/213, fol. 83.

sufficient for life in London by the end of the eighteenth century. According to one anonymous pamphleteer writing in 1767, the notion that fifty pounds a year was a fitting wage for clerical workers was 'as absurd and impudent, as it is false and malignant'.[43] The author went on to calculate a budget which depended on living in the meanest parts of London, being clothed in plain style, staying just clean enough to keep one's place and taking little opportunity for leisure but yet still being left with little to put aside against sickness or old age.[44]

Thus, junior men leaving the office early might have gone on to a second job, kept an interest in their previous employment or business or spent time managing investments that might have supplemented their incomes. Evidence relating to the cohort of 1783 is rather sketchy, but in the early nineteenth century the Bank made registration of additional employment compulsory. At that time a number of the cohort of 1783 were still employed by the institution and some registered second jobs. Henry Vonholte, Christopher Olier and William Mullens were coal merchants. Isaac Cooper and Charles Stuart were wine merchants. Thomas Reid was a tobacconist. Other men acknowledged jobs which seem more obviously to be amenable to part-time working. William Caulier was a pen cutter. Jeremiah Kelly was an agent to a Yorkshire carpet manufacturer. Thomas Brennand performed the same function for Mr Greenwood, a dealer in patent medicines.[45] Other men had second jobs within the Bank, particularly, as we shall see, in managing accounts.[46] For these men, once their regular working day ended, usually around two or three in the afternoon, they were employed, at a small additional salary, in posting bills and notes into the Discount Ledgers. This was work that could not start until late in the working day and had to be completed prior to the start of the next working day, which sometimes necessitated working into the late evening.[47]

Insurance records indicate that clerks also made investments to supplement their incomes. John Holland and Jacob Coulthard, both clerks at the Bank, together insured various properties and businesses in Lad Lane, including the tap house of the Swan Inn, a barber shop, a counting house, stables and lodging rooms.[48] Others had more modest property

43. Anon., *Considerations on the Expediency of Raising Wages*, p. 5.
44. Ibid., pp. 5–10.
45. BEA, M5/691, Register of clerks in business, passim.
46. See chapter 5.
47. See, for example, BEA, M5/213, fols. 6–7.
48. London Metropolitan Archive (hereafter LMA), MS 11936/427/740354.

portfolios. Seawallis Larchin owned a house in Chelsea that was, in 1786, valued at £300. It was standing empty at the time but had been rented out to a Captain Pakenham.[49] Thomas Nisbett, of the Three Per Cent Consols Office, owned a house in Gracechurch Street, which in 1794 was valued at £800 and rented to a haberdasher.[50]

The departure of many of the clerks either to attend to their other business interests or to spend the afternoon at leisure indicates the extent to which business had slowed in many parts of the Bank by the mid-afternoon. Yet, the banking hall remained open until 5:00 P.M. and the vaults and warehouse remained accessible, as did the majority of ledgers. As we shall see in the next chapter, the business of managing the Bank's accounts continued and even increased towards the end of the day. More-over, the business of closing up the offices and locking away cash and paper money remained to be done. These tasks were left in the hands of men who were always junior in post: the clerks-in-waiting. The depar-ture of the senior men, therefore, raises questions about the quality of the management of the Bank, the ways in which supervision operated and the possible risks of leaving the Bank in the hands of the more junior men.

The Question of Management

The highest levels of management at the Bank of England were the gov-ernor, deputy governor and 24 directors. These men were elected from amongst the most prominent shareholders with the qualifying share-holding for a governor being £4,000. It was £3,000 for a deputy gover-nor and £2,000 for a director.[51] Together they formed the Court of Direc-tors and committed themselves by oath to 'be "indifferent and equall to all manner of persons" and to give their best advice and assistance for the support and good government of the corporation'.[52] None were paid employees, although the governor and the deputy governor each received an allowance of £200 per annum, while each director received £150 per annum.[53] The directors tended to be affluent businessmen, often bankers or merchants. Although some of the more prominent directors inevitably had close links to government, relatively few of them were, or became,

---

49. LMA, MS 11936/341/526365.

50. LMA, MS 11936/399/634968.

51. Elizabeth Hennessy, 'The Governors, Directors and Management of the Bank of England', in Roberts and Kynaston, *Bank of England*, p. 185.

52. Ibid.

53. Acres, *Bank of England from Within*, 1:91.

Members of Parliament (MPs). Indeed, of the 133 men who became directors between 1735 and 1792, only fifteen became MPs.[54] On average, a directorship was attained when a man was in his mid-forties, and those who rose to the governorship were generally in their mid- to late fifties.[55] They were men who were clearly successful in other aspects of their life, but they were often, as Bagehot later described them, 'amateurs'.[56] Their roles within the Bank depended very much on their willingness to learn about and involve themselves in its business. Some were exceptionally diligent. Others failed to attend meetings and made little contribution to the operation of the institution.

The Bank's bye-laws stipulated that not more than sixteen of those who had been directors in each year could stand for re-election in the following year.[57] In practice, however, it was usually only the relatively junior directors who stepped down, and once a director had served as either deputy governor or governor he was said to have 'passed the chairs' and was no longer required to step down.[58] Some directors, therefore, gave long and unbroken service to the Bank. Clapham's analysis noted several who served for over thirty years, including, during the late eighteenth century, Samuel Beachcroft, who served, albeit with a couple of short breaks, from 1760 to 1796, and Richard Neave began as a director in 1763 and continued until well into the nineteenth century. One of the Inspectors, Samuel Bosanquet, commenced his directorship in 1771 and was still serving in 1806.[59]

Although the Court of Directors met weekly, day-to-day management was dominated by the Bank's senior men and the various committees that were appointed to superintend business and make strategic decisions. The Bank's governor had a general oversight, and the various preserved governors' diaries record involvement in a wide variety of business. James Sperling was governor between 1773 and 1775, and the majority of his time, as recorded in the diary, was spent in attending the prime minister, receiving information about outstanding debts, considering petitions and managing property.[60] Samuel Beachcroft was governor from 1775 to 1777, and his diary reveals similar concerns but also a willingness to get involved

54. Kynaston, *Time's Last Sand*, p. 47.
55. Ibid., p. 45.
56. Quoted in Kynaston, *Time's Last Sand*, p. 208.
57. Acres, *Bank of England from Within*, 1:90.
58. Hennessy, 'Governors', p. 189.
59. Clapham, *Bank of England*, 1:199.
60. BEA, M5/450, Governor's Diary—James Sperling, passim.

with more of the day-to-day management, including the disciplining of clerks and approving the choice of curtains for the Bullion Office.[61]

The committees also had significant responsibility for day-to-day affairs. The Committee for Building was responsible for the maintenance of the current buildings and new accommodations under construction.[62] The Committee in Waiting was constantly constituted to superintend the day-to-day running of the Bank. It comprised a rota of directors who were expected to attend daily to oversee the management of the Bank, including advances and discounts. There were two standing committees during the 1780s—the Committee for House and Servants and the Committee for the Accounts and for the Treasury, usually known as the Committee of Treasury.[63] The former was established to manage the appointment and disciplining of staff and included eighteen of the directors.

It was the Treasury Committee, however, that was most prominent. Its membership was the governor, deputy governor and a selection of senior directors, usually those who had 'passed the chairs'.[64] It was regarded by one critic of the Bank, Alderman William Pickett, as a 'dark and concealed system of management' which sat and made decisions 'without the deliberation of the whole Court'.[65] The Committee's Minutes certainly show it to have been taking significant decisions. In April 1783, for example, in the closing months of the War of American Independence, the Committee discussed variously loans to the East India Company (EIC), negotiations with Lord North and Lord John Cavendish (then chancellor of the Exchequer), the state of the coinage, attempts to import gold from Lisbon and the procurement of guineas from Holland.[66] The latter actions related to a serious bullion shortage experienced by the Bank during the early 1780s and as a consequence of the War of American Independence.[67] As these examples show, throughout the Committee of Treasury's Minutes, the close relationship with the business of government is obvious.

61. BEA, M5/451, passim.

62. BEA, M5/748. The Committee for Building Minutes are also available in digitised form: https://www.bankofengland.co.uk/archive/committee-for-building-minutes.

63. BEA, M5/376. No Minutes for the Committee of Treasury survive before 1779, from 1779 BEA, Minutes of the Committee of the Treasury, G8.

64. In 1783 the Treasury Committee was Edward Payne, Samuel Beachcroft, Peter Gaussen, Daniel Booth, William Ewer and Edward Darell. BEA, G4/23, fol. 363.

65. William Pickett, *An apology to the Public for a continued Intrusion on their Notice with an Appeal to the free and independent Proprietors of Bank Stock, demonstrating that it is highly proper for them to examine into the State of their Affairs* (London, 1788), p. 36.

66. BEA, G8/2–3, Minutes of the Committee of the Treasury, unpaginated.

67. Kynaston, *Time's Last Sand*, p. 56.

Yet, they also illustrate the limits of the Bank's willingness to accommodate the state. Indeed, the bullion shortage so concerned the directors at that time that they refused for a period of six months to authorise the Bank's usual advances to government. As Kynaston argues, in doing so they 'played a difficult hand with considerable adroitness'.[68] The Bank's refusal to fund the loan meant that the state became dependent on the resources of the money market. There followed a tightening of credit which eased the bullion drain. This episode was identified by Feaveryear as the first identifiable occasion on which the Bank attempted to control the money markets.[69]

Clapham accepted Pickett's account of the prominence of the Treasury Committee. He found that some 'important business' was not presented to the Court of Directors and that the Court's Minutes showed little active discussion of the business that was presented to them.[70] The Court of Directors, Clapham concluded, were 'not at all eager or enterprising'.[71] Yet, even the record of meetings of the Treasury Committee shows it to have been particularly active only at times of crisis or economic stress. Notably, it met sixteen times in April 1783, including several times on a Saturday, and an average of 8.6 times a month in the five months preceding. After the end of the war, however, the frequency of the meetings changed. The Committee met only an average of two times per month in the six months from October 1783 to March 1784.[72] During the times that the business was proceeding as normal, there is every indication that directorship was rather 'light touch'.

The Bank's shareholders might have been expected to act to hold the directorate accountable for their actions, or indeed their lack of action. Those shareholders eligible to attend could express their views in the General Court, which met four times a year and as needed to consider the renewal of the charter or when a vacancy in the directorate occurred.[73] Yet, during the early 1780s, only around 100 to 130 of the more than 2,000 shareholders eligible to vote attended meetings.[74] Thus, although the shareholders theoretically had the right to influence the management

68. Ibid., p. 57.

69. A. E. Feaveryear, *The Pound Sterling: A History of English Money* (Oxford, 1931), pp. 176–177; Kynaston, *Time's Last Sand*, p. 57.

70. Clapham, *Bank of England*, 1:202.

71. Ibid., 1:173.

72. BEA, G8/2–3, unpaginated.

73. Hennessy, 'Governors', p. 189.

74. Clapham, *Bank of England*, 1:201.

decisions taken by the Bank, they did not exercise it, at least not while things were going well and dividends were being paid regularly.

The Bank's directors, therefore, made strategic and high-level decisions when required, but the quality of their management was not consistent, their attention was often divided between the Bank and their own business concerns and they were certainly less active at times when there was no obvious threat to the institution. The shareholders, who might have held the directors to account, generally failed to exercise their rights. Much of the management of day-to-day business, therefore, fell to the clerks. As does a civil service, they remained the permanent, knowledgeable and skilled presence required to compensate for the sometimes inadequate attentions of their masters.

Rising through the Ranks

Although we have seen that senior clerks were sometimes neglectful of their roles and junior clerks were not always mindful of their subordinate positions, the Inspection still revealed a clear hierarchy at the Bank. The term 'management' was used, albeit sparingly, in the Committee of Inspection's Minutes, indicating that there was an expectation that business be organised and ordered.[75] The term 'manager' was not used at all, but the report contains the term 'supervisor,' especially with regard to the transfer offices, and speaks of the superintendence of business. It also makes numerous mentions of the terms 'superior' and 'chief', with regard to chief men, and as a common description for the head of an office.[76]

Notwithstanding some resistance to the hierarchical structure from junior men, the senior clerks generally found it straight-forward to articulate the theoretical structure and organisation of their departments. As we have seen, when Abraham Newland, the chief cashier, was called before the Committee of Inspection, he presented a list of the offices under his control. Payne, the chief accountant, did likewise for the offices under his control. In a modern business these structures would be expressed as organisational flowcharts. A 'descriptive, linguistic system' of analysis, however, is typical throughout the Inspectors' report and is the way inspections were conducted within the Bank and elsewhere over the next century or so.[77] Consistent with that approach, the chief men's overviews

75. BEA, M5/212, fols. 1,123, 136; BEA, M5/213, fols. 173, 179.

76. BEA, M5/212; BEA, M5/213, passim.

77. A. McKinlay and R. G. Wilson, '"Small Acts of Cunning": Bureaucracy, Inspection and the Career, c. 1890–1914', *Critical Perspectives on Accounting*, 17 (2006), p. 658.

were further explored in specific interviews about the way particular offices worked and interacted with each other. Thus, Mr Newland supplemented his testimony by describing the hierarchies in the offices under his control:

> [He] was called in & ask'd in what light he consider'd the Clearers: He said, the two Juniors are accountable to Mr Pamphilion the senior Clearer & are bound to follow his directions; their Office is separate from the Bill Office & they are accountable only to himself as Chief Cashier. Mr Newland inform'd the Committee that the OutTellers are not immediately under the Senior OutTeller so as to be oblig'd to follow his directions; but are accountable to Mr Church in the first instance. That the InTellers are immediately under Mr Campe, the senior, & he is expected to attend to their good behaviour.[78]

It is also possible to read between the lines of the Inspectors' reports and find evidence of the control that the senior men exercised, or failed to exercise, over some aspects of their subordinates' lives. We have already seen that Mr Vickery made the lives of the men in his office difficult at times. Other senior men noted their capacity to give men leave to be absent or depart the office early.[79] During the latter stages of the Inspection we can also observe concern with whether better working conditions could be secured by making presents to senior men. Thus, Mr Gribble of the Accountants Office told the Inspectors that he had never heard 'of any presents being made to the Heads of the Office by an inferior Clerk for any indulgence'.[80] All his fellows who were asked made the same statement, but given that the Inspectors asked this question on several occasions, there must have been some suspicion that it was, or had been, the practice in some offices.

The men, therefore, understood, in a variety of ways, that there was a reporting structure outside of the directorship, and discussion of obligations and indulgences, along with the use of words like 'accountable' and 'obliged', confirms that the senior men were, in theory at least, responsible for the organisation and efficiency of their part of the business, empowered to issue instructions and could expect those instructions to be heeded. Equally, the Committee of Inspection overtly acknowledged the hierarchies that existed by always turning first to the senior men in each

78. BEA, M5/212, fol. 29.
79. See, for example, BEA, M5/212, fol. 36.
80. BEA, M5/213, fol. 5.

office. In doing so they validated the managerial system that had been put in place.

The men who attained higher offices in the Bank rose through the ranks. The institution operated an internal labour market, in which men were recruited only at entry level and on an initial £50 per year salary. Records relating to employment and training practices do not survive for the period under consideration, but the Bank does hold some incidental records from the early eighteenth century and comprehensive records from the early nineteenth century. The processes themselves were of long-standing, having been brought in soon after the Bank opened in order to avoid recruiting men who were unfit for the role.[81] Thus, it is possible to use records relating to other points during the long eighteenth century to make some assumptions about the backgrounds and capacities on entry of the clerks employed in 1783.

The opportunity to work at the Bank was determined by patronage, and thus the first hurdle an applicant would have encountered was making contact with one of the directors to seek their nomination for a post.[82] For some men this would have meant a straight-forward exploitation of a personal connection. Mr Gould's petition was supported by R. Reynell, a kinsman of Gould's who had, he claimed, spoken to one of the directors 'yesterday in the House of Commons with Relation to [Gould's] indeavours to be A servant to the Bank'.[83] For others it would have been a more complicated affair and one that might have involved payment of a considerable sum. In his diary Samuel Harrison described his application process as a financial transaction. He recorded,

> Mr Madden, who had often promised to get me into the Bank, hearing with astonishment I was possessed of £100 at once set to work, and actually to the disbelief of my mother got me a nomination for which I gladly paid him the £100 and £20 more. I had then letters to write to the Governor, Deputy Governor and twenty-four directors soliciting their votes.[84]

The necessity of a personal recommendation meant that access to a position at the Bank was about who an applicant knew, or was able to

81. Anne L. Murphy, 'Learning the Business of Banking: The Recruitment and Training of the Bank of England's First Tellers': *Business History*, 52 (2010), pp. 150–168.

82. For details of directors' nominations, see BEA, M5/686, Directors' nominations, 1756–1809.

83. BEA, 6A31/1, Petition of Mr Gould.

84. 'Diary of Samuel Harrison', quoted in *Old Lady*, 5:12–13.

make contact with, rather than what they knew.[85] This system of patronage was exercised by the patron not always for pecuniary gain but, as Bowen asserts with regard to the EIC, in order to provide for kin, friends and associates.[86] Such systems of support for individuals, especially at critical points in their life cycle, was typical in the pre-modern world.[87] But that does not mean that employment practices at the Bank were poorly considered. Nor should the value of personal connections be dismissed. As a means of attempting to ensure candidates possessed the integrity required for positions of trust, a personal recommendation continued to be a requirement for employment in industries like banking and insurance into the twentieth century.[88]

Although patronage secured an introduction to the Bank, nomination was just the start of the process. Men had to demonstrate that they had, or were capable of acquiring, the requisite skills and that their backgrounds held no hint of poor behaviour, profligacy, temptation for fraud or embezzlement or previous political or religious activism. In the latter respect, the directorate had been shocked to discover a 'Papist' employee in 1746, and since that time there had been rules preventing the employment of Catholics.[89] Later in the eighteenth century, as the threat of revolution loomed, men were asked to declare whether they belonged to any political associations or clubs.[90] A concern with the financial stability of the men employed was equally understandable given the temptations available to Bank employees. The directors were wary of employing men with outstanding debts, although they did accept applications from discharged bankrupts. In doing so they were following English law which granted bankrupts who fully cooperated with the Commission of Bankruptcy a full discharge of their debts and a small stipend, thus allowing them to rebuild their lives.[91]

85. This was typical of employment practices in other similar businesses. See, for example, Bowen, *Business of Empire*, p. 141; Supple, *Royal Exchange Assurance*, p. 71.

86. Bowen, *Business of Empire*, p. 122.

87. For a useful discussion, see Ilana Krausman Ben-Amos, *The Culture of Giving: Informal Support and Gift-Exchange in Early Modern England* (Cambridge, 2008), pp. 45–81. See also Brewer, *Sinews of Power*, p. 74.

88. Gregory Anderson, *Victorian Clerks* (Manchester, UK, 1976), p. 12.

89. Acres, *Bank of England from Within*, 1:227.

90. Anne L. Murphy, '"Writes a Fair Hand and Appears to Be Well Qualified": Recruiting Bank of England Clerks at the Start of the Nineteenth Century', *Financial History Review*, 22 (2015), p. 21.

91. Emily Kadens, 'The Last Bankrupt Hanged: Balancing Incentives in the Development of Bankruptcy Law', *Duke Law Journal*, 59 (2010), p. 1261. See also Julian Hoppit, *Risk and Failure in English Business, 1700–1800* (Cambridge, 1987); Jérôme

To support their nomination, applicants were expected to prepare a petition. The few petitions that survive are from earlier in the eighteenth century, but they are instructive about the type of skills that were considered valuable. Peter Saffree was 'very sencible [the work] requires Good hands and such as are Expert at business'.[92] Nathaniel Gary noted that he had been 'bred a Goldsmith' in the service of his father. Gary had for twelve years worked in the Exchequer, the Malt Lottery Office and the Classis Lottery of 1711 Office.[93] Robert Beachcroft's petition claimed he was 'bred to Buisness, booke keeping and telling money &c.'.[94] Stafford Briscoe explained that he had been apprenticed as a goldsmith and practiced that trade for many years. He further claimed to have resided in most of the main towns for commerce in Spain, Holland and France and to have a working knowledge of French and Spanish 'sufficient to write or translate any Letters or Bills'.[95] The breadth of Mr Briscoe's experience should not surprise. For many in London's mercantile class, an apprenticeship that included a sojourn abroad and the acquisition of foreign languages was common.[96]

As Stafford Briscoe's application indicates, applicants were likely to have acquired their skills at the expense of a previous employer. Indeed, the directors appear to have preferred to employ men with some work experience. Records from the early nineteenth century show that the average age of candidates was between 18 and 21, suggesting a prior working life of between three and seven years, assuming a school-leaving age of around 14 or 15.[97] Although evidence is not plentiful, the Bank does appear to have been unusual in preferring to recruit men with work experience. Bowen's study of the EIC, for example, suggests some candidates for employment were often just fifteen or sixteen years of age.[98] Sayers also emphasised the employment of school leavers at Lloyds Bank.[99] Checkland likewise noted the use of an apprenticeship system in the Scottish banks from the early nineteenth century, with the National Bank, at

Sgard, 'Bankruptcy, Fresh Start and Debt Renegotiation in England and France (17th to 18th Century)', in Thomas Max Safley, ed., *The History of Bankruptcy: Economic, Social and Cultural Implications in Early Modern Europe* (Abingdon, UK, 2013), pp. 229–241.

92. BEA 6A31/1, Petition of Peter Saffree junior.

93. BEA, 6A31/1, Petition of Nathaniel Gary.

94. BEA 6A31/1, Petition of Robert Beachcroft.

95. BEA 6A31/1, Petition of Stafford Briscoe.

96. Gauci, *Emporium of the World*, p. 112.

97. Murphy, 'Writes a Fair Hand', p. 32.

98. Bowen, *Business of Empire*, p. 141.

99. R. S. Sayers, *Lloyds Bank in the History of English Banking* (London, 1957), p. 68.

least, stipulating that its clerks should be no younger than 15 but no older than 20 years of age.[100]

One reason for the Bank's approach may have been that the school education available during the eighteenth century was often inadequate to the task of instilling the skills needed for clerical work. Traditional grammar schools still concentrated on offering a classical education. A more 'modern' education might have included English and mathematics, perhaps with some attention to the humanities, foreign languages and those other socially valuable skills of drawing and dancing. Commercial schools placed more emphasis on the skills that were required of Bank clerks: being able to write a good hand and basic maths and bookkeeping. Yet, in all areas of education, abuses and neglect were common, and provision at secondary and higher levels was generally poor.[101] Consequently, only a very small proportion of the population would have had more than a few years of formal schooling.[102] It is perhaps not surprising, therefore, that the Bank's directors preferred another employer to bear the costs of the transition from education to work.

Evidence from the early nineteenth century, however, suggests that even this approach could not ensure that highly qualified candidates were available to the Bank.[103] Candidates were subjected to practical tests designed to reveal key shortcomings. The first was a handwriting test. Good penmanship was required, meaning the candidate had to display a neat, legible hand, the ability to write without leaving blots on the paper, and the ability to copy without error. Indeed, errors were to be avoided at all costs because of the potential association of the erasure of errors with fraud.[104] Speed was also important, and the committees overseeing employment of clerks during the nineteenth century were looking for neat and expeditious hands.[105] With regard to accounts, candidates had to be competent in simple mathematics and understand double entry

---

100. S. G. Checkland, *Scottish Banking: A History, 1695-1973* (London, 1975), p. 393.

101. Paul Langford, *A Polite and Commercial People: England 1727-1783* (Oxford, 1998), pp. 79–88; David Mitch, 'Education and Skill of the British Labour Force', in R. Floud and P. Johnson, eds., *The Cambridge Economic History of Modern Britain*, vol. 1, *Industrialisation, 1700-1860* (Cambridge, 2004), pp. 346–347.

102. Patrick Wallis, 'Labour Markets and Training', in R. Floud, J. Humphries and P. Johnson, eds., *The Cambridge Economic History of Modern Britain*, vol. 1, *1700-1870* (Cambridge, 2014), p. 201.

103. BEA, M5/406, Committee for Examining Candidates.

104. I. Jeacle, 'The Bank Clerk in Victorian Society: The Case of Hoare and Company', *Journal of Management History*, 16 (2010), p. 315.

105. Murphy, 'Writes a Fair Hand', p. 35.

bookkeeping. The Bank's test of competency involved the addition of columns of figures. Again, the ideal was a man who could work with accuracy and speed. The final test involved the handling of money. Candidates had to be able to recognise numerous different forms of specie and notes and understand their value and thus were asked to compute a number of 'parcels' of cash. Competence was measured by speed (in number of minutes taken) and accuracy (by number of parcels computed incorrectly). Although it was relatively straight-forward to find men with good penmanship and basic mathematical competence, it was with the last of these tests that candidates particularly struggled. Only 20 out of the 594 individuals who took the test between 1800 and 1815 managed to complete it without error.[106] And it is unlikely that the previous generation of men were any more competent with such tasks on entry to the Bank.

Given that the human capital available to the Bank, therefore, lacked experience and relevant skills on initial appointment, the institution had to ensure that on-the-job training was available to new men. This, however, was not a formalised process. Rather, it appears that new clerks learned their roles under the supervision of a senior man. No trace of any more formal measures being established can be found.[107] Equally, it is not made clear how long it was before men were considered fully competent, but it has been possible to trace the amount of time the men employed in 1783 had waited for their first salary increment. This shows that, on average, the first pay raise came after 3.5 years of service, which perhaps indicates a minimum period of service before clerks were considered fully competent in their work.[108] At the EIC, clerks were asked to work for three years before receiving a salary, which offers some corroboration to the suggestion that this was a minimum requirement.[109]

It was the fate of some workers in eighteenth-century offices to remain in a junior position even after an initial training period had been completed. Boot's study of the salary structure at the Bank of Scotland revealed that salaries there changed little between the year a clerk was appointed and the year he died or retired.[110] Bowen has argued that most clerical staff at the EIC ended their careers where they began, spending years in a particular office and having their rate of promotion determined by the

106. Ibid., p. 36.

107. This was also the case at the EIC. See Bowen, *Business of Empire*, p. 143.

108. See appendix 1. Calculation based on a sample of 287 out of 321 cases.

109. Bowen, *Business of Empire*, p. 141.

110. H. M. Boot, 'Salaries and Career Earnings in the Bank of Scotland, 1730–1880', *Economic History Review*, 44 (1991), p. 645.

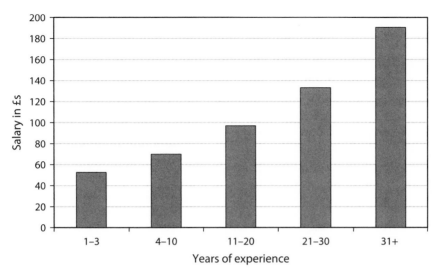

FIGURE 4.3. Average salary of cohort of 1783 by length of experience.
Source: BEA, Minutes of the Court of Directors, Book V, G4/23, fols. 368–373;
Book W, G4/24, fols. 54–58; Staff Salary Ledgers, E41/1–18.
Note: The Bank's total clerical wage bill for 1783 was £31,085.

death or departure of those higher up the career ladder.[111] This was not necessarily true for the cohort employed at the Bank at the time of the Inspection. They served the institution at a time of great expansion, and as the number of offices and employees increased, so did opportunities to move into junior or middle management.

As figures 4.3 and 4.4 demonstrate, after around three years of service they could expect their pay to rise broadly in line with their age and experience. Indeed, age was a significant identifier of seniority, and this is consistent with the early modern view that age brought wisdom.[112] After around ten years of service, clerks received an average salary of £80 per annum. At twenty-five years of service, clerks earned around £150 per year. However, although prospects for promotion were reasonable, the most senior posts became free only occasionally; thus it was the rare man who moved into the position of chief cashier or accountant. Moreover, because promotion was still dependent on age and length of experience, rather than just capacity, and because men were generally in their twenties when

111. Bowen, *Business of Empire*, pp. 141–142.

112. S. Sweeting, 'Capitalism, the State and Things: The Port of London, *circa* 1730–1800' (unpublished PhD thesis, University of Warwick, 2014), p. 120; Keith Thomas, 'Age and Authority in Early Modern England', *Proceedings of the British Academy*, 62 (1976), pp. 205–248.

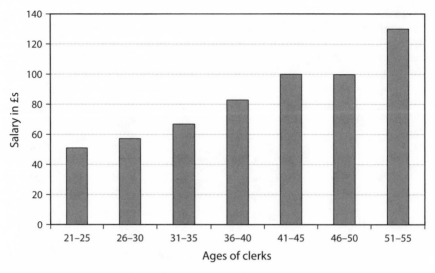

FIGURE 4.4. Average salary of cohort of 1783 by age.
Source: BEA, Minutes of the Court of Directors, Book V, G4/23, fols. 368–373;
Book W, G4/24, fols. 54–58; Staff Salary Ledgers, E41/1–18.
Note: It has not been possible to trace the ages of men employed before 1758;
therefore, data in this chart are based on 259 observations and men aged 55 or
younger.

they started work at the Bank, they often were over the age of 50 before they
started to earn a salary in excess of £100 a year.

The highest-paid men in 1783 were Robert Lewin, the Bank's secretary; John Payne, the chief accountant; and Abraham Newland, the chief
cashier, all of whom earned £250 a year. Newland had been working at the
Bank for thirty-six years in 1783 and Payne for thirty-eight years. Lewin
had been with the Bank nearly sixty years, having been employed in 1724.
Payne's deputies, William Edwards and Joseph Betsworth, earned £170 a
year and had twenty-four and thirty-one years' experience, respectively.
Nine men occupied senior positions in the Cashiers Office under Abraham
Newland. They were each paid £200 a year and had worked in the Bank
for an average of thirty-four years.[113]

How those men rose to the highest offices in the Bank cannot precisely
be known, but the career trajectory of Mr Walsh of the Three Per Cent
Consols Office, which was taken note of by the Inspectors, is instructive.

113. The pay profile at the Bank was similar to that at the EIC. The starting salary at the
EIC was £40 a year, and men with 25 years' experience earned around £160 a year in 1800.
Figures do not include perquisites and gratuities. Boot, 'Real Incomes', p. 643. For further
discussions of the incomes of the middling sorts, see Boot, 'Salaries and Career Earnings'.

Walsh was regarded by Samuel Bosanquet as 'very intelligent, very able, and the only one fit for a head yet seen'.[114] Walsh told the Committee

> that he had been 12 years in the Bank, & for the last 4 years one of the
> 3 Chief Clerks of this Office, being appointed Assistant to Mr Miller &
> Mr Vickery. That when he first came into the Bank, he was placed in
> the department of the Chief Cashier where he went through the Offices
> of OutTeller & InTeller, & was some time at one of the Cash books &
> assisted in the Bullion Office at the time of taking in the deficient Gold
> Coin; he was afterwards removed into the Accountants Office, which he
> went through; & from thence to the 3 P C^t Consols, where he has seen
> every part of the business before he was appointed one of the Chief
> Clerks.[115]

Yet, while Mr Walsh might have gained significant knowledge of the inner workings of the Bank, he was not necessarily being trained for a management role. As Sidney Pollard argued, this was a time when 'formal management training was so rare as to be negligible'.[116] Management technique was not a particular concern of the Bank's directors. Indeed, as Hennessy found, meaningful changes in managerial style at the Bank did not occur until the late nineteenth century and, in some respects, rather later than that.[117] Nor did the Inspectors take a particular interest in management style, but they were, nonetheless, concerned with the types of men appointed into senior positions. In their final report they reflected on how men rose to prominence and recommended that promotions be given greater consideration than they were currently given. They remained convinced that promotion should be governed by seniority, as that was 'fair & equitable', but they acknowledged that it 'will not apply in all cases, nor ought it to be resorted to where particular Talents are required'.[118]

The question of the degree to which the Inspectors viewed a want of managerial talent a problem is difficult to answer. Although there were several comments relating to lack of subordination from the junior clerks and lack of attention from their seniors in the Minutes, their final report was measured and their comments relating to promotion were framed as recommendations rather than required changes. Likewise, it is clear that

114. BEA, M5/471.

115. BEA, M5/213, fol. 78.

116. Sidney Pollard, *The Genesis of Modern Management: A Study of the Industrial Revolution in Great Britain* (Cambridge, MA, 1965), p. 147.

117. Hennessy, 'Governors', pp. 202–213.

118. BEA, M5/213, fol. 175.

they did recognise talent during their examinations of the clerks. Samuel Bosanquet's notes featured a number of men who he perceived were well-qualified, competent and had the right temperament for supervision. Thus, he wrote of Mr Coxeter as 'precise—a gentleman, seems qualified for a supervisor' and of Mr Turner as 'very intelligent & a good head of the [Three Per Cent Reduced] office'.[119] Bosanquet was also discerning in his assessments, noting that Mr Selby was 'very intelligent and civil man cautious what he says—but appears not fit for a head'.[120] Moreover, inadequate control may have been a concern for the Inspectors, but this does not mean that managerial oversight was always lacking or that it was ineffective.

Sticks and Carrots

Various mechanisms operated to ensure that men were working to satisfactory standards. The need to adhere to certain deadlines required attention and diligence from the clerks. We have seen throughout the working day that clerks operated within time constraints that included opening and closing of offices, cut-off times for certain activities and requirements to transfer documents and ledgers between offices for the purpose of updating the Bank's record. It has likewise been noted that the Bank imposed its time discipline on its customers and the investing public who went there to buy, sell and transfer shares or government securities and to collect their dividends. The consequences of missing deadlines were, in some cases, customer complaints and, in other cases, the requirement to put in additional hours or work late.

Although we have seen some incidence of unauthorised absence, especially in the transfer offices, checks were made to ensure that men were at their desks when they were supposed to be. Like all large-scale workshops and early factories, the Bank kept an appearance book to record the clerks' arrival times. Matthias Alcock, the principal door-keeper and the man charged with keeping that book, told the Inspectors that he drew 'a line every day about 10 minutes after 9, to mark the names of those who do not come to their time'.[121] Tardiness was not ignored, and the Inspectors reinforced the expectation of punctuality. In their interviews with each senior man, they asked for an account of their staff, which included details of

119. BEA, M5/471, unpaginated.
120. Ibid.
121. BEA, M5/213, fol. 165.

their time-keeping.[122] This would seem to indicate that supervisors were mindful of punctuality and admonished unauthorised absence.

Checks and balances were in place throughout the Bank to identify errors or attempts to defraud the Bank. These were not always sufficient to remove temptation, as noted in chapter 2 in the case of Charles Clutterbuck. Nor were they always sufficient to catch errors, and the Inspectors made numerous adjustments to working practices to improve checks and balances. Thus, tellers were asked to 'sign their initials in each other's books for such sums as they receive in Money or Notes from one to another in the course of the day's business'.[123] Further checks were introduced in the Discount Office, and the Inspectors discussed the appointment of an additional clerk to check entries of money paid into the Bank, a process that was apparently liable to error as there had been hitherto no independent way to ascertain that the money had been credited to the correct account.[124] Clearly, such checks and balances were a tried and tested method of identifying errors before they led to significant problems.

Knowing there was an independent check on their ledgers may have ensured the diligence of many clerks, but there were additional incentives to careful work. The Bank maintained lists of rules which guided the clerks' work and behaviour in the office. These may not have been brought regularly to the attention of the clerks.[125] It was noted, for example, how rules about acting as jobbers and brokers had been ignored or forgotten by the transfer office clerks. Nonetheless, the clerks did receive an annual reminder of their commitment to their employer. At their election, or initial employment, each clerk was required to swear an oath that they would be 'true and faithful' to their employer and 'faithfully and truly execute and discharge' their duties.[126] They committed to keeping the Bank's business private, including the understanding that they should not 'make knowne, publish or deliver out any accompt, paper, minute, order or transaction of the Bank'.[127] Technically, clerks were re-elected each year and, therefore, renewed their oaths each year as well.[128]

The Committee for House and Servants was nominally responsible for staff discipline and certainly took note of minor infractions. The

---

122. BEA, M5/212, fol. 85.
123. Ibid., fol. 41.
124. Ibid., fols. 57, 84.
125. Acres, *Bank of England from Within*, 1:226.
126. Ibid., p. 132.
127. Ibid.
128. Ibid.

Committee was obliged to regularly report to the Court of Directors, although this generally consisted of a formulaic confirmation that the chief cashier and the chief accountant had 'no complaint' regarding the men in their charge.[129] There is evidence to show that the Bank's governor involved himself in the disciplining of employees. Thus, Samuel Beachcroft's diary notes a number of records of the admonishment of clerks, including that of 'Mr Tudman for taking a Bank Note that was forged'.[130] Errors of this nature could lead to wages being stopped to compensate the Bank for any losses. Thus, in June 1780 the out-teller Thomas Smith was ordered to make good a deficit of £10 found in his cash bag.[131] The directors also took action to protect the institution against larger losses caused by the negligence or criminal behaviour of the clerks.

Each clerk was expected to provide the Bank with personal security backed by an independent bond guarantor. These bonds started at £500 for junior clerks and rose to a maximum of £5,000, depending on responsibility. The Bank was diligent both in maintaining up-to-date records for guarantors and pursuing compensation in the event of large losses resulting from errors or dishonesty.[132] The case of William Kingston is illustrative of the institution's determination to secure redress. At the time of the Inspection, Kingston was a Consols clerk who had forged a will to gain control of the estate of William Talbot, an estate primarily encompassing £3,700 in the three per cent consols. The case was complicated by two factors. First, Kingston did not pursue the fraud during the course of his duties at the Bank, and second, he died soon after perpetrating his fraud. Nonetheless, the directors chose to pursue the bond-holder, and it was the opinion of Freshfields, the Bank's solicitors, that there was not much

> reason to doubt that the words of the Bond are sufficient to extend to the loss, which, in this instance, the Bank has sustained. The words are very general and extensive, and seem chosen with a view to cover every loss which may be sustained by any act or neglect of the Clerk either in, or during his service.[133]

It was, therefore, a significant undertaking to act as guarantor for a clerk. Guarantors were unlikely to be able to escape their obligations, and failure

129. See BEA, G4/23, fols. 218, 238, 260, 288, 310, 333, 357, 385.

130. BEA, M5/451, fol. 18.

131. BEA, G4/23, fol. 96.

132. Ibid., p. 133.

133. BEA, F6/68, Freshfields Papers relating to Bank staff: William Kingston, Clerk, Consols Office.

to honour the bond could lead to imprisonment for debt. Given that guarantors were very often family or close connections of the clerks, this would seem to be an additional incentive for the clerk to act in the best interests of their employer, or at least not to act against the interests of their bond guarantor.

Dismissal was an option in cases of serious infractions of the rules, but this was not often used. Only thirteen dismissals can be traced among those employed in 1783, just over 4 per cent of the total number of employees.[134] Furthermore, the Bank's directors did show some willingness to forgive past indiscretions. In August 1775 the friends of Benjamin Vowell appealed on his behalf for his reinstatement in the Bank, his previous bad behaviour, which had occasioned his suspension on 2 June that year, having been caused by the 'Loss of a Wife [which] had brought him to drink'.[135] Samuel Beachcroft, the governor, promised to put the matter to the Court of Directors. Vowell was duly reinstated but appears not to have learned his lesson, and clearly the directors' capacity for forgiveness stretched only so far. Vowell was dismissed from the Bank's service in June 1776.[136] As we shall see in the next chapter, forgiveness was never an option in cases of dishonesty against the Bank. Fraudsters and embezzlers, when caught, were prosecuted and the ultimate penalty imposed.

Managerial oversight was not the only mechanism by which the integrity and diligence of clerks were encouraged. The basic wage was not a great incentive for honest and diligent behaviour in the early years of a clerk's employment. Nonetheless, it was a regular wage in a prestigious environment and the prospect of a lifetime's earnings which would, in most cases, ensure a comfortable lifestyle in mid- and later life. It was also employment in which the hours, in most cases, were reasonable and, as previously shown, could provide opportunity for taking on additional work to supplement a salary. Equally, although the clerks were not permitted to take annual holidays and generally worked a six-day week, around fifty public holidays were kept at the Bank, thus allowing some breaks in the working year.[137] Salaries were supplemented by gratuities from customers and corporate customers, especially for those clerks in customer-facing roles.[138] The Bank also paid gratuities in recognition of

---

134. BEA, E41, Establishment Department: Salary Ledgers, passim; BEA, E20, Establishment Department: House Lists, passim.

135. BEA, M5/451, fol. 26.

136. BEA, G4/22, fols. 117, 182.

137. Ibid., p. 231.

138. See 'The Customer Experience' in chapter 2.

'extra service' given by some of the clerks.[139] Thus, in April 1783 it paid out £1,565 to more than fifty clerks in individual amounts ranging from £200 to Abraham Newland and £150 to John Payne, the chief accountant, to £10 each for a number of more junior men.[140]

The Bank did not make formal arrangements for the payment of benefits to clerks who were unable to work, nor at this time did it offer a guaranteed pension on retirement. Nonetheless, the institution generally did provide a financial safety net for its workers. It was usually generous to clerks whose need was great. For example, two of the cohort of 1783 who left the Bank owing to what the records describe as 'mental derangement' were treated well. The dependents of both John Bell and Francis Symondson were provided with pensions. In Symondson's case, this amounted to £280 per year paid to his wife and child.[141] Although the Bank did not guarantee pensions, it frequently made generous arrangements for those who retired from the Bank's service. Few can have done better than John Best. Employed by the Bank in February 1763, he resigned in June 1768 and was awarded a pension of £40 per year, which he continued to draw until his death in 1793.[142] Those who served the Bank for longer periods of time generally drew pensions equivalent to, or sometimes in excess of, their final salaries. Thus, Edward Martin, who resigned in 1815 after working for the Bank for forty-two years, retired on a pension of £280 per year. Richard Marston resigned in 1835 after serving for fifty-three years. His final salary was £310, and he was awarded a pension of £350 per year.[143] In practice, only those men who were dismissed left the Bank without a substantial gift or pension. The Bank's outgoings in respect of pensions were not great, however. Indeed, most clerks died within five years of retirement.[144]

In addition to the payments of pensions, some generosity was shown towards widows and orphans of the Bank's clerks, but this usually took the form of one-off payments rather than the provision of a regular annuity. Thus, £200 was paid to the daughter of Henry Davies in 1804, some four years after Davies's death. William Walton's widow received a £500 gift from the directors soon after his death. John Barnard's widow, Ann, was awarded just £100 on his death in 1807.[145] The clerks also made their

139. BEA, G4/23, fol. 359.
140. Ibid.
141. BEA, E41/1, passim.
142. Ibid., fol. 62.
143. Ibid., passim.
144. BEA, E46, List of Staff Receiving Pensions.
145. BEA, E41/1, passim.

own arrangements for the maintenance and relief of their widows and dependents. They set up a fund in 1764, the aim of which was to provide an income of £20 per annum for the widows of those men who had been subscribers for ten years or more.[146] The subscriptions raised were invested in the public funds under the trusteeship of four of the principal officers in the Bank. Those men who acted in ways that jeopardised their employment at the Bank were, therefore, compromising a steady wage in their early career, a comfortable middle-age and financial security post-retirement.

By the early afternoon, the pace of work in the Bank had slowed considerably and the heart of the City moved away from Threadneedle Street. Clerks were able to take some time away from their desks, and some of the offices most closely associated with the work of the City closed their doors. The senior men considered their work to be done and left the Bank in the hands of the more junior clerks. The Inspectors feared that this left the Bank vulnerable, and so they required henceforth a senior presence until the Bank closed for the day. In their final report they recommended 'a better defined system of subordination' among the clerks with the intention of creating 'a chain of obedience, from the Juniors towards the Heads of their respective Offices'.[147]

In addition to requiring greater managerial diligence from the senior men, the Inspectors reflected upon how such men rose to prominence and recommended that the directors on appointing committees 'pay great attention to the abilities & characters of those they nominate; & at the time of Election, to their performances: for though amongst so great a number it cannot be expected that all shall be equally capable, yet care should be taken not to elect such as are apparently liable to exception'.[148] As we have seen, the Inspectors also felt that promotions required greater consideration and attention paid to the capacities of the individual, not just their level of seniority.

Some thought, therefore, was given to the factors that would contribute to the effective running and overall security of the institution. The conclusions reached were that the men in managerial roles mattered. Those men who rose to high office had to be selected on merit and not just seniority, they had to have authority and they had to be prepared to

146. Acres, *Bank of England from Within*, 1:231.
147. BEA, M5/213, fol. 173.
148. Ibid., fols. 174–175.

demonstrate authority. Nonetheless, it has also been noted that, in the absence of effective managerial oversight, there were other mechanisms that kept men honest and working in the interests of the Bank. These included the various checks and balances that operated in each office and were strengthened by the independent bond guarantors, usually family and friends, who could be called on in case of costly errors or dishonesty by the clerks. It was, perhaps, self-interest that kept clerks honest and diligent. Aside from the penalties that could be enacted against those who, through incompetence or deceit, cost the institution money, a lifetime's earnings in the employ of a prestigious organisation was a powerful incentive for virtuous behaviour.

CHAPTER FIVE

Accounting for Public Confidence

AT AROUND FIVE O'CLOCK each evening, notaries came to the Bank to inspect various accounts held by overseas customers. Notaries, not to be confused with scriveners, were 'specifically concerned with the legal minutiae of money dealings already completed'.[1] Their role was not codified in English law, but a late eighteenth-century description suggests that their office was 'to attest deeds or writings, to make them authentic in another country, but principally in business relating to merchants'.[2] Their presence at the Bank at the latter end of the day was particularly noted by the clerks who kept the various transfer books. Mr Selby of the Three Per Cent Consols Office told the Inspectors that, in relation to 'the foreign Accounts . . . Notaries come to inspect . . . the Ledgers, in order to certify the Sums standing in any particular names'. He added that 'the Notaries generally come about 5 o'clock & expect to find the Articles posted'.[3] Clerks at the Bank Stock transfer books and the Three Per Cent Reduced Office similarly noted the presence of notaries at around five in the evening.[4]

Since another of the specialist legal functions of the notary was to protest bills of exchange, there was also a notary charged by the Bank with managing this process.[5] In preparation for his arrival, one of the clerks in the Cashiers Department took from the out-teller who stayed late each

1. Pressnell, *Country Banking*, p. 38.
2. *British Dictionary* (1797), quoted in Roy Edgar Samuel, 'Anglo-Jewish Notaries and Scriveners', *Transactions (Jewish Historical Society of England)*, 17 (1951–1952), p. 113.
3. BEA, M5/213, fol. 69.
4. Ibid., fols. 33, 44.
5. Pressnell, *Country Banking*, p. 287.

day 'all Calls remaining in his hands unpaid' and a list was prepared of those 'for the Notary, who comes at 6 o'clock'.[6] The notary then 'takes an account himself every night in a book of the Bills to be noted, which are all those remaining unpaid in the Discount Account, all foreign Bills on sundry Accounts and such inland Bills & Notes as have been order'd by the proprietors to be noted. These bills he takes away with him & returns them the next morning'.[7] The work of the notaries and its meaning have not been noticed by other historians of the Bank, and, indeed, the work of the notary has not attracted much attention from British historians.[8] Nonetheless, their presence at the Bank is another indicator of the extent to which the institution's reputation and relationship with its customers depended on accurate and timely record-keeping. The presence of the notaries and their role in scrutinising the Bank's records thus sets the scene for the themes of this chapter.

Despite debate about the significance of double entry bookkeeping for the emergence of capitalism, the accuracy and integrity of accounting processes have long been acknowledged as indicative of the level of trust that might be reposed in an individual or institution.[9] Jacob Soll has also argued for the ways in which 'good accounting practices' have enabled trust in governments and has suggested that lack of accountability has produced 'financial chaos, economic crimes, civil unrest, and worse'.[10] What is being argued here is not that a position of financial strength was the basis for trust. Rather, it was the practices by which the financial position of the individual or institution were recorded that mattered. Bookkeeping specifically, because it was formal, precise and based in a 'rule-bound system

6. BEA, M5/212, fol. 15.

7. Ibid., fol. 17.

8. Overviews may be found in H. C. Gutteridge, 'The Origin and Historical Development of the Profession of Notaries Public in England', in *Cambridge Legal Essays Written in Honour of and Presented to Doctor Bond, Professor Buckland and Professor Kenny* (Cambridge, 1926), pp. 123–137; J. S. Purvis, 'The Notary Public in England', *Archivum*, 12 (1962), pp. 121–126.

9. See, for example, Bruce G. Carruthers and Wendy Epseland, 'Accounting for Rationality: Double-Entry Bookkeeping and the Rhetoric of Economic Rationality', *American Journal of Sociology*, 97 (1991), pp. 31–69; William Deringer, *Calculated Values: Finance, Politics and the Quantitative Age* (Cambridge, MA, 2018); Frederic C. Lane, 'Double Entry Bookkeeping and Resident Merchants', *Journal of European Economic History*, 6 (1977), pp. 177–191; Mary Poovey, *A History of the Modern Fact: Problems of Knowledge in the Sciences of Wealth and Society* (Chicago, 1998); Roxburgh, *Representing Public Credit*; B. S. Yamey, 'Accounting and the Rise of Capitalism: Further Notes on a Theme by Sombart', *Journal of Accounting Research*, 2 (1964), pp. 117–136.

10. Jacob Soll, *The Reckoning: Financial Accountability and the Rise and Fall of Nations* (New York, 2014), p. xii.

of arithmetic', seemed to offer guarantees of authenticity and integrity.[11] Moreover, the zero balance function in double entry bookkeeping 'helps to convey a sort of virtue, insofar as this balance is seen as having been arrived at in a disinterested manner'.[12]

Accounting undoubtedly was a key technology at the Bank of England, and the institution had been using complex double entry bookkeeping systems since its inception in 1694.[13] Including the General Ledger and Stock and Annuity Ledgers, the Bank maintained a wide variety of cash books, accounts, ledgers relating to the issuance of banknotes, lists of lost notes, details of discounted bills, bullion ledgers and a variety of different registers covering all aspects of its business.[14] The full range of accounting instruments, including waste books, journals and day books, were used by the clerks. For example, the in-tellers kept individual accounts that they made up each day detailing cash they received as an initial balance from the warehouse, funds received from customers and funds paid out.[15] Likewise, the clerks who attended the Exchequer kept 'a kind of Waste-book' in which was entered the day's transactions maintaining an account between the clerk and the Bank that allowed the former to account for the funds issued to him at the start of the day and those remaining in his hands at its close.[16] It was previously noted that the clerks' work was subject to an outwardly robust range of checks and balances. The Bank's ledgers were very well kept, and it is rare to see an error or an erasure. The integrity of the record was further underpinned by the tests to which the clerks were subject prior to their employment and which ensured the neatness and legibility of their writing and their competence with numbers.[17]

Equally, the Bank had generally effective methods of storing and archiving records, something of which the Inspectors took notice. By the mid-1770s there was a purpose-built archive in the four-storey, fire-proof library building.[18] When they visited the library as part of their

11. Poovey, *Modern Fact*, p. 30.

12. Roxburgh, *Representing Public Credit*, p. 91.

13. Elizabeth Hennessy, 'The Governors, Directors and Management of the Bank of England', in Roberts and Kynaston, *Bank of England*, p. 214. For a discussion of book-keeping as a key technology, especially in European state-formation, see Pepijn Brandon, 'Accounting for Power: Bookkeeping and the Rationalization of Dutch Naval Administration', in Jeff Fynn-Paul, ed., *War, Entrepreneurs and the State in Europe and the Mediterranean, 1300–1800* (Leiden, 2014), p. 151.

14. For a short digest of the surviving ledgers, see Clapham, *Bank of England*, 1:303.

15. BEA, M5/212, fols. 5–6.

16. Ibid., fol. 140.

17. See 'Rising through the Ranks' in chapter 4.

18. Abramson, *Building the Bank*, p. 66.

investigations, the Inspectors found the books were by 'no means to be in a perishing condition, but the papers very dry. They found a great number of files of money tickets, of orders for making out Bank Post-bills, & of other papers of the same kind, which lie about the floor & take up a good deal of room'.[19] They made recommendations in their final report about the rationalisation of the archive, noting that many of the records could be 'destroyed without any possible injury or inconvenience to the Bank' in order to make room for future records. They further required that 'the Books & papers to be arranged in regular order, marked with their contents and dates, & the catalogue of them kept up, so as that immediate reference may be had to any of them when required'.[20] The clear implication of this form of organisation was to ensure preparedness for ease of inspection, error-checking or gathering of evidence should it be required.

Many, although by no means all, of the Bank's bookkeeping processes took place within public view. The banking hall and transfer offices were open spaces to which the public had access and could observe the clerks at work and in which the ledgers were on show. The Bank's integrity was also written on the ledgers and in their existence as objects. Many of the ledgers in which customers' and public creditors' accounts were recorded were weighty, large, folio-sized volumes. On each was stamped the image of Britannia, which, as previously argued, symbolised the connection between Bank and state. Moreover, as Roxburgh argues, 'the placement of the giant tomes in public view represented a practice of accounting that was done behind the scenes'.[21] The Bank's customers and public creditors, or their nominees, could not only observe the ledgers being used but also scrutinise their contents. Those nominees, like the notaries, performed the necessary checks on behalf of their clients; and by their physical presence, they reminded the clerks and directors that scrutiny was in operation. Additionally, accounts were kept in such a way as to facilitate scrutiny. Thus, accounts that indicated a customer's holdings—for example, a drawing account or stock ledger—were regularly tallied so that their position could be seen at a glance.

The Bank's competence in managing its own credit was recognised by contemporaries, including Defoe, who praised the Bank for its perfectly kept ledgers.[22] Lord North in 1781 noted the institution's 'prudent man-

19. BEA, M5/213, fol. 167.
20. Ibid., fol. 176.
21. Roxburgh, *Representing Public Credit*, p. 91.
22. Quoted in Roxburgh, *Representing Public Credit*, p. 68.

agement . . . judicious conduct, wise plans, and exact punctuality'.[23] The very existence of these systems says something of the Bank's precocity as an eighteenth-century business. The level and complexity of its work could not be managed without robust accounting systems. This is especially clear in the management of the national debt, and it set the Bank apart from some departments of the state which were notoriously chaotic.[24] Indeed, while the Bank maintained something close to best practice in the management of its accounts, 'little progress was made in increasing the rigor and professionalism of state accounting procedures through much of the eighteenth century'.[25] Likewise, it was not until the early nineteenth century that annual accounts of government finances were available for the public to scrutinise.[26] Accounting should, however, not just be seen as a matter of administration; it also reflected the means of organising and enforcing power within the institution.[27] The Bank's accounting processes, through its checks and balances, allowed oversight of the work and integrity of the clerks.

The primary purpose of this chapter is to understand the Bank's accounts and accounting practices as factors that were essential to the maintenance of confidence both in the institution and in the public funds. It considers the work of the Accountants Department, its processes, checks and balances, and interactions with other Bank offices. This work extended over the course of the day, taking place as records and ledgers were made available by other offices, and intensified towards evening as clerks sought to update records that would be required for the start of the following working day. The chapter also examines the working conditions for the accountants and the consequences for their health of spending hours each day at their desks hunched over their ledgers. Finally, the accuracy and integrity of the clerks' work will be tested through an exploration of the crimes of fraud and embezzlement. Examination of how such crimes were committed and detected reveals much about the effectiveness of the Bank's accounting processes.

23. William Cobbett, speech of 13 June 1781, in Cobbett, *Parliamentary History*, 22:518.

24. Brandon, 'Accounting for Power', p. 152.

25. Deringer, *Calculated Values*, p. 273.

26. Ibid., p. 274.

27. Anthony G. Hopwood, 'The Archaeology of Accounting Systems', in N. Macintosh and T. Hopper, eds., *Accounting, the Social and the Political: Classics, Contemporary and Beyond* (Amsterdam, 2005), pp. 73–84.

The Accountants Department

The Bank's chief accountant at the time of the Inspection was John Payne. His department covered both the transfer offices, discussed in chapter 3, and a number of other offices primarily charged with the keeping of the Bank's various accounts. When Mr Payne first appeared in front of the Inspectors, he, like Mr Newland, presented a list of the offices under his control. The list read as follows:

1. The Clerks who enter the Credits and post the payments of the Specie and Cash-notes, that is, Bank notes. [The chief clerk of this office was Thomas Pollard.]
2. The Clerks who do the same business in the 7 days sight notes. [The chief clerk was William Aldridge.]
3. The Clerks who transact the business of the Bills and Notes discounted. [Thomas Pollard was also in charge in this office.]
4. The Clerks in the Drawing Office who post all the Articles in the Accounts of those that keep Cash at the Bank, fully and distinctly. This is a complete Check upon the same Accounts as they are kept in the Hall, where only the Page of the Cash book and the sum are regarded. [The chief clerk was Joseph Betsworth.]

   The 3 following Persons are stationed in the Accountants Office, because they have a general Connexion with the Specie & Cash notes, the Drawing Accounts, & the Bills & Notes discounted; but their peculiar Business is distinct from those Branches viz:

5. Thomas Beardsley. . . . Writer of the Journal.
6. John Newton & George Armstrong. Enterers, seriation of the Bills and Notes discounted, both as they are discounted, & as they are paid.

[Offices seven to eleven inclusive on the list were the transfer offices.][28]

12. Chancery Office, where the Accounts of all the Suitors in Chancery are kept of which a Balance is taken every year. The number of Accounts is now about 2600. [E. Smith was the nominal head of this office but was noted as 'allways absent'. Thomas Landifield was the acting head.]
13. Cheque Office, Their ledgers are a Duplicate of the Dividend books in the several Annuity Offices by which they are enabled to

28. See 'Managing the Market' in chapter 3.

examine all the paid Warrants, to see that they correspond with such Dividend books. They sort the paid Warrants placing them in numerical order & at a proper time when they are agreed send them to the Exchequer. [Bryan Baillie was the chief clerk.]

14. Account of the Exchequer Bills. This contains an Entry of the Bills in circulation, & of the Supply bills as they are <u>issued</u> from the Exchequer. Also the Entry of the Bills in circulation, as they are <u>set off</u> for cancelling at the Exchequer, with the Premium due thereon from day to day; & of the Supply bills, as they are either discharged by Cash or exchanged for other Supply bills in the current year, with the Premium due thereon. Kept by the Accountant General & Checked by the Deputy Accountant.

15. General Ledger, posted from the General Cash book by the Deputy Accountant.[29]

Perhaps having learned from observing the progress of the Inspection through the Cashiers Office during the previous eight months, Payne also presented the Inspectors with written accounts of the work in his office to supplement his oral testimony. Unfortunately, nothing of these papers appears to have survived beyond their titles:

- An Account of Cash-books & Note Ledgers with a specimen of the latter from the Accountants Office,
- An Account of the business of the Drawing Office in the Accountants Office,
- An Account of the process of a Dividend, &
- An Account of the business of transferring in the Annuity Offices.

Like the employees of other offices in the Bank, the accountants began work at 9:00 A.M.; but, unlike the other employees, some accountants were still at their desks late into the evening. Their work was inextricably linked with that of the Cashiers Department since it was either the updating of accounts to which funds had been added or withdrawn, the preparation of balances or the checking of ledgers. Much of the work was dull and repetitive, involving transferring amounts to and from various ledgers and then performing checks to see that the corresponding ledgers balanced. Men like Mr Laverick, who had been working at the Bank for twenty years, spent his day 'abstracting the old Notes unpaid from the old Ledgers into Clearing books'.[30] Mr Thomas's job involved

29. BEA, M5/212, fols. 204–206.
30. BEA, M5/213, fol. 4.

adding up the cash books worked in the hall. He noted that the books had been through several processes before they reached him—day 1 in the hall, day 2 in the Accountants Office to post amounts to accounts, day 3 with the accountants in the Cheque Office and then day 4 with Mr Thomas.[31] Mr Holdsworth managed the recording of cash notes following the day of issue. He also detailed the several interlinking steps that were required. Thus, the credit was entered into the note ledger from the cash book kept in the banking hall. The amount of notes was then 'cast up . . . in small books kept for the purpose' and checked against the G cash book.[32] The debits, or banknotes paid, were likewise posted from the cash books to the note ledgers, and 'every one is set against the respective Note to which it belongs'.[33]

As we have seen, given the sums of money that were in the hands of some clerks, a great deal of emphasis was placed on personal responsibility for cash and notes. There were, thus, a number of ways of transferring responsibility between individuals and desks. The use of 'spoilt notes' is mentioned to transfer balances between ledgers.[34] Clerks signing for receipt of funds in the day books of one of their fellows is also noted.[35] The role of the Clearer was specifically constituted to manage transfer of responsibility for the out-tellers when they returned from their walks. There were three Clearers based in the banking hall. The out-tellers delivered notes, warrants and drafts directly to the Clearers, although the latter had first to be checked by the Drawing Office. Cash was paid into an in-teller, and a ticket was then issued that allowed the out-teller to procure a 'spoilt note' for the appropriate amount. Once all the paper had been delivered to the Clearer, the out-teller's account was balanced.[36] It then became the Clearers' responsibility to manage the ensuing debits and credits with other offices in the Bank.

In addition to these attempts to create an audit trail that could pinpoint individual responsibility for losses, the Bank's processes encompassed a number of checks to ensure that overall amounts were correct. Thus, the clerks at the cash books in the Drawing Office and in the Warrant Office were all obliged to 'check their entrys with the Clearers books'.[37] With

31. Ibid., fol. 3.
32. BEA, M5/212, fol. 208.
33. Ibid.
34. Ibid., fol. 133.
35. Ibid., fol. 30.
36. Ibid., fol. 7.
37. Ibid., fol. 10.

regard to Bank post bills, the clerks took a weekly balance which recorded the amount of notes in circulation, and 'every six months [they] take out an Account, from all books in use, of the Notes outstanding, & compare it with the weekly account'.[38] Mr Newton, who was in charge of the D cash book, told the Inspectors his book was 'an effectual check upon the account of Bills & Notes discounted, & reference is constantly had to it in case of failures or any disagreement in the Accounts'.[39] Mr Betsworth, the chief man in the Drawing Office, revealed that 'the principal part of the Work consists of a check upon [the Drawing Office in the banking hall]'.[40] In addition, a 'general balance' was taken once a quarter from the Accountants Office ledgers as well as from the banking hall ledgers and the two were compared. Then, every six months the list was 'copied out fair in a book with the addition of the Titles of all the Accounts' and was then sent 'into the Parlour to be lodged in the Iron Closet'.[41] This latter process was an additional precaution against the potential loss of records since it was noted that it had only been required since the Gordon riots of 1780.[42]

While much of the accountants' work was, by the late eighteenth century, concerned with the maintenance of accounts with the public, various ledgers were also kept that recorded the Bank's accounts with the state. This included accounts of all the various public funds, an 'Exchequer Audit Roll account & the Accounts of all Annuities & Dividends paid', and an account of Exchequer bills 'which shows an exact State of all the Exchequer bills, in the possession of the Bank, on the Land & Malt Taxes'.[43] Exchequer bills were short-term promissory notes issued for the term of one year, although they were renewable.[44] Through its management of Exchequer bills, the Bank held a 'quasi-monopoly' over short-term government borrowing.[45] By the later eighteenth century it was a fund that ran into the millions, with £6.5 million created and £5.9 million redeemed in 1783 and £5.6 million created and £6.8 million redeemed in 1784.[46]

38. Ibid., fol. 210.
39. BEA, M5/213, fol. 9.
40. BEA, M5/212, fol. 215.
41. Ibid.
42. Ibid.
43. BEA, M5/213, fols. 10, 18.
44. Clapham, *Bank of England*, 1:210.
45. Dickson, *Financial Revolution*, p. 360. See also Cox, *Marketing Sovereign Promises*, pp. 61–62.
46. Mitchell and Deane, *Abstract*, p. 405.

The Bank also kept accounts which were 'exact counterparts of those kept by the Accountant General of the Court of Chancery'.[47] The accounts consisted of monies under the control of the accountant general and the capital and securities of the various suitors of the Court.[48] Official accounts were also kept at the Bank, including accounts relating to the Excise, Customs, the Army and the Navy. Receivers of the Land Tax also kept accounts with the Bank and relied on the chief cashier to make payments for them to the Exchequer.[49] As Clapham asserts, there was no requirement that all such accounts be kept at the Bank, but many were, and during the 1780s some departmental accounts were formally transferred to the institution.[50]

The clerks also described methods of reporting to the state. Thus, a general balance of the Chancery accounts was generated in October, 'after which it is signed by the Head of [the Chancery Office], & then certified by the Chief Accountant of the Bank, when it is sent to the Accountant General of the Court of Chancery, who delivers it to the Lord Chancellor'.[51] The Chief Cashier's office managed all monies issued from the Treasury for paying dividends. These funds were recorded in the Audit Roll; on the credit side was entered 'every Article received from Government for the payment of Dividends on the several different kinds of Government Annuities', and on the debit side was entered the dividends paid.[52] The Audit Roll was made up and settled with the Exchequer every two years.[53] Individual accounts of unpaid dividend warrants were more regularly reported to the Exchequer. Their compilation was dependent upon the fund. Thus, for the Three Per Cent Reduced fund, this was 'annually as soon after the 30th Septr as the accounts can be got ready'.[54] For the three per cent consols, the work was begun 'on the 1st or 2nd of January & made up as soon after as can be, but it is generally 5 or 6 months before it is completed'.[55] Mr Walsh later explained that this was because it was 'not sufficient in this Office to make a List of the Dividends unpaid for the last 2 half years

47. BEA, M5/213, fol. 115.
48. Ibid., fols. 115–116.
49. BEA, M5/212, fol. 137.
50. Clapham, *Bank of England*, 1:151; Bowen, 'Bank of England', p. 11. Not all such accounts are easy to recognise since many were held in the name of the fund-holder rather than the name of the fund.
51. BEA, M5/213, fol. 115.
52. BEA, M5/212, fol. 135.
53. Ibid., fol. 136.
54. BEA, M5/213, fol. 52.
55. Ibid., fol. 62.

only, but it is necessary to extract those likewise that remain unpaid in the 6 preceding ones'.[56]

Although identified in this account, unpaid dividends remained in the hands of the Bank at this time. There was no attempt to locate the public creditors concerned, and thus there was a considerable accumulation of funds: £292,000 in 1774 and £547,000 in 1789.[57] In 1790 William Pitt, then prime minister, introduced a bill in the House of Commons to claim £500,000 of the unclaimed dividends. The Bank's directors put up strong resistance to this, arguing that 'the money which it is proposed to be taken from them is private property of which they are in possession on account, and for the benefit of those to whom the same belongs'.[58] The action proposed was, therefore, 'extraordinary . . . [and] repugnant to the rights of those with whose property the petitioners are entrusted'.[59] They went so far as to suggest the action would be 'productive of great alarm and perhaps occasion public disturbances'.[60] The Commons were, however, little moved by such claims, and it was ultimately only by offering an interest-free advance of £500,000 to the government that the removal of the unpaid dividends was avoided. Subsequent to this, the Bank, for the first time, published a list of persons with unclaimed dividends.[61]

The overarching record of the Bank's accounts was the General Ledger. This was maintained by Mr Edwards, the deputy accountant, and locked with a padlock when not in use.[62] It was not accessed by any other clerk 'except Mr Beardsley, who helps to prick the Ledger'.[63] Pricking (poking small holes into the pages of the ledger) ensured that lines were straight. As Roxburgh asserts, this helped to ensure that the correct figures were added or subtracted and thus was vital to the integrity of the record.[64] The General Balance was made up every night after five o'clock. It recorded all payments and receipts made that day, and it drew its information from the Hall Balance Book, in which was recorded balances from

56. Ibid., fol. 79.

57. S. H. Preston, 'Unclaimed Stocks, Dividends, and Bank Deposits', *Chambers's Journal of Popular Literature, Science and Arts*, 8 (1891), pp. 21–24.

58. Quoted in Acres, *Bank of England from Within*, 1:265.

59. Ibid.

60. Ibid.

61. Bank of England, *The names and descriptions of the proprietors of unclaimed dividends on Bank stock, which became due before the 10th October 1780, and remained unpaid the 30th September 1790* (London, 1791).

62. BEA, M5/213, fol. 17.

63. Ibid.

64. Roxburgh, *Representing Public Credit*, p. 93.

'the 6 Bank Note Cash Books; the 4 Cash Books kept in the Drawing Office; the Chancery Book, letter Z; the G Cash Book; the Bank Stock Dividend Warrants paid; & the Exchequer & Cash Office Account'.[65] In addition, Edwards checked 'all the Great Accounts . . . such as Cash, Bullion Exchequer bills deposited, Bills discounted' on a weekly basis and took balances of all the accounts recorded in the General Ledger six times a year 'but without balancing the Accounts themselves in the said Ledger'.[66] Edwards also noted how the Bank's financial position was presented to the directors, explaining that two half-year balances were taken, each just prior to the payment of the half-yearly dividend on Bank stock. Those balances were 'laid before the Directors; & the Accounts are all closed, & a general Balance Sheet entered in the Ledger itself once a year'.[67] Presentation of the Bank's financial position was, therefore, regularly made to the directorate, although the Bank was not required to publish its balance sheet until the mid-nineteenth century.[68]

Working Conditions

The accountants' work mostly took place in offices out of public view. The office was likely to have been crowded with clerks sitting at rows of desks. The work conducted in those offices was detailed and repetitive and required clerks to remain seated at their desks for the majority of the day, a practice that, if not during the late eighteenth century, was, by the early nineteenth century, understood to be deleterious to general health. By that time physicians had begun to take notice of cramps and even paralyses of the writing arm.[69] The condition was associated not just with writing but with the volume and intensity of the work, such as would have been the case for men in the Accountants Office. Repetitive strain might have been the most debilitating work-related injury that clerks faced, but the implication from later studies of the health of office workers is that the clerk's life might also have led to an accumulation of niggling pains and irritating ailments. C. T. Thackrah observed in 1831 that clerks suffered from poor muscle tone, aches and pains, digestive problems and poor circulation

65. BEA, M5/212, fol. 82.

66. BEA, M5/213, fol. 16.

67. Ibid., fol. 16.

68. The Charter renewal of 1833 required the Bank to make a weekly return of its 'bullion, securities, circulation and deposits' to Parliament and publish a monthly return in the *London Gazette*. Kynaston, *Time's Last Sand*, p. 127.

69. Eve Rosenhaft, 'Hands and Minds: Clerical Work in the First "Information Society"', *International Instituut voor Sociale Geschiedenis*, 48 (2003), p. 41.

due to long hours, a lack of exercise and confined working conditions. He noted that 'though urgent disease is not generally produced, yet a continuance of employment in its fullest extent never fails to impair the constitution and render the individual sickly for life'.[70]

Moreover, while the general longevity of the Bank's clerks must be acknowledged, the buildings did not always provide a healthy workplace.[71] Indeed, although the premises were purpose-built, architectural style had sometimes won out over practicality. For example, because a number of the offices were lit from windows above, the sunlight shone down on ledgers, making it difficult to read them and impairing the eyesight of some clerks. When he was governor, Samuel Beachcroft ordered the colouring of the key lights in the dome 'by way of trial to prevent the great glare of light on the Books'.[72] The Inspectors were also informed about offices that, 'not having any chimnies or other apertures for the admission of fresh Air, are so unwholesome as greatly prejudice the health of the Persons employed in them'.[73] At the time of the Inspection, Mr Millington, the head of the Bank Stock Office, was at home very ill and unlikely to recover. His colleagues attributed his illness to the 'closeness' of the office.[74] It was also noted that 'the Library is so cold & damp for the greatest part of the year, that the Clerks are afraid of continuing there the necessary time for doing the business required'.[75]

The long hours, stress and pressure of clerical work could also take its toll on mental health. In their testimonies to the Committee of Inspection, clerks at the Bank often mentioned long hours in terms that indicated their unhappiness with such modes of working, and they pointed to the pressure of serving the public.[76] Such, and indeed worse, complaints appear to have been common among clerical workers. Charles Lamb, who had worked at the East India Company (EIC), remembered lying awake at night worrying about figures added incorrectly or mistakes in ledgers.[77]

70. Quoted in Anderson, *Victorian Clerks*, p. 17.

71. Of the 321 men employed in 1783, the career paths of 286 can be traced. Of those, 154 died while still in service, but they had served an average of thirty years in the Bank prior to their deaths. The 108 men who retired generally did so after thirty-five years of service. Given that the average age of the cohort at employment was twenty-seven, these men lived into their late fifties or early sixties at least.

72. BEA, M5/451, fol. 30.

73. BEA, M5/213, fol. 22.

74. Ibid., fol. 21.

75. Ibid., fol. 164.

76. See, for example, the testimony of Mr Miller to the Committee of Inspection. BEA, M5/213, fol. 61.

77. R. Vallance and J. Hampden, eds., *Charles Lamb: Essays* (London, 1963), p. 157.

Bowen's account of the management of EIC business notes the 'rising tide of paper' requiring a level of sustained attention to detail which might lead to exhaustion and work-related stress.[78] Rosenhaft's account of German clerical workers also notes the mental strain arising from the constant need for accuracy and the scrutiny of critical eyes on one's work. There were also the constraints of confidentiality to deal with and the consequent check on speech and action.[79] Rosenhaft cites feelings of 'embarrassment, worry and strife' relating to the stresses of clerical work.[80]

The stresses of work at the Bank were compounded for some clerks by very long working days. Certainly, some of the accountants' offices were 'esteemed easy, & are therefore commonly given to those who have served many years in the House'.[81] Other offices completed their work by 3:00 P.M., allowing the men to leave work either for leisure or to go to a second job. There were, however, numerous tasks that had to be completed by the end of each day and which required clerks to stay later. Indeed, it may be argued that a 'second shift' of work commenced at around 2:00 P.M., after customer footfall slowed, and carried on sometimes until the late evening. Clerks who worked at this time were charged with ensuring that various accounts were completed and up to date for the start of the next business day.

In the transfer offices, for example, after the 3:00 P.M. closure, an abstract of all the transfers made that day was created. The abstract was then duplicated and the sums of the two lists compared to check accuracy. As has been noted, the duplicates were sent out of the Bank every evening.[82] A total of twenty-one duplicates were made in the Bank each day.[83] Their purpose was to ensure that the accounts of the public creditors could still be kept accurately in the event of an accident at the Bank that led to the destruction of the original records. Late afternoon work also included posting bills and notes into the discount ledgers. Mr Southey told the Inspectors that this work had to be done late in the day because it required the prior completion of the discounting business.[84] In the late afternoon processes, each bill or note was first 'journalised' and then posted in the discount ledgers to the account of the person by whom it was payable.[85] The warrants from the Discount Office were also journalised

78. Bowen, *Business of Empire*, p. 147.
79. Rosenhaft, 'Hands and Minds', p. 39.
80. Ibid.
81. BEA, M5/213, fol. 11.
82. Ibid., fols. 32, 36.
83. Ibid., fol. 39.
84. Ibid., fol. 6.
85. BEA, M5/212, fol. 212.

and posted to the account of the discounter in the same ledgers. The process then had to encompass notes and bills redeemed. This was done with the aid of the 'Article Book', which was kept by the Clearers in the banking hall and which contained an account of all notes and bills sent out each day for payment. This book became available when the day ended for the Clearers in the early afternoon. The total balances of all discounters were then checked against the Article Book and the amounts posted against the individual accounts in the ledgers.[86] The completion of the work prior to the next working day allowed the ledgers to be made available to the directors' committee-in-waiting to facilitate their day-to-day decision-making.

Sixteen clerks were employed to complete these tasks, and it was the practice of the Bank to appoint clerks from among those whose main jobs finished in the early afternoon. Each was allowed £18 and 5 shillings per annum in addition to their main salaries.[87] They certainly earned their money. Mr Southey reported 'that the work of entering the Discounts & of the payments is extremely heavy—on a moderate day he never gets away 'till 6 or 7 o'clock, & frequently he is much later: many of the other Gentlemen, particularly those who post the payments upon, must remain 2 hours longer'.[88] Mr Bentley similarly noted that his work 'never takes him up less time than two hours & a half or three hours, but very frequently 4 or 5. That he is very seldom out of the Office before 8 at night, if the business is heavy much later, & on a Saturday generally 'till 10 or 11 o'clock'.[89]

Interestingly, having had the opportunity to reveal their working conditions to the Inspectors, the junior clerks in the Accountant's Office sought to secure better conditions. They petitioned the Court of Directors for 'an increase in their annual allowance for doing this extra work'.[90] The Inspectors were asked for their opinion and offered one that was wholeheartedly in support of an uplift in remuneration. They recorded the following:

> That the 16 Clerks employed in the Accountants Office upon the Business of entering & posting discounted Bills into the Discount Ledgers appear to the Committee to be paid very inadequately to the additional trouble & labour bestowed by them in doing this Business, receiving the sum of £300 only, which divided among the whole number amounts to about £18.5 each in addition to their Salary, although they work in an

86. Ibid., fol. 213.
87. BEA, M5/213, fol. 6.
88. Ibid.
89. Ibid., fol. 7.
90. Ibid., fol. 48.

Office which does not partake in the smallest degree of any present or gratuity given by the Publick, & are allways kept 'till a very late hour at night: & that it be recommended to the Governor & Committee of Treasury to take their case into consideration.[91]

It is of interest that these particular clerks framed their request not around a removal of work or the employment of additional hands but rather an increase in the pay for hours worked. They clearly recognised that their work was disadvantageous compared with that of the other clerks in two respects. First, since they did not work in roles that offered direct service to the public or other institutions, they could not participate in the receipt of gratuities. Second, they were not able to undertake external second jobs as did many of their counterparts. Arguably, therefore, these clerks were seeking payment sufficient to compensate for these lost opportunities. In doing so, they demonstrated an ability to think of their time as a medium for exchange, and a willingness to allow the Bank to purchase their time at any hour of the day or evening with sufficient monetary compensation. The Inspectors' willingness to support their claims is less easy to explain. Perhaps they recognised the validity of the clerks' claims, but they might also have been conscious of the very great trust that was placed in men who worked late into the evening, usually with little supervision, and their capacity to do great damage if they were so minded. As noted above, it is likely, therefore, that they viewed additional compensation as essential to keeping such men diligent and honest.

Losing Control

One test of the effectiveness of accounting systems at the Bank is to ask whether they could be deployed to identify crimes of deception or indeed exploited by those determined to defraud the institution or its customers. Prior to the explosion of banknote forgery that followed the introduction of £1 and £2 notes in 1797, there was a small but steady number of cases of deception involving the Bank that were heard at the Old Bailey each year.[92] Most were committed by those external to the Bank, but its clerks also transgressed occasionally.[93] This type of crime was not necessarily

91. Ibid.

92. Tim Hitchcock, Robert Shoemaker, Clive Emsley, Sharon Howard and Jamie McLaughlin, et al., *The Old Bailey Proceedings Online, 1674–1913*, www.oldbaileyonline .org, version 7.0, 24 March 2012.

93. For an overview of clerks' criminality during this period, see Acres, *Bank of England from Within*, 1:232.

difficult to perpetrate. Banknotes and other paper instruments of exchange were relatively easy to alter or counterfeit.[94] Moreover, since the Bank saw such a heavy footfall of customers, it was impossible for clerks to know everyone. Immediate identification of those impersonating customers or public creditors was, therefore, challenging.

The penalties imposed upon forgers and fraudsters were, however, severe. A capital statute had protected Bank of England paper since 1697, and in 1729 a statute was passed that made forgery, counterfeiting, assisting or uttering 'any deed, will, testament, bond, writing obligatory, bill of exchange, promissory note for payment of money, indorsement or assignment of any bill of exchange, or promissory note for payment of money, or acquittance or receipt, either for money or goods' a felony without benefit of clergy.[95] Moreover, this statute was 'sweeping and general', and unlike many other felony statutes, the penalty of death was often imposed.[96] Indeed, throughout the long eighteenth century, 'a small but steady stream of forgers died upon the gallows'.[97]

As a matter of course, the Bank made efforts to protect against forgery and fraud. There were numerous records and processes which sought to aid identification of customers. The 'Firm Book', for example, preserved a record of all the signatures of persons holding accounts with the Bank.[98] Other processes were intended to ensure that parties could be traced. Thus, a 'Permit Book' was kept as a register of those allowed to draw on any individual who kept an account with the Bank. This was also possible in the case of bills but required a power of attorney to be lodged with the Drawing Office.[99] Indorsements were also used in situations where individuals were not known to the clerks. Thus, when the individual came into the Drawing Office to present a draft for payment, they were required to indorse the draft. Once the payment had been made, the draft was then entered into one of the various cash books, immediately posted to the drawing ledger with a cross-reference to the relevant cash book so that records were kept up to date.[100]

94. Mockford, 'Exactly as Banknotes Are'; Virginia Hewitt, 'Beware of Imitations: The Campaign for a New Bank of England Note, 1797–1821', *The Numismatic Chronicle*, 158 (1998), pp. 197–222.

95. Randall McGowen, 'From Pillory to Gallows: The Punishment of Forgery in the Age of the Financial Revolution', *Past and Present*, 165 (1999), p. 129.

96. Ibid., p. 109.

97. Ibid.

98. BEA, M5/212, fol. 83.

99. Ibid.

100. Ibid., fols. 79–80.

Nonetheless, there were also points at which the Bank's processes lacked rigour. We have seen, for example, issues with both the preparation and storage of notes that created risks of forgery and theft.[101] Although checking signatures was a tried and tested way to ascertain identity, when examined, clerks, in the transfer offices at least, admitted that it was not their practice 'to compare the signatures of all persons transferring Stock with their acceptances, in order to see if the writings are alike answered'.[102] The failure to check signatures in the transfer offices was the result of an overwhelming amount of work and a desire to serve the public in a timely fashion, and it was symptomatic of processes elsewhere in the institution. There was simply not enough time for all possible checks to be enacted.

Where deception occurred, the Bank was dogged in pursuing prosecution and often sought to exact the highest penalty.[103] Indeed, although referring to the Restriction Period, McGowen argues that 'the gallows played the pivotal role' in the Bank's strategy for dealing with deception.[104] This involved the Bank in more than just the identification of criminal behaviour. Within the contemporary prosecution system, victims of crime were obliged to seize the perpetrator, investigate the crime and bear at least some of the costs of prosecution.[105] As a case recorded in Samuel Beachcroft's diary illustrates, the institution was prepared to go to great lengths in such investigations. Thus, on 3 June 1775 there was delivered to Mr Martin, a clerk at the Bank, a forged note which had been taken by a Mr Clark in Northampton. Mr Martin's following investigations took him to Scotland and the Netherlands in his attempts to identify the forgeries and track down the counterfeiters.[106]

There is no question that the Bank's ledgers and accounts and the clerks who kept them formed a key part of its investigations of crime and its evidence-giving in court. Thus, in the case of John Matthison (alias Maxwell), heard at the Old Bailey in May 1779, a forged note was identified by Francis Martin, deputy secretary to the Bank, by comparison with the Bank's books. When asked whether the note was genuine, Martin stated, 'I believe it to be a false one; I have examined this note with our books; I do not find such a note issued out of the Bank that day. I have

101. See chapter 2.

102. BEA, M5/213, fol. 30.

103. Deirdre Palk, ed., *Prisoners' Letters to the Bank of England, 1781–1827* (London, 2007), p. viii.

104. Randall McGowen, 'Managing the Gallows: The Bank of England and the Death Penalty, 1797–1821', *Law and History Review*, 25 (2007), p. 243.

105. McGowen, 'Policing of Forgery', p. 83.

106. BEA, M5/451, fols. 15–21.

examined both the cash book and the note ledger'.[107] Further evidence relating to the quality of the paper on which the note was printed and the cashier's signature was presented in this case. In both instances it was clear that the court placed trust in the expertise and integrity of the clerks and the records that they maintained.[108]

In the case of John Vestenburg, heard at the Old Bailey in 1772, a number of clerks were called to testify about the Bank's accounting processes as a way of identifying the fraud. Vestenburg was accused, but ultimately acquitted, of involvement in the forgery of a draft for £5,000. The clerks giving evidence in this case referred variously to methods of keeping customer accounts in the Drawing Office, the issuance of cheques and the maintenance of customer bank books. Since the fraud referred to a draft drawn up in 1765, the clerks also referred to the preservation of records that had allowed them to trace the crime. These included tickets instructing the tellers to make payments and the historical accounts of the person who had been defrauded.[109] Equally, the case of Thomas Sherwood, convicted in 1778 of forging a power of attorney, saw Bank clerks produce in court the relevant three per cent consols transfer book and the Minute Book of the Court of Directors, which recorded permission to make the disputed transfer.[110] The Bank's records and its keeping of those records, therefore, were trusted sufficiently to support the prosecution of those charged with deception.

This did not mean, however, that they were infallible. The case of John Smith, heard in 1782, demonstrated that, with such a common name, mistakes could certainly occur. It transpired that a transfer of £200 had been placed into the account of the wrong John Smith. The man who benefitted from this, instead of pointing out the error, accepted the dividend for the higher amount and then sold out his stock. But when the case came to trial, he was found not guilty because 'the clerks of the Bank made a mistake, and that mistake enabled them to offer this man more than belonged to him, . . . he dishonestly took more than belonged to him; but he, from the circumstances of the case, never personated any man'.[111]

107. *Old Bailey Proceedings Online* (www.oldbaileyonline.org, version 8.0, 28 November 2021), May 1779, trial of John Matthison, otherwise Maxwell (t17790519-24).

108. Ibid.

109. *Old Bailey Proceedings Online* (www.oldbaileyonline.org, version 8.0, 11 December 2021), April 1772, trial of John Vestenburg (t17720429-78).

110. *Old Bailey Proceedings Online* (www.oldbaileyonline.org, version 8.0, 11 December 2021), February 1778, trial of Thomas Sherwood (t17780218-14).

111. *Old Bailey Proceedings Online* (www.oldbaileyonline.org, version 8.0, 11 December 2021), December 1782, trial of John Smith (t17821204-79).

Errors that facilitated fraud were relatively rare. Deliberate impersonation of a fund-holder or their nominee was, however, more common. One of the most celebrated was that of Sophia Pringle. Pringle's fraud was motivated by an inability to support herself and her lover, who had become too ill to work. She therefore hatched a plan to defraud her father's lodger, William Winterburne, by forging a power of attorney and then procuring the services of a broker to sell £100 of stock in Winterburne's name. This attempt was successful. Pringle then made a second attempt to sell additional stock a week later. Having appeared to the broker earlier 'in the habit of a servant', she returned with a 'muff and feathers'. This was sufficient to arouse the suspicions of the broker, who informed the Bank. Pringle was apprehended, tried and executed.[112]

The prosecution of Henry Berthaud demonstrates the extent to which it was difficult for some fund-holders to protect themselves against such crimes. Berthaud had offered to accompany the illiterate Mark Groves to the Bank of England and assist him in the purchase of £100 in unspecified stock. Berthaud conducted the business but retained the receipt. He later returned to the Bank and sold the stock, signing Groves's name for it. Groves realised he had been defrauded only later when he went to enquire at the Bank and found no funds in his name.[113] Similarly, Thomas Eaton testified at the Old Bailey that John Ash had impersonated him in order to gain control of £750 of Bank shares. When Eaton had gone to the Bank to collect his dividend,

> and while he was in the act of receiving it, he perceived the prisoner close to his elbow, the prisoner was a journeyman Baker, and was at that the paying his adresses to a niece of Mr. Eaton's, seeing the prisoner at his elbow he thought it odd, but he only said, you want to see what I am worth.[114]

However, having observed Eaton's worth and his signature, Ash returned to the Bank and identified himself as Eaton to sell out the shares. These cases illustrate the complexities of managing a public debt owned by thousands of individual creditors. The identities of individuals frequently had to be taken on trust. This made deliberate exploitation, such as that

---

112. Deirdre Palk, 'Sophia Pringle', *London Lives, 1690–1800*, accessed 26 November 2021 (www.londonlives.org, version 1.1, 17 June 2012).

113. *Old Bailey Proceedings Online* (www.oldbaileyonline.org, version 8.0, 11 December 2021), September 1782, trial of Henry Berthaud (t17820911-107).

114. *Old Bailey Proceedings Online* (www.oldbaileyonline.org, version 8.0, 11 December 2021), January 1784, trial of John Ash (t17840114-53).

conducted by Pringle, Berthaud and Ash, possible based on reasonable knowledge of a public creditor's holdings. Detection relied upon the original fund-holder making inquiries or, as in the case of Pringle, financial professionals becoming aware of anomalous behaviour and acting on their suspicions.

Members of the public committing such crimes had to rely upon their knowledge of individual public creditors and sometimes, as in the case of Ash, observation of the Bank's processes. Clerks knew the systems in the Bank, and inevitably they also learned how to identify and exploit the loopholes in those systems. Few acted upon that knowledge, but those who did often did significant damage before they were apprehended. A particularly notable case is that of Robert Aslett, who had served as secretary to the Committee of Inspection. Aslett had been praised by the Inspectors for his diligence and subsequently rose to high office in the Bank, becoming 'second cashier' and, as Acres suggests, being expected to take over from Abraham Newland as chief cashier in due course.[115] Yet, Aslett was a speculator and lost considerable amounts of money in the funds. In order to cover his losses, he misappropriated thousands of pounds in Exchequer bills.[116] His crime was possible because he was solely in charge of the purchase of Exchequer bills, owing to what was by 1803 'the great age and growing infirmities of Mr. Newland, the principal Cashier'.[117] This was despite the 1783–1784 Inspection and subsequent inspections that highlighted the importance of 'superintending care' of the Bank's clerks.[118] In fact, it was only subsequent to Aslett's frauds that a system of 'dual control' was introduced, in which no single clerk could have sole control over any item that had monetary value.[119]

The subsequent history of another clerk working at the time of the Inspection provides a perspective on how one of the more junior men could manipulate the Bank's records. Francis Fonton was not particularly noticed by the Inspectors but appears to have been generally regarded as a good clerk. However, around 1788 or 1789 he met the wife of a sea captain who, while her husband was away, amused herself by following an itinerate basket-maker turned preacher.[120] Fonton was married at the

115. Acres, *Bank of England from Within*, 2:364.

116. Ibid., 2:364–367.

117. *Old Bailey Proceedings Online* (www.oldbaileyonline.org, version 8.0, 12 December 2021), July 1803, trial of Robert Aslett (t18030706-34).

118. BEA, M5/213, fol. 174.

119. Giuseppi, *Bank of England*, p. 84.

120. Anon., *Genuine and Impartial Memoirs of Francis Fonton, late of the Bank of England* (London, 1790), p. 11.

time, although little is found about his wife. He was a dissenter and, in the aftermath of his conviction, professed some Antinomian religious views, possibly picked up from this preacher or other explorations in religion. Fonton began an affair with the sea captain's wife, and she assured him that, thanks to the ministrations of their preacher, they could do as they pleased in the evening but then rise in the morning to 'prayer in the chapel of the basket-maker' and, presumably, forgiveness of their sins.[121] Fonton took full advantage of this and of two other women living in the sea captain's house, kept there apparently for the 'basest of purposes'.[122]

Fonton was soon offering to help his lover increase her fortune. She had saved £200, and he offered to put it into the stocks for her. The receipt she was given for her money was fake. The surviving sources are not clear on why Fonton defrauded his lover, but we may speculate that he used the money to fund his lifestyle. The pamphlet detailing Fonton's life also lists others whom he similarly defrauded, including a milk-maid, a brick-maker and a cow-keeper; the latter was described as having lost his mind when he discovered that he had been defrauded out of £300. Mr Blades, one of the City officers, also gave Fonton power of attorney to act as his agent, and he sustained a loss of £600.[123]

Fonton was not convicted for these crimes. However, he was apprehended for a fraud against William Papps, conducted in May 1789. Papps, who had used Fonton as a broker before, asked him to purchase £50 in the 4 per cent annuities. Fonton agreed to do this and some days later called Papps into the Bank to sign an acceptance for the stock. What Papps actually signed was a transfer of £450 from his account to another man, John Pierce. Fonton then gave Papps a receipt for the £50, and so Papps initially had no reason to doubt the transaction.[124] At a trial prosecuted by the famous William Garrow, Fonton was found guilty of a crime described as 'the most injurious to a commercial country like this'. The point was further made that it was Fonton's situation at the Bank which allowed him to know 'every minutiae in the business . . . and that knowledge you have applied to a purpose the most base and nefarious'.[125]

Like Aslett, Fonton exploited gaps in the Bank's processes to commit his crimes. In particular, Fonton was able to identify deceased public

121. Ibid., p. 12.
122. Ibid., p. 13.
123. Ibid., p. 15.
124. *Old Bailey Proceedings Online* (www.oldbaileyonline.org, version 8.0, 15 December 2021), September 1790, trial of Francis Fonton (t17900915-37).
125. Anon., *Genuine and Impartial Memoirs of Francis Fonton*, p. 35.

creditors, access dividend warrants and sign them on another's behalf, and issue receipts for stock. The inscribed system of stock holding practiced at the Bank compounded the problem. A system in which the Bank was the only holder of the legal record of ownership of stocks was always going to be open to manipulation by someone who was so inclined. And crimes would be discoverable only when the original fund-holder questioned their account. Finally, of course, Fonton had to be physically in a position to commit his crimes. It was his job within the Dividend Offices that allowed him easy access to not only the records but also the customers, the people whom he would defraud.

The Inspectors found that the integrity of the Bank's accounts and the clerks who managed them stood up to scrutiny the majority of the time. There were numerous checks and balances, which seemed to effectively prevent, or at least identify, errors or deliberate attempts to manipulate the record. As in other areas of the Bank, however, there remained concerns about security. In this case, the Inspectors' particular worry was the storage of the unpaid dividend warrants, which 'were placed (to the amount of £75,000) in a wooden Cupboard under one lock, to which each of the Clerks has a key'.[126] This struck the Inspectors as surprising given that the Cheque Office, in which the warrants were stored, had been established as the result of a previous case of embezzlement. In order to keep greater control over the warrants in the future, the Inspectors ordered more effective checks on the unpaid warrants and the removal of the Cheque Office to a different part of the Bank where it would be more secure and an iron safe could be installed.[127]

One risk that could not be eliminated, however, was the clerks themselves. The previous chapter discussed the precautions that were taken in the employment of the men. The requirement that each clerk provide guarantors against losses they might incur during the course of their work has also been noted. Further, the Committee for House and Servants, one of the standing committees of the Bank, took responsibility for the oversight of the clerks and monitored their diligence and behaviour both at work and outside of work, when called so to do. Acres notes, for example, dismissals for 'rioting and drunkenness' outside of the Bank—in 1736, Edward Stone was dismissed as a result of his gambling habit.[128] Yet, as

---

126. BEA, M5/213, fol. 142.
127. Ibid., fols. 144–145.
128. Acres, *Bank of England from Within*, 1:226.

the cases of Aslett and Fonton show, sometimes risky behaviour was not obvious until it was too late.

Moreover, the temptations of life in London were many. As some of the men in the Accountants Office worked into the late evening, other clerks would have left the Bank for the day. They may have lingered on their way home to enjoy the opportunities the city afforded. They would have found plenty to entertain them. Shops stayed open until around 10.00 P.M. Evening theatre and opera finished at around eleven. A visitor to London in 1770 found the London's streets as crowded at midnight as they were at midday.[129] The gaming tables in some less respectable establishments awaited others. In the wake of Charles Clutterbuck's fraud, the *London Chronicle*'s correspondent reported observing 'several clerks belonging to banking and merchant houses, who are in the custom of frequenting such tables, and sacrificing their time, their character and their fortunes, to the meanest gratifications'.[130]

129. Georg Christoph Lichtenberg, *Visits to England*, quoted in Acres, *Bank of England from Within*, 1:226.
130. Andrew, "'How Frail Are *Lovers Vows*'", p. 186.

CHAPTER SIX

Guarding the Guardian of Public Credit

THE GREATEST PHYSICAL THREAT to the Bank came during the Gordon riots. The riots were unprecedentedly bloody with some estimates suggesting that up to 700 people had been killed or wounded. Twenty-five individuals were subsequently hanged for offences against property.[1] One observer, a military volunteer, wrote of the 'atmosphere red as blood with the ascending fires, muskets firing in every part, and consequently women and children lying sprawling in the streets; all the lower order of people stark mad with liquor, huzzaing and parading with flags'.[2] Amongst the destruction, on the night of 7 June 1780, in the 'most revolutionary phase' of the Gordon riots, attempts were made to storm the Bank of England.[3] The first came a little after 8:00 P.M., the second after 10:00 P.M. and finally in the early hours of the morning 'a large party of rioters [approached from] Cheapside in order to attack the Bank, several of them armed with muskets. . . . The mob was so great that they beat off the Horse Guards but the Foot, by keeping a constant fire, dispersed them'.[4] Among those who stood alongside the Horse and Foot Guards that night were the political radical John Wilkes and the Bank's own staff.[5] Legend has it that the latter's guns were loaded with bullets cast from the melted down ink-stands

1. Ian Haywood and John Seed, 'Introduction', in Ian Haywood and John Seed, eds., *The Gordon Riots: Politics, Culture and Insurrection in Late Eighteenth-Century Britain* (Cambridge, 2012), p. 7.

2. Nicholas Rogers, *Crowds, Culture and Politics in Georgian Britain* (Oxford, 1998), p. 152.

3. Haywood and Seed, 'Introduction', p. 6.

4. *London Chronicle*, quoted in Abramson, *Building the Bank*, pp. 83–84.

5. Ian Gilmour, *Riot, Risings and Revolution: Governance and Violence in Eighteenth-Century England* (London, 1995), p. 355; Acres, *Bank of England from Within*, 1:208–209.

from their desks.[6] By the end of the night, hundreds of the rioters were dead and areas of the City left in ruins, but the Bank remained safe and indeed opened for business (although a much-reduced business) the next day.[7]

The conflict serves as a powerful reminder that we should not underestimate the Bank's vulnerability, as essentially a public space, to attack by riotous crowds, nor should we overestimate the support for the institution. Moreover, the attack on the Bank was not just an anomaly in a set of actions more properly directed at the symbols of state repression.[8] Certainly some of the rioters may have been spurred on by rumours that the Bank contained a quantity of Popish money, but a number of factors also made it a legitimate target. Since it was regularly active in the courts, as it sought to protect both its business and the financial system against the activities of coiners and forgers, the Bank was viewed as a symbol of both authority and repression. Historians also acknowledge a strong 'class' bias in attacks on Catholics and other targets. As Rudé suggested, there was, in the actions of the rioters, 'a groping desire to settle accounts with the rich, if only for a day'.[9] In this respect, the Bank was a natural target. It had, for a long time, been the focus of resentment among those of London's middling sorts who were losing ground to the monied men and indeed among a broader section of society who suffered the burden of taxation that resulted from the wars of the period. And while it is certainly going too far to suggest that the mob understood that 'whoever is master of the bank and the tower will soon become master of the city, and whoever is master of the city will soon be the master of Great Britain', the rioters must have seen the Bank as a strong symbol of political and economic power.[10]

The purpose of this chapter is to consider how the Bank was secured against such threats, particularly in the aftermath of the Gordon riots. What follows will outline the evening and night-time routines, from locking away the Bank's records to procedures followed by the institution's

6. Acres, *Bank of England from Within*, 1:210. As Acres asserts, it seems unlikely that the Bank would have had to resort to such measures since it kept a reasonably well-stocked armoury.

7. Haywood and Seed, 'Introduction', p. 7.

8. See, for example, Clapham, *Bank of England*, 1:184–185; Acres, *Bank of England from Within*, 1:208–210.

9. G.F.E. Rudé, 'The Gordon Riots: A Study of the Rioters and Their Victims', *Transactions of the Royal Historical Society*, 6 (1956), p. 109; Gilmour, *Riot, Risings and Revolution*, p. 361.

10. Watson, biographer of Lord George Gordon, quoted in Abramson, *Building the Bank*, p. 84.

watchmen. It will demonstrate the measures taken against catastrophic threats like riot and arson. Yet, we must also acknowledge that, despite the drama of June 1780, mundane risks, such as neglected candles and misplaced keys, were far more regular and pressing problems at the Bank. This chapter will also return to themes that have been considered throughout concerning the Bank's relationship with its customers, the state and the public creditors and the messages of probity contained in its visible routines of organisation and management. The size and complexity of the Bank also continued to create what by now are familiar problems to us. Well-designed routines, once again, had been compromised by the press of business and the need to deal with the everyday life of a complex organisation.

Fortifying the Bank?

Daniel Abramson has argued that the Gordon riots revealed the Bank's dependence on the state for its security. He cites the immediacy of the response to the disturbance and the size of the force stationed at the Bank in the immediate aftermath of the riots: 534 Foot Guards, which was the largest armed force in the City.[11] In some respects, he was right. The defence provided to the Bank on the night of 7 June 1780 and subsequently stands as a powerful statement of Parliament's willingness and desire to protect the country's chief financial institution. It also reflects a widely held view of 'the confusion that must have ensued, the ruin that would have been spread, the distresses in which orphans, widows, natives and foreigners, persons of all ranks and conditions . . . would have been involved, by the annihilation of so many hundreds of millions of property, and the total abolition of all public credit!'[12] But Abramson's assessment of the Bank's dependence on the state-backed force is too simplistic. As discussed above, the institution's reputation rested upon an intimate relationship with the public that was based upon transparency, access and a very carefully mediated relationship with government. In the aftermath of the riots, therefore, difficult choices had to be made.

The directors clearly contemplated a response that included fortification of their buildings. Immediately following the disturbances, they consulted with a military engineer, Lieutenant Colonel Hugh Debieg, regarding possible improvements to the site's defences. Debieg argued

---

11. Abramson, *Building the Bank*, p. 86.
12. *Gentleman's Magazine*, July 1780, quoted in Haywood and Seed, 'Introduction', p. 8.

for a number of changes to the site, including enclosing the Bank within 'strong and high' walls topped by 'flanking towers sufficiently high to command the roofs'.[13] He also advised the purchase and demolition of adjacent buildings, especially St Christopher's church, which was located to the immediate left of the Bank in Threadneedle Street. Debieg's view was that these changes would enable the Bank's staff to defend it against attack at least until troops could be sent to its protection.[14] That a military engineer was consulted is testament to the seriousness with which the directors regarded the defence of the Bank, but the idea of turning it into a fortress went a step too far. Undoubtedly, the directors were mindful of the expense. Debieg estimated that the proposed changes would cost around £30,000.[15] But the directors were also keenly aware of the Bank's status as a public institution. As such, it had to be accessible to London's financial community and the investing public and had to be seen to be accessible. Thus, the fortification of the Bank was rejected.

On the other hand, the takeover of St Christopher's did go ahead, prompted at least in part by the needs of security. Being directly adjacent to the Bank, the church seemed to offer a means of easy access for persons intending harm to the institution. This led the directors to ask that they be allowed to purchase those parts of the church immediately adjoining the Bank's buildings and that some doors and lower windows of the church be blocked. However, the concerns of space were also in the directors' minds, and in March 1781 the Bank switched tack and petitioned Parliament to be granted the church in its entirety. The parishioners protested, but their numbers had been eroded by the Bank's systematic purchase of houses in the vicinity, and their bishop, Robert Lowth, supported the Bank's cause. There had been ninety-two houses in the parish of St Christopher's in 1734 when the Bank moved into Threadneedle Street.[16] The Bank calculated that by the time it had taken down the houses purchased during the early 1780s, the number of parishioners would not exceed ten. Thus, the parish of St Christopher's was merged with the adjoining parish of St Margaret Lothbury in 1781.[17] In 1782 the Bank paid £4,462 for the parish lands and compensated the vicar of the church with an annual sum of £38 during his life and the sextoness, Susanna Sculthorp, with a one-off sum of 20

13. Quoted in Abramson, *Building the Bank*, p. 86.
14. Ibid.
15. Ibid.
16. See 'Threadneedle Street' in chapter 1.
17. John Deacon, 'The Story of St. Christopher-Le-Stocks', *The Old Lady of Thread-needle Street* 58 (1982), pp. 76–78.

guineas.[18] Soon after, the demolition of St Christopher's and the repurposing of its site began. Although the church was removed, and in spite of its need for space, the Bank never did build over St Christopher's burial ground. Indeed, the human remains were not removed until a further redevelopment of the Bank during the mid-nineteenth century.[19] But while the dead slept undisturbed, the destruction of St Christopher's marked the removal of one of the last key points of resistance against the Bank's control of its immediate physical environment.

One reason for the Bank's desire for additional space was to accommodate the Foot Guard that became a permanent feature of the Bank's night-time security arrangements. It had remained at the Bank twenty-four hours a day in the immediate aftermath of the riots and had been regarded as a necessary measure. The Guard had then been removed in the autumn of 1780 on account of the City's elections to Parliament. In late September, as the election concluded, the Bank's governor, Daniel Booth, requested resumption of the Guard, writing to Colonel Hyde:

> Sir,
>
> I am desired by the Court of Directors of the Bank of
> England, (as the election of members of Parliament for the
> City of London finally closed yesterday at three o'clock in
> the afternoon) to request the favor, that a Guard of 30 men,
> may be ordered this evening to the Bank; and as it seems
> to be the opinion of the Gentlemen, Directors of the Bank,
> that a Guard in the daytime is not now necessary (if you
> have no material objection) they rather wish they may come
> early in the evening and return in the morning.[20]

This request was agreed to, and for the next 193 years, until 1973, a troop of around thirty Guards was stationed at the Bank each night.[21]

Not all in London supported the Guard's presence at the Bank. Indeed, it was resented by both the City Corporation and the local populace. This was, in part, because on their march from Westminster via the busy streets of The Strand, Fleet Street and Cheapside, they went two abreast, jostling the public out of their way. Their march was satirised by James

18. BEA, G4/23, fols. 323, 341.

19. At that point the remains were transferred to Nunhead Cemetery, near Peckham Rye. Deacon, 'St. Christopher-Le-Stocks', p. 78.

20. BEA, G4/23, fol. 115.

21. Kynaston, *Time's Last Sand*, p. 54. See also BEA, 17A100/1, The Bank Picquet: Its function and history 1963.

FIGURE 6.1. James Gillray, *A March to the Bank* (1787).
Source: Bank of England Museum accession 0274 (ii). © Bank of England.

Gillray, who in 1787 presented an arrogant, strutting Guard trampling over those who dared to get in their way, whether men, women or children (figure 6.1).[22] This negative view was reinforced the following year when one evening, a guard, Joseph Mitton, bayoneted and killed a member of the public who was too slow to get out of the Guard's path. Mitton was arrested and tried for murder but convicted only of common assault because the judge deemed his actions not to have arisen from any preconceived malice.[23]

Leaving aside specific grievances against the Guard, resentment also centered on the mere presence of a military force protecting a civilian institution. In particular, the Corporation of London considered the Guard both unconstitutional and an infringement on the City's ancient privileges.[24] The aldermen understood that the Bank was not merely reacting to the

22. Vic Gatrell, *City of Laughter: Sex and Satire in Eighteenth-Century London* (London, 2006), pp. 279–280.
23. Acres, *Bank of England from Within*, 1:223.
24. Ibid., p. 224.

immediate imperatives of the Gordon riots. They undoubtedly sympathised. In the aftermath of those disturbances, many had become concerned about rising crime, a concern that was to grow over the course of the 1780s as a perceived crime wave hit London.[25] The City's aldermen were also fully aware of the increasing burden of managing the criminal population as a consequence of the break in transportation during the War of American Independence. Arguments about what could be done, however, were politically contentious and rested on where control of the City should lie, especially if a military force was brought in to maintain order. For this reason, the aldermen have been judged as obstructive of solutions to the City's policing, more focused on protecting their privileges than residents and businessowners.[26] Harris argues persuasively that this was not the case and that the City authorities certainly understood the issues but sought civil solutions and ultimately more enlightened responses to rising crime.[27]

Yet, although perhaps motivated by the same concerns, the Bank's directors refused to trust a civil force for the protection of their interests. The Lord Mayor and Court of Aldermen made several advances to the Bank in an attempt to either have the Guard removed or to be able to provide a troop from the City of London's own militia. An approach by Alderman Watson in July 1788 was not met by any sympathy from the Bank's directors. They replied

> that [they] could not be induced to say, they thought the Guard unnecessary as they had great reason to believe it was highly approved in foreign countries, and there considered as a great security to the property of the Stock-holders; who deemed a Guard, established from the King's own Guards, as a greater security than any private Guard. And that the majority of the Proprietors appeared to be pleased with it.[28]

There, it seems, was an end to the argument. Shareholders and public creditors, both domestic and foreign, approved of the Guard, and thus it would stay in spite of the City's objections.

We must wonder, however, whether the shareholders were so pleased with the fact that, once at the Bank, the Guard was not visible. After

---

25. Andrew T. Harris, *Policing the City: Crime and Legal Authority in London, 1780–1840* (Columbus, OH, 2004), p. 38.

26. Ibid., p. 39.

27. Harris, *Policing the City*, pp. 39–40.

28. BEA, M6/19, Memorandum regarding the introduction and continuance of the King's Guard.

initially being stationed in St Christopher's Church, the Guard was provided with its own barracks in 1782. On 30 May 1782 the Committee of Buildings ordered 'that the door and window frames of the external openings of the empty house in Princes Street adjoining to Mr Newlands, be taken away, and the said openings be bricked up, in a substantial manner, and such other works done thereto, as may be necessary for the reception of the guards'.[29] Thereafter the soldiers remained in what eventually became purpose-built barracks each night rather than patrolling the area around the Bank. They were there in case of attack rather than to serve as a regular defence force.

Moreover, given the occasional complaints made by the Bank about the quality and attentiveness of the Guard, one might also wonder whether they would have been in a fit state to respond in an emergency. Acres records occasions when the officer was absent at night or brought unauthorized persons to the barracks. In April 1793 a more serious complaint was made when two gentlemen who had come into the Bank to dine with the Guard's officer became abusive, broke bottles and glasses and started a fight with the officer himself 'in the Bank yard'.[30] It seems unlikely that the officer was a totally innocent, or indeed sober, participant in the brawl. Thus, while having an armed force, sober or otherwise, was undoubtedly a deterrent to serious threats, the Bank's staff had to rely on other systems to manage security throughout the night.

Locking Up

While the Foot Guard settled into their barracks, the process of locking up within the Bank commenced. Throughout the day the Bank's papers, books and ledgers were needed. They sat on desks or were stored on shelves or in open repositories so as to be within reach. This was necessary to provide customers with a timely service and, as has been established above, was a significant indicator of the transparency of the Bank's processes in support of its primary businesses. Yet, while there were good reasons for the records to be openly available all day, they needed to be made secure when the institution closed. It is important to remember, however, that the working day at the Bank did not finish at 5:00 P.M. As we saw in the previous chapter, the business continued into the early, and sometimes late, evening as clerks worked to update records ahead of the

29. Ibid.
30. Acres, *Bank of England from Within*, 1:222.

start of the next working day. This involved routines that differed from office to office, that sometimes could not be completed on time and that were always overseen by the more junior men in the Bank's employ—those who formed the cohort of clerks-in-waiting. They had the responsibility of securing the records, ledgers, cash and notes that represented millions of pounds in value, but they were not men in supervisory roles.

In their investigations, the Inspectors appear to have judged the effectiveness of the clerks-in-waiting and the routines they supervised by several measures. They were understandably concerned with physical security in the disposal of records and valuables. They were interested to see the operation of checks and balances so as to ensure that no individual had sole control of security procedures, and they wanted to know who was accountable and to gain a clear sense of who had final responsibility for locking up. Systems were working well in some offices. In his description of the storage of banknotes, Mr Phillips, principal of the O cash book, told the Inspectors that the notes left in each book were counted by a clerk from a different book, under the direction of one of the cashiers. The notes were then locked away in the warehouse. One clerk from each book attended the putting away of the books, and one clerk from each book remained every night until the general balance was made up.[31]

Thomas Holmes, recorded as having been at the Bank for nineteen years, had acted as clerk-in-waiting for the Drawing Office on the evening of 24 November 1783. He was equally clear about procedures. It had been his responsibility to lock up the Drawing Ledgers, the General and Dividend Ledgers, the Journal and the 'tin box' (probably the box in which papers and notes were conveyed to the Exchequer).[32] These items were locked in the strong room, and then the key was delivered to the apartment of the chief accountant. Holmes also shows us how procedures were improving as a response of the Inspection. He noted that 'within the last fortnight an order has been given for the Clerk in Waiting to sign his name every evening in a book kept for the purpose, as an acknowledgement that he has safely deposited all the effects above'.[33]

On the other hand, procedures in the Discount Office, perennially vulnerable because of the records it contained, were more complex. Mr Lewin, who had been the clerk-in-waiting for the Discount Office on the evening of 10 April 1783, informed the Inspectors that business there seldom

---

31. BEA, M5/212, fols. 101–102.

32. BEA, M5/213, fols. 13–14. See chapter 1 for reference to work at the Exchequer.

33. Ibid., fol. 14.

finished before 7:00 or 8:00 P.M. and sometimes the clerks stayed later. Once Lewin's work was finished, the key to the iron chest in which the bills were stored would be delivered to the apartment of the chief accountant or deputy accountant; in their absence, it might be handed over to a servant.[34] A late finish, therefore, meant less certainty about who took control of the keys at the end of the day. Further testimonies revealed additional issues in the Discount Office. Abraham Newland was called in and asked what he thought of the locking-up processes 'on those nights when the business finishes late'.[35] He judged that the storage of the bills was insecure, and thus a 'place for securing these Bills & Notes with 2 different Locks to it ought to be provided & 2 Clerks be directed to remain every night 'till they are all lock'd up, each Clerk taking a key, & leaving them 'till next morning, at such different places as the Committee shall think fit'.[36] He further argued that the Discount Office was not a fit place for the repository for the bills and notes as it was too isolated. He preferred that it be sited somewhere more public.[37]

The complexity of business and a later finish also created problems for the out-tellers. Out-telling, as we saw in chapter 1, was a job undertaken in the morning, but an out-teller-in-waiting was obliged to remain in the Bank every day until 6:00 P.M. 'to receive payment of such Bills as have been brought in by the OutTellers unpaid & are afterwards taken up at the Bank by the persons they are upon'.[38] Because this work was not completed until later in the evening, it was impossible for the out-teller's funds to be locked away as normal but was 'customary for him to deliver his money tied up in a bag, weighed & ticketed, to the Clearer with his Notes & other Effects, & the Clearer sends the bag to the Cashier in waiting who locks it up in the Warehouse all night'.[39] Weighing and ticketing was a systematic procedure, but the passing of the out-teller's bag through several hands prior to locking up implied a problematic lack of accountability for its contents.

Failures in the Bank's processes were compounded by the complications of the technology of security. Historians have located the emergence of a modern security industry during the 1770s but do not seem to have found the sources that might allow an exploration of how these new technologies

34. BEA, M5/212, fols. 65–66.
35. BEA, M5/212, fol. 63.
36. Ibid.
37. Ibid.
38. BEA, M5/212, fol. 7.
39. BEA, M5/212, fol. 8.

were implemented.[40] The Committee of Inspection's Minutes provide just such an opportunity. They show that, by some standards, the technology of security used at the Bank was sophisticated. Locking drawers, cupboards, bookcases, chests and safes were used to store papers and cash during the day and at night. There were also vaults and the 'warehouse', in which were stored unsigned notes, cash, bullion and other papers and in which key ledgers, cash and notes in use were locked overnight. Most of the individual office doors had locks, and some of those doors, including those of the Bullion Office and the warehouse, were constructed of iron rather than wood.[41] The Bank's General Ledger was also padlocked 'to prevent it being opened or looked into'.[42]

Yet, while acting as a strong deterrent to an opportunist, it is not certain that all locking devices would have been sufficiently complex to challenge a determined and sophisticated thief. As Joseph Bramah showed, most eighteenth-century locks were of simple construction and depended upon 'applying a lever to an interior bolt by means of a communication from without'.[43] Such devices were not difficult to force and offered only the illusion of security. Moreover, even complex mechanisms, which included a higher number or greater complexity of 'wards' or obstructions to opening, offered no real barrier to the determined lock-breaker, according to Bramah. 'For though an artful and judicious arrangement of the wards . . . may render the passage to the bolt so intricate or perplexed, as to exclude every instrument but its proper key', a skilled workman would still be able to break the lock.[44]

There is no record of the types of locks generally used at the Bank, but it is clear that the Inspectors were unconvinced of their quality in at least some cases. The Bank's wooden drawers and cupboards were condemned as being too easy to break into. The chest in the Discount Office was 'very light, weak, not fix'd to the floor, & in all respects insufficient for the security of so large a property as is frequently there deposited'.[45] The chests

40. For example, David Churchill, 'Security and Visions of the Criminal: Technology, Professional Criminality and Social Change in Victorian and Edwardian Britain', *British Journal of Criminology*, 56 (2016), pp. 857–876. A similar argument has been made by Peter Linebaugh, who dates the emergence of new theory and practice to the period following the Gordon riots. Peter Linebaugh, *The London Hanged* (London, 2006), p. 365.

41. BEA, M5/213, fol. 180.

42. BEA, M5/213, fol. 13.

43. Joseph Bramah, *The Petition and Case of Joseph Bramah . . . Inventor of the PATENT LOCKS for the Security of Life and Property* (London, 1798), p. 7.

44. Ibid., p. 8.

45. BEA, M5/212, fol. 62.

used for the storage of keys in the Chief Cashier's office were regarded as 'very insecure', and the Committee ordered them to be replaced.[46] Since all clerks had access to particular areas or stores in the Bank, it would have been extremely difficult to trace errors or attempts to defraud the Bank. Equally, it was almost impossible to pin down whose responsibility it was to lock up. Although the responsibility nominally lay in the hands of the clerks-in-waiting, with so many others having access to keys, the clerks-in-waiting could never be positively identified as having been the last persons to access a storage unit or office. Further, the watchmen also had access to the keys of certain offices overnight, as they needed them to gain entry for cleaning.

Keys, in fact, presented a particular problem within this system. The burden of trust was high, and yet accountability was low. This was in stark contrast to the typical Georgian household, which often had just one set of keys, a measure which restricted access to, and monitored movements within, the house.[47] Household keys were kept in the hands of its head, and access to keys corresponded to the seniority and responsibility of servants and other members of the household.[48] Keys, therefore, were a symbol of power and not just over the means of access to spaces.[49] And yet, many of the Bank's keys were in the hands of junior or unsupervised clerks. In addition to the keys that provided access to particular offices, keys were given to individual clerks for their desks or lockers. There were also, in some offices, common closets or drawers to which all clerks had a key. In the Discount Office, for example, some bills were stored overnight in an iron chest which itself was stored in a closet, but the key to the closet was stored in a common drawer to which all discount clerks had access.[50] One of the most obvious faults in the system was the storage of keys to the chest in the Chief Cashier's office. This chest had two locks, but there were three keys in the Bank for each lock. The three keys to one lock were kept by the tellers, and the three keys to the other lock were kept by the cashiers. The keys were transferred between the two groups as needed with the only restriction being that, at the end of the day, one key had to be left with the teller-in-waiting and one with the cashier-in-waiting.[51] At

46. BEA, M5/213, fol. 169.

47. Amanda Vickery, *Behind Closed Doors: At Home in Georgian England* (New Haven, CT, 2009), pp. 43–44.

48. Linebaugh, *London Hanged*, p. 366.

49. Ibid.

50. BEA, M5/212, fol. 52.

51. Ibid., fol. 196.

that time the chest was locked, but all the keys remained in various desks in the banking hall. The Committee of Inspection decried the practice, noting that at the time of their inquiry, the chest contained 'Loan receipts &, other articles, to the amount of upwards of four millions'.[52]

Storage of keys when not in use was another worry. At the end of the day's business, keys to all the offices of the Bank were supposed to be delivered by the clerks to the gate porter's lodge, where they were held during the evening. To each was attached a brass label to indicate the office to which it belonged. They were hung up in the passage of the gate porter's lodge, excepting the keys of the Chief Cashier's and Discount offices, which were hung up in the kitchen. These keys could be taken by any of the porters, watchmen or clerks during the evening and were generally collected by a watchman, the porters or indeed the first clerk from each office to attend in the morning.[53] Mr Watkins noted that it was usual, but not compulsory, for people to check either with him or with his wife before taking any keys from his house.[54] Other keys were taken home by clerks in the evening. There were, for example, two keys to the iron chest in the Bill Office. One was locked up overnight in the vault, but the other was taken home by the clerk-in-waiting.[55] In spite of that clerk having possession of the key all night, the Committee were informed that he still could not have been held responsible for the contents of the iron chest because that chest frequently remained unlocked and in use even after the clerk left the Bank for the day and was only finally locked by the other key, that which was stored in the vault overnight.[56]

Likewise, the disposal of duplicate keys was seen to be a problem. These were stored in two little chests in the Chief Cashier's office, and the Committee noticed that 'access being had to one of these little Iron Chests gives a compleat opportunity of opening the Bullion Office, Warehouse, & Safe in the great Parlour, access to the other gives the same opportunity, as well as to the great Iron Chest in Mr Newland's Office'.[57] They concluded that anyone who could get into those little chests would then have access to all the valuable property in the Bank, with the only exceptions being property stored in the vaults. The solution to this was that the duplicate keys were 'sealed up, numbered, & the descriptions put on them, [and] . . .

52. Ibid.
53. Ibid., fols. 187, 197.
54. Ibid., fol. 188.
55. Ibid., fol. 13.
56. Ibid., fol. 24.
57. Ibid., fol. 180.

deposited in the Safe in the Committee room'.[58] The reader might be interested to know that the packages survive unopened, at the time of writing, in the Bank's museum.

The Committee of Inspection was quick to recognise that the trust reposed in locking closets, safes, drawers and offices was generally compromised not by the ingenuity of thieves but instead by lax management of the technologies of security and, in particular, the storage and disposal of keys. The Inspectors' solutions were to alter security systems by removing some keys from circulation, reinforcing the notion that responsibility for managing keys rested with the senior staff, commissioning new small iron chests to be manufactured and placed at the houses of the chief cashier and the chief accountant so that the keys to the Bank could, each night, be deposited there, and manufacturing a lockable cupboard for the storage of the keys at the gate porter's house.[59] There was, however, only so much that could be done in the management of the technology of security. There were points of weakness that were more difficult to address, especially during the early evening.

The first line of defence for the Bank was its perimeter. Some of its access points were shut and locked as soon as was practicable in the late afternoon or evening. Thus, the bullion cartway was locked at around 3:00 P.M., and the gates to the transfer office were locked at half past three.[60] The front gates were supposed to be shut each evening at five during the winter and six during the summer months.[61] Yet, because business carried on much beyond the hours that the Bank was open, and because visitors and residents continued to come and go throughout the evening, this meant that the front gate stood ajar; and, it appears that the two watchmen who were supposed to be stationed at the gate were sometimes neglectful. The Committee took particular note of an incident in which 'Mr Newland [the chief cashier] with another person came in at the gate, passed through the Hall, & went into the Chief Cashier's Office & after staying there a considerable time to look out some papers returned again to the gate, which he found in the same situation, without being perceived by any person in the Bank'.[62] Mr Watkins, the head gate porter, accounted for the lapse in security by saying he had been ill

---

58. BEA, M5/213, fols. 180–181.

59. BEA, M5/212, fols. 198–200. See appendix 4 for the full text of the Inspectors' report on security.

60. Ibid., fol. 191.

61. Ibid., fol. 189.

62. Ibid., fol. 191.

and confined to his apartment.[63] The Committee do not appear to have asked the obvious questions about why the absence of the head gate porter should have been seen as a reasonable explanation for such a lapse, and where the appointed watchmen had been at the time. Nor is it recorded that they asked who was in charge in Mr Watkins's absence. Such lapses were undoubtedly common throughout the evening as visitors came and went and the Bank's clerks left for the evening. The Bank, therefore, was not fully secure until the gates were finally locked at 11.00 P.M.

The Bank's Watch

Once the clerks had left and the residents of the Bank had retired, the institution was in the hands of the watchmen. Fifteen watchmen were employed at a salary of £20 a year, and the Bank retained four supernumeraries who attended each evening to see if they were needed. They were paid a guinea a quarter retaining fee, and if they were required to work, they were paid 1 shilling per night.[64] That shilling was deducted from the pay of the man who was absent. Many of the watchmen also would have had second jobs during the day, and the Bank's men were better paid than their City counterparts. Yet, as we have already seen, by the latter part of the eighteenth century the rising cost of living had begun to seriously erode real wages and the watchmen were experiencing periodic hardship.[65] In a petition presented to the Court of Directors in March 1774, the watchmen requested relief owing to the 'great hardships themselves and families were reduced to by the extreme dearness of the necessaries of life'.[66] The Court agreed but did not order a permanent uplift in salaries. Instead, they ordered the sum of 45 guineas to be equally divided among the fifteen watchmen and 8 guineas to be divided among the four supernumerary watchmen.[67] Similar gratuities were given during other periods of particular economic distress.[68]

Nonetheless, while the basic wage paid by the Bank might not always have been sufficient for life in London, it did have the distinction of being a regular wage and one paid in cash. The directors were also benevolent

63. Ibid., fol. 192.

64. Ibid., fol. 186.

65. L. D. Schwartz, *London in the Age of Industrialisation: Entrepreneurs, Labour Force and Living Conditions, 1700–1850* (Cambridge, 1992), pp. 171–172.

66. BEA, G4/22, fol. 8.

67. Ibid.

68. Acres, *Bank of England from Within*, 1:236.

where they believed it was deserved. In November 1775, Mr McFarland, 'a poor sick watchman', was granted 2 guineas. After his death, McFarland's widow was granted 3 guineas of the full 5 guineas, 'as accustom'd to allow on these occasions', 2 guineas having been advanced previously to help with the funeral expenses.[69] There were also opportunities for additional earnings, which are revealed to us through exercises undertaken during the early nineteenth century to adjust remuneration away from reliance on perquisites. A table of earnings produced in 1805 listed additional pay for working on holidays and Sundays, at 2 shillings 6 pence per day. The value of this work to each man was, however, 'uncertain as it depends upon their taking the duty'.[70]

At the time of the Inspection, perquisites were available to those responsible for security at the Bank. These offerings included being able to take and sell worn-out pens and receiving the stubs of candles used during the watchmen's shifts. A dinner was provided for the watchmen, and each evening between eight and nine o'clock one of their number was allowed to go 'to a neighbouring alehouse and bring or order in six quarts of drink, being a Pint apiece for each man and no more'.[71] Accommodation was provided in the Bank for the door-keepers and the gate porter, and those who were resident were made allowances of coal and candles and could also charge to the Bank 'tinware, turnery and upholstery' for use in their own residences.[72] Some staff were also provided with outer clothing suitable to their positions. The gate porter, for example, was given a 'crimson cloth gowne lined with orange, and a large Bamboo cane with a silver head'.[73] The watchman stationed in the Bartholomew Lane passage was allowed a great coat and a pair of pantaloons at Christmas each year.[74] The Bank also paid regular and generous gratuities: £3 3 shillings each year for the regular watchmen and £2 2 shillings for the supernumeraries.[75] They were also granted a Christmas box by the directors, and the Bank's own clerks also seem to have sometimes offered Christmas boxes and tips to the watchmen, porters and door-keepers.[76]

---

69. BEA, M5/451, fols. 39, 43, 41.

70. BEA, M6/117, List of porters and watchmen with details of their wages and allowances, 1805.

71. Quoted in Acres, *Bank of England from Within*, 1:235.

72. Acres, *Bank of England from Within*, 2:377, 2:382–383.

73. Ibid., 1:144.

74. BEA, M5/607, fol. 12.

75. See, for example, BEA, G4/23, fol. 359.

76. Acres, *Bank of England from Within*, 2:378.

This gifting differed from the gratuities that the Bank made to the clerks, because gifts were made to all watchmen equally and regularly. They were not, then, gifts in recognition of performance but rather would have been regarded as regular and, it is important to understand, expected supplements to wages.[77] As Margot Finn argues, gifts and monetary support were commonly presented to servants and employees and represented social obligation and charity but were also intended to create ties of loyalty.[78] It was perhaps these regular gifts that kept the watchmen and porters active in the Bank's service and desirous of keeping their positions. Yet, as already demonstrated, for an institution attempting to establish its reforming credentials, systems of perquisites and gratuities created problems. Thus, perquisites began to be phased out by the early nineteenth century, with salaries elevated to compensate for any losses.

In order to earn their wage, the watchmen were expected to ensure that all parts of the building were safe and no unauthorised persons remained in the Bank. They were also expected to be vigilant against any threats, and 'upon any noise of fire or calamitous accident' they were required to ring the 'Great Bell' to raise the alarm.[79] They assembled around one hour after the front gates were first shut, thus at 6:00 P.M. in the winter and 7:00 P.M. in the summer. Of the fifteen watchmen, not all were on duty at any one time. Between six or seven o'clock and ten o'clock there were two men at the front gate, one in the banking hall, one in the Rotunda and another stationed in 'the passage', which ran between the Bullion Office and Bartholomew Lane. After 10:00 P.M., there was one man in the front lodge, one in the banking hall, one in the Rotunda and one in 'the passage'.[80] Each man was relieved every two hours, and the men not on duty could occupy themselves in rest and refreshment as they pleased until their duties of cleaning and preparing offices commenced in the morning.

The threats against which the Bank's watch guarded were not negligible. In 1785 the 'violence of nocturnal depredators' was bemoaned by *The Times*, which described them as having 'grown so daring and insolent, that no time, place, or occasion, can afford protection against them'.[81] It was not just individual criminals who were feared. The Gordon riots had left a mark on the collective memory. The coming of peace in 1783 and consequent demobilisation of the armed forces had, as it always did at the

77. Schwartz, *London in the Age of Industrialisation*, p. 158.
78. Finn, *Character of Credit*, p. 84.
79. Acres, *Bank of England from Within*, 1:235.
80. BEA, M5/212, fol. 185.
81. *The Times*, quoted in Harris, *Policing the City*, p. 41.

end of war, increased the fear of crime.[82] Compounding the problem, as noted earlier, was the cessation of transportation of criminals to America. The effects of this were felt especially in London, where the concentration of population and the numbers of criminal acts presented particular issues. The City aldermen in 1786 estimated an additional 4,000 persons remained in the country who 'in the Judgement of the Law were proper to have been sent out of it'.[83]

There had been some improvements in London's night-time environment. Street lighting, powered by oil rather than candles, extended throughout the City, mostly on main thoroughfares but also by now in courts and alleys. It is questionable how much light was given by streets lamps, but they were supplemented by the light from houses and shops in the early evening, and contemporaries argued that better-lit streets had reduced crime, especially assaults and robberies.[84] The City's own watch had been reformed and was now staffed by salaried men rather than householders working in rotation. The expectation of the role was that watchmen would see that entrances to domestic and business buildings were secure, check the state of the street lighting, call the hour or half-hour as a means of reassuring local residents and as a warning to miscreants in the area, and apprehend anybody committing a crime or behaving suspiciously.[85] They may also have interacted with the Bank's watch. In 1776 Edward Sprigs, one of the City's watchmen who worked in the vicinity of the Bank, petitioned for a gratuity to be granted by the Bank's directors in respect of a year's attendance on magistrates with 'common women'. Sprigs was awarded 3 guineas for his service to the Bank and later secured employment as one of the institution's watchmen.[86]

Yet, notwithstanding the competence of its individual members, the City's watch was generally not regarded as capable of dealing with serious threat.[87] The French traveller Pierre Jean Grosley wrote that London was 'guarded during the night only by old men chosen from the dregs of the

82. Douglas Hay, 'War, Dearth and Theft in the Eighteenth Century: The Record of the English Courts', *Past and Present*, 95 (1982), pp. 117–160.

83. Quoted in Harris, *Policing the City*, p. 42.

84. J. M. Beattie, *Policing and Punishment in London, 1660–1750: Urban Crime and the Limits of Terror* (Oxford, 2001), pp. 222–225; Cruikshank and Burton, *Georgian City*, pp. 9–10.

85. Harris, *Policing the City*, p. 13.

86. BEA, M5/451, fol. 55.

87. Beattie, *Policing and Punishment*, pp. 170–172; 222–225; Cruikshank and Burton, *Georgian City*, pp. 9–10.

people, who have no other arms but a lanthorn and a pole'.[88] The author of *Outlines for a Plan for Patroling and Watching the City of London* was more measured but observed, 'The incessant Fatigue of Watching every Night, must inevitably be productive of a Langour little Compatible with the vigilant Exertion to be expected from a useful Guard'.[89] Further, the pay offered to City watchmen was not sufficient to inspire vigilance. At around £13 per annum, it was barely enough to support a family and thus too low to attract the right sort of men since 'watching all and every Night makes it impossible for industrious Handicraftsmen or Manufacturers, to accept of being employed as Watchmen'.[90] Young and able-bodied men would also have been working during the day and thus would have eschewed such night-time employment.

The capacity of the Bank's own watch to do a better job was questionable. They were not necessarily any more youthful or sprightly than their City counterparts. Certainly, many men were retained until their late old age. Hence, at Michaelmas 1777 William Banning and his wife, the gate porter and housekeeper, were let go because they had 'grown old and worn out in the service of the Bank'.[91] In spite of occasional action to retire elderly men, there was no systematic action taken to improve the physical capacity of the watch until the early nineteenth century when some porters, including the 77-year-old Nathaniel Neale, were let go owing to their infirmity. At the same time, an order of the Court of Directors was made, stipulating that 'in future the age of Porters and Watchmen when taken into the service of the Bank to be not less than 25 nor more than 40'.[92] That order was revised in 1809 to one which required men to produce a certificate of their age and a certificate from a 'respectable Medical Man' as to their being in a 'good state of health and free from any bodily infirmity'.[93]

The watch was armed with half-pikes and had access to firearms.[94] The Bank possessed thirty-one muskets with bayonets and 'other accoutrements'.[95] These were kept in the gate porter's lodge and were cleaned and

88. Grosley, *Tour to London*, quoted in R. Shoemaker, *The London Mob: Violence and Disorder in Eighteenth-Century England* (London, 2004), p. 22.

89. Quoted in Elaine A. Reynolds, *Before the Bobbies: The Night Watch and Police Reform in Metropolitan London, 1720–1830* (London, 1998), p. 72.

90. Beattie, *Policing and Punishment*, p. 198.

91. BEA, G4/22, fol. 268. The Bannings were awarded a pension of £35 per annum.

92. Acres, *Bank of England from Within*, 1:380; BEA, M5/607, fol. 1.

93. BEA, M5/607, fol. 1.

94. Acres, *Bank of England from Within*, 1:235.

95. BEA, M5/212, fol. 192.

maintained once a year by an armourer. However, although the porter kept powder and ball at the ready, it does not seem as though the weapons were always loaded. Indeed, William Watkins, the principal gate porter, specifically noted that they had been taken down and loaded 'at the time of the Riots of 1780'.[96] Furthermore, having access to a firearm was one thing; knowing how to use one was quite another. While some of the watchmen might have had previous military service, there is no guarantee they would have been familiar with and able to use a gun. Schwoerer cites long-standing reluctance to allow guns into the hands of the lower sorts, even before consideration of public safety, and how the costs of such weapons would have prevented the poor from owning them.[97] It is unlikely, therefore, that the Bank's watchmen would have been particularly effective against a serious threat.

The storage of guns at the Bank was precautionary, but the threat of riot was real and present. London during the eighteenth century was a crowded and disputatious environment. Shoemaker refers to this period as 'quintessentially the century of the mob'.[98] Although rioting was less prevalent after the unprecedented violence of the Gordon riots, Londoners needed little excuse to take to the streets both in dispute and in celebration. They did so at any time of the day, but studies have shown that crowds—and in particular, riotous crowds—were more likely to gather in the evenings.[99] Harrison, although referring to Bristol rather than London, asserts several reasons for this, including the awareness of leaders of groups that meetings needed to be called outside of working hours, the convenient cover of darkness for riotous actions and the fact that darkness offered no hindrance to the actions of rioting mobs.[100] Equally, celebratory gatherings were usually accompanied by illuminations of some sort which required darkness to be seen to full effect.

It was this particular expression of support for a cause that may explain one of the peculiarities of the Bank's construction. As has been noted, the Bank's street-facing walls had no windows at the ground-floor level. This was undoubtedly to limit points of easy access to the buildings. Nonetheless, it is also likely to have reflected an awareness that the smashing of

96. Ibid.

97. Lois G. Schwoerer, *Gun Culture in Early Modern England* (Charlottesville, VA, 2016), pp. 46–64.

98. Shoemaker, *London Mob*, p. 111.

99. Mark Harrison, 'The Ordering of the Urban Environment: Time, Work and the Occurrence of Crowds 1790–1835', *Past and Present*, 110 (1986), pp. 134–168.

100. Ibid., p. 161.

windows was a typical action of a discontented crowd. In particular, since the setting of lights in windows was a common way of celebrating good news or signalling approval of a particular cause in Georgian England, crowds regularly broke the windows in those buildings where owners refused to illuminate.[101] 'Pulling down houses' was another risk during periods of unrest. This indicated not the physical destruction of the house but rather the destruction of doors and windows and the removal and burning of fixtures and fittings.[102] Such actions would have been highly damaging to the Bank's business. Little wonder, then, that it was judged wise to create a building with as few points of vulnerability and ingress as possible at ground level.

Fire!

The one constant, serious threat to the Bank's existence was fire. Although fire was a possibility any time of the day, the risk increased during the evening and at night when candles and fires for heating would have been most frequently lit and fewer people were around to notice and deal with a blaze before it got out of control. The risk of fire was certainly one of the biggest physical threats that the institution faced, and thus fire prevention was one of the watchmen's main roles, although performed with limited reach. The Bank was housed in a very large building, and not all of the spaces were regularly patrolled at night. Chimneys, hearths and stoves improperly attended to in the offices presented a hazard. Clerks had to work by candle-light, especially in the winter months. The porters and watchmen too carried candles, and there is mention in the Bank's records of them neglecting naked flames in what were deemed to be hazardous areas.[103] Since the Bank provided apartments for the chief accountant and the deputy accountant, the two door-keepers and the gate porter, it also faced the threat of a domestic fire spreading to the offices. Indeed, the Inspectors specifically pointed to the dangerous location of the Cheque Office, which, in their opinion, was exposed to considerable risk. This was because it was sited over the gate porter's lodge, 'where fires are constantly kept a great part of the year'.[104]

Risks also came from outside the Bank. Arson was a possibility, whether by deliberate attack from a disgruntled employee or customer

101. Shoemaker, *London Mob*, pp. 119–121.
102. Ibid., p. 125.
103. Acres, *Bank of England from Within*, 1:298.
104. BEA, M5/213, fol. 144.

or as the result of protest. Indeed, during the later eighteenth century, arson became more and more common, especially in conjunction with labour and social unrest.[105] Because of the narrow streets surrounding some of the Bank's boundaries, there was also a risk of fire, either caused deliberately or accidentally, spreading from adjacent buildings. Acres notes that fears were heightened by fires in Cornhill in 1748, when around 100 houses had been destroyed, and in Sweetings Alley near the Royal Exchange in 1759.[106] Although outside of our period, the progress of the fire at the Royal Exchange in 1838 is particularly instructive. Occurring at night and not being noticed until the early hours of the morning, the blaze was already out of control by the time it was spotted. Despite the prompt attendance of the London Fire Engine Establishment, formed in 1833, there was little that could be done. The weather was against the fire-fighters. It was January, and the water from their attempts to quench the flames merely froze on the pavements and turned to ice, further hampering efforts. The Royal Exchange was destroyed.[107]

Fire threatened the Bank in two ways. First, it could have led to the destruction of buildings or objects within those buildings with a consequent loss of assets and possibly business. Secondly, and perhaps much more importantly, fire could have caused the loss of records and information. It has been shown that the Bank kept the only legally binding record of ownership of shares and government debt. In consequence, stock ledgers, transfer books and dividend lists either were all irreplaceable or would have required a significant amount of work to reconstruct. The impact on public trust that could have resulted from such a loss of records must be considered, as well as the impact on the relationship with the Exchequer. The latter point was specifically highlighted by the Inspectors in their discussion of the Cheque Office, where the dividend warrants that had been paid were stored prior to return to the Exchequer and where 'old unpaid or Back Warrants, down to within 4 or 5 years of the running Dividend, are kept'.[108] The Inspectors were shocked to find that the storage of these documents was badly organised in part because of the problems of space and the large number of stored documents, 'the place not being large enough to contain them all, some are in an outer room adjoining, within a low wooden partition, & others in the open Lobby, where they are

105. R. Pearson, *Insuring the Industrial Revolution: Fire Insurance in Great Britain, 1700–1850* (Aldershot, UK, 2004), p. 3.

106. Acres, *Bank of England from Within*, 1:191, n. 1.

107. Ann Saunders, *The Royal Exchange* (London, 1991), p. 33.

108. BEA, M5/213, fol. 142.

much exposed to accidents'.[109] Should the documents be lost, the Inspectors noted, 'it would raise an almost insuperable difficulty in settling with the Exchequer; where they scrupulously require every single Warrant to be produced'.[110]

Chapter 1 noted that the Bank's directors were active in their pursuit of fire-prevention measures.[111] These measures included buying up property around the Bank to facilitate the widening of thoroughfares in order to permit access and prevent the spread of any fires from nearby buildings. As part of Robert Taylor's improvements to the Bank during the 1770s, a four-storey, fire-proof library was added. Its principal use was the storage of records.[112] The prevention of loss from fire was also part of specific night-time routines. Notably, the safety of records was of such importance that duplicate abstracts of each day's stock transfers were made and sent out of the Bank to the counting house of Edward Payne, one of the senior directors.[113] In addition, some records retained within the Bank were kept in wheeled 'trucks' overnight and were thus 'ready to wheel away in case of Accidents'.[114]

In spite of its caution regarding records, the Bank does not appear to have insured its main premises.[115] The reason for this is likely that a key selling point of fire insurance was that it came with the services of an insurance company fire brigade, and the Bank had already been making its own fire-fighting arrangements.[116] Indeed, one of its first acts on establishment had been the purchase of the necessaries for securing Mercer's Hall, the Bank's first home, against fire. This included the purchase of a fire engine.[117]

The Bank's directors were unquestionably wise to make their own fire-fighting arrangements. Fire brigades were established in London, particularly by the insurance offices, and each parish was supposed to be responsible

109. Ibid., fol. 143.

110. Ibid., fol. 144.

111. See 'Threadneedle Street' in chapter 1.

112. Abramson, *Building the Bank*, p. 66.

113. BEA, M5/213, fols. 37–38.

114. BEA, M5/212, fol. 148.

115. The directors did insure property owned by the Bank and rented out. Thus, the Sun Fire Insurance Office recorded the Bank's policy insuring a 'House only in Castle Alley Cornhill in the tenure of William James Stockbroker' to a value not exceeding £2,000. In another instance, the Governor & Company of the Bank of England insured 'their House only in Bank Street Cornhill in the tenure of Susanna Burchall & Co. Milliners'. LMA, MS 11936/253/376126; LMA, MS 11936/276/417355/359.

116. B. Wright, *Insurance Fire Brigades, 1680–1929: The Birth of the British Fire Service* (Stroud, UK, 2008), p. 39.

117. Acres, *Bank of England from Within*, 1:48.

for the maintenance of fire-fighting equipment, such as ladders, buckets, hoses and even engines. But in reality, most means of fighting fires were inadequate. Parishes often failed to maintain their equipment, few were trained to operate it and water supplies were frequently inadequate for the purpose of fighting fires.[118] Engines could also take a considerable time to reach a blaze. Moreover, insurance company firemen may have been generally brave and hardy, but they were apparently a hard-drinking and sometimes reckless breed. Dismissals for drunkenness, absenteeism and other misbehaviours were frequent.[119] Such behaviour made their performance when fighting fires rather variable. In consequence, a number of London companies either set up their own fire brigades, including the twelve livery companies, or at least maintained their own fire-fighting equipment, as did the East India Company and the Bank.[120]

By the time of the Committee of Inspection's report, in 1783, the Bank owned four fire engines. The exact construction of the Bank's machines is not known, but during the 1780s they were manufactured and maintained by John Bristow. They probably worked along the lines of the engine invented in 1726 by Thomas Newsham, which was fitted with a large air-vessel to ensure a continuous stream of water and pumps arranged at the side to maintain water pressure.[121] This type of engine could be fitted with long lengths of hose in order to project water to great heights.[122] The engines were made in several sizes, with the smallest being compact enough to be carried like a sedan chair. Given the size of its buildings, the Bank undoubtedly had to purchase larger models which were capable of pumping around 770 litres of water a minute a distance of around 35 metres.[123]

Fire engines were costly to purchase and also required regular maintenance to ensure they remained in good working order.[124] Major main-

118. Pearson, *Insuring the Industrial Revolution*, p. 83; Wright, *Insurance Fire Brigades*, p. 44.

119. Pearson, *Insuring the Industrial Revolution*, p. 81; Wright, *Insurance Fire Brigades*, p. 59.

120. Pearson, *Insuring the Industrial Revolution*, p. 83; M. Makepeace, *The East India Company's London Workers: Management of the Warehouse Labourers, 1800–1858* (Woodbridge, UK, 2010), p. 27. See also Sweeting, 'Capitalism, the State and Things'.

121. BEA, M5/376, 2 July 1783. Bristow's engine was also used by the Sun Fire Insurance Office during the late eighteenth and early nineteenth centuries. Wright, *Insurance Fire Brigades*, p. 109.

122. J.B.P. Karslake, 'Early London Fire-Appliances', *The Antiquaries Journal*, 9 (1929), pp. 229–238.

123. Wright, *Insurance Fire Brigades*, p. 125.

124. Wright estimates engine costs to have been between £120 and £150 in the early nineteenth century. Wright, *Insurance Fire Brigades*, p. 109.

tenance and repairs seem to have been made by the engine-makers themselves, and payments to them appear regularly in the Minutes of the Committee for House and Servants.[125] But the Bank's watchmen also performed routine maintenance and tested the engines on the first Thursday of every month.[126] This is likely to have been in the evening, when the Bank's courtyards were free of customers. As testament to the effort and perhaps danger involved in the pumping of water using a fire engine, Samuel Beachcroft's diary records an accident in which Nicholas Hodges, one of the watchmen, was hurt whilst playing the engine and, in consequence, confined for eight weeks in the hospital.[127]

Aside from ensuring the engines were in good working order, the efficiency of the Bank's fire-fighting arrangements was dependent upon a water supply, and clearly the Bank had experienced problems in that regard. Samuel Bosanquet recorded in his notebook that, at the time of the Gordon riots, the cisterns in the fore-yard had been entirely empty.[128] Mr Watkins also noted that when he first arrived at the Bank, the cisterns were not well supplied, but in more recent years he said that the problem had not occurred and he did 'not remember any want for a considerable time past'.[129] The difficulties of securing supply was one reason the Court of Directors, in response to a memorandum from the Ward of Cornhill proposing the erection of an 18,000-gallon tank by St Peter's church for the 'more effective extinguishing of any fire', ordered that a £50 donation be made towards the costs.[130]

The considerations of fire prevention and fire-fighting draw our attention once again to the Bank's need to control its environment. The life of the City had the potential to compromise the security of the Bank in numerous ways, from violent unrest and deliberate attack to the accidental fire that could spread and cause untold damage. The precautions taken by the Bank show the concern for its buildings, fixtures and fittings but also for the records and ledgers upon which the public debt and the economy of London were based. These steps demonstrate the effective organisation and administrative efficiency for which the institutions of eighteenth-century Britain are rightly praised. But they also encourage us to consider

---

125. In July 1783, for example, £19 10 shillings was paid to John Bristow, the Bank's engine-maker. BEA, M5/376, 2 July 1783.

126. BEA, M5/212, fol. 192.

127. BEA, M5/451, fol. 33.

128. BEA, M5/471, unpaginated.

129. BEA, M5/212, fol. 193.

130. BEA, G4/23, fol. 198.

the sometimes insecure foundations on which this efficiency was built and how much trust was reposed in relatively poorly paid employees.

While the most visible symbol of the Bank's security, the Foot Guards, slept in their barracks, life bustled on quietly within the Bank. The watchmen continued their patrols throughout the night, catching what sleep they could when they were off duty. They could never be described as a fighting force, but their presence helped to keep the Bank safe from the key night-time threat of fire. And their patrols might have deterred anyone who regarded the Bank as an easy target. They were not paid well, but the salary was regular and in cash and supplemented by systems of gifting and perquisites, which helped to engender loyalty. The Bank invested in fire engines and guns, although the need for them hardly ever arose. Nascent technologies of security were also employed to some good effect, and, following the Inspection, routines for locking up were improved, the disposal of keys was made more effective and the senior men were, once more, reminded of their responsibility for the Bank's security. Most nights were orderly and peaceful.

As dawn broke, the Foot Guard returned to their barracks in Westminster and the Bank's watchmen rose to start the process of cleaning and laying the fires in the offices. Soon after, the gates were opened and first clerks arrived back in their offices to begin another day. The process of life at the Bank began again.

Conclusion

IN MARCH 1784 the work of the Committee of Inspection came to an end. During the course of their investigations, the Inspectors found a dedication to public service, processes that generally worked well and a business that, taken all together, was capable of supporting an already vast and growing public debt and the economy of what was, at the time, the largest city in the world. They had also found much to concern them, particularly relating to security, efficiency and accountability. Some of these issues they were unwilling to deal with. Thus, it continued to be permissible to accept gratuities from customers into the nineteenth century. Moreover, not all security risks were eliminated, as the crimes of clerks like Francis Fonton and Robert Aslett make clear. But the Inspectors did make significant changes to a number of processes within the Bank, including the issue of banknotes, the management of transfers of the public debt and the issuance of dividends. They changed the layout of offices, revised filing systems and improved security from the routines of locking up the Bank to the distribution of keys.

They also reflected on the Bank's employees. Their final report focused particularly on the clerks, 'the number of whom certainly renders them an object of considerable moment'.[1] The Inspectors took notice of the lack of subordination of the junior men and the lack of attention of their senior colleagues. They further desired that the chief men would take more control in the future and be held accountable for the conduct of the men who reported to them. And they asked the Court of Directors to be more mindful of both the 'abilities & characters of those they nominate' and those who were promoted into positions of seniority.[2]

1. BEA, M5/213, fol. 173.
2. Ibid., fols. 174–175.

As they concluded their business, the Inspectors thanked the Committee of Treasury and the Court of Directors 'for the attention we have experienced from them, & . . . for the candour with which our Reports have been received'.[3] And they made it clear that whatever shortcomings they had identified in the course of their investigations, they remained convinced of the value and virtue of the Bank of England. Their expression of that value and virtue bears repeating:

> When we contemplate the immense importance of the Bank of England not only to the City of London, in points highly essential to the promotion & extension of its Commerce, but to the Nation at large, as the grand Palladium of Public Credit, we cannot but be thoroughly persuaded that an Object so great in itself & so interesting to all Ranks of the Community, must necessarily excite care & solicitude in every breast, for the wise administration of its Affairs, but principally and directly in theirs who are entrusted with the immediate management of them: We deem it therefore superfluous to say a single word to the Court with a view of inculcating a religious Veneration for the glorious fabrick, or of recommending a steady and unremitting attention to its sacred Preservation.[4]

If the intention of the Bank directors in setting up the Committee was to avoid the fate of the East India Company, this statement seems to indicate that the Inspectors thought their work was done.

The Court of Directors clearly appreciated that work. The Committee of Inspection was not disbanded after 1784. It continued, ultimately becoming a permanent fixture of the Bank's management techniques and separating into several committees responsible for individual offices within the Bank. The agendas remained similar. The Committees concerned themselves with absences, the enforcement of discipline and the elimination of inefficiencies and errors.[5] There obviously remained a need for such regular oversight not only as procedures grew lax and knowledge of the rules grew dim with the passage of time but also as the wars against Revolutionary and Napoleonic France resulted in a vast increase in business. Hence, in 1804 a minute of the Court of Directors noted that business was once again being 'very improperly executed' and sought to

3. Ibid., fol. 174.
4. Ibid., fols. 178–179.
5. BEA, 9A312/1, Accountant's Discount Office Rules and Orders; BEA, C29/43, Orders of the Court and Committee of Inspection for the Discount Office Hall, passim.

remind the heads of the various offices that the Court would henceforth hold them responsible for

> the due execution of the business of their respective Offices: and for the conduct of the Clerks employed under them; That if any of the Clerks do not perform the work assigned to them in a satisfactory manner, or if they absent themselves, without leave of the Head of their Office, or if they remit or neglect the orders of their supervisors, or are inattentive to the established Rules of their Offices, or if they in any manner behave improperly, it is in all such cases, the duty of the head, or Chief Clerk, to report on their conduct . . . in order that [they] may be immediately suspended or dismissed.[6]

Obviously, the Bank's senior men were not prompted to make long-term changes in their behaviour by the Inspection of 1783–1784.

Whatever the outcome, for the historian, the Committee of Inspection's reports provide a fascinating window into the eighteenth-century Bank of England. They reveal that, without question, the Bank provided a solid foundation for the management of the public debt. There were certainly risks to which public creditors were exposed. Their identities could be stolen with relative ease, but cases of this happening were rare, primarily because the institution pursued forgers and fraudsters energetically and generally sought the ultimate penalty against those who were apprehended. Moreover, processes were generally sound and operated with a transparency that helped to engender trust in both the Bank and the state. It has also been shown that this trust was underpinned not only by the physical form of the Bank but also by the symbols it used, like that of Britannia, which operated to tie its fate to that of the state.

In its management of the short- and long-term public debt, the Bank was acting on behalf of the state. Although it has not previously been viewed in these terms, the institution was the state's most prominent contractor. It provided the services and the administrative competency and efficiency that the Treasury could not deliver at that time. No matter how trenchant its critics, the Bank was embedded in the business of state finance and, after nearly a century of operating in this way, it would have been impossible to alter that fact. There were, as we have observed, compromises in this arrangement. The housing of the secondary market in the long-term debt within its walls and the Bank's inability to prevent its clerks from acting as brokers and jobbers compromised its impartiality.

6. BEA, G4/30, fols. 235–236.

And yet the provision of a market space in which the public creditors' business could be done swiftly and efficiently and in which the value of the debt could be debated openly was also a great benefit. It helped to underpin the credible commitment which supported the British state's ability to borrow.

The Committee's reports also revealed the extent to which the life of the Bank and its internal rhythms were bound up with those of the City, sometimes reluctantly, but often willingly, embraced. It was vulnerable to encroachments and at risk from its environment, and we have seen how it sought to protect itself, especially during the hours of darkness. During the day it was a public space, a place for merchants, business-owners and many of London's middling sorts to see and a place where they might wish to be seen. The footfall in its offices ebbed and flowed with the other business of the City and the rhythms of the day. It was a site where important business relationships were formed and maintained, and where the economy of London could be regulated and stimulated. And it was a site where trust was enacted in many ways, not always in the anonymous forms that some historians have assumed characterised the later eighteenth century.

Throughout the foregoing discussion, the Bank's clerks have been prominent. The many impeccably preserved records at the Bank have allowed us to detail their work and elements of their lives outside work. For the first time it has been possible to see how banking and bankers during the eighteenth century operated, from the issuance of notes and the extension of credit to the management of money and the maintenance of the accounts in which were preserved detailed and comprehensive records of ownership and relationships. We have seen the organisational skills that were needed to connect processes across the Bank, and it has been possible to observe where the human capital on which the Bank relied fell short, failed or were turned to dishonest purposes.

The value that the Bank's clerks placed on their working lives is difficult to fathom. For many, a long working life was merely the measure of the pressure of supporting a family in London. For them, specialisation at the Bank had made the experience of clerical work mundane. Yet, the business was also pressurised and management techniques ensured that there were significant financial penalties for errors and incompetence. Certainly, Charles Lamb—writer, sometimes clerk at the East India Company and someone who as a young man would have been the contemporary of some of those clerks working in 1783—offered a rather bittersweet reflection on his time employed in clerical labour. He opened his essay 'The Superannuated Man' by lamenting his lost youthful freedom and the wasted years spent in the 'irksome confinement of an office'.[7] Throughout his working years he was conscious of an inaptitude for business and was often kept awake at night by the imaginary terrors of 'false entries, errors in my accounts and the like'.[8] On retirement, he revelled in the ability to once more call his time his own.

But for a time at least he missed the routine of the working week and the companionship of those with whom he had worked so many years, and on a visit to his old office he was resentful of the man who had taken his place and his desk.[9] Many of the Bank's clerks clung to their posts, often working long into their old age in spite of the generous pensions offered by the Bank, thus indicating that their work was important to them. Many struggled to place their sons at the Bank so that the next generation could enjoy the benefits of work in the country's chief financial institution. Some men certainly made lasting friendships and regretted the loss of the working environment when it came to retirement. Abraham Newland, for example, fondly remembered his time at the Bank and, at his death, left significant legacies to former colleagues.

The value we as historians should place on the work completed by the gentlemen of the Bank of England is much less ambiguous. The needs of the fiscal-military state were met nowhere more obviously than in the vast expansion of business undertaken by the Bank and, it is important to state, in its ability to stand as intermediary between the state and those who lent it money. The clerks were the foundation on which that business rested.

7. Charles Lamb, 'The Superannuated Man', in *The Last Essays of Elia*, with an introduction and notes by Alfred Ainger (London, 1883), p. 259.

8. Ibid., p. 261.

9. Ibid., p. 264.

Appendices

Directors and Staff at the Bank of England, April 1783

Governor:	Richard Neave
Deputy Governor:	George Peters
Directors:	Samuel Beachcroft
	Thomas Boddington
	Roger Bochin
	Daniel Booth
	Samuel Bosanquet*
	Lyde Browne
	Edward Darell
	Thomas Dea*
	Peter Gaussen
	Daniel Giles
	George Hayter
	Edward Payne
	Henry Plant
	Thomas Raikes
	Godfrey Thornton
	Benjamin Winthrop*
	Richard Clay
	William Cooke
	George Drake
	William Ewer
	William Halhed
	Thomas Scott Jackson
	William Snell
	Mark Weyland

* Members of the Committee of Inspection

Office	Name	Salary (£s per annum)
Accountants Office	John Payne	250
	William Edwards	170
	Joseph Betsworth	170
	Samuel Bayntun	140
	David Williams	120
	Samuel Ewer	110
	John Newton, jun	110
	Thomas Holmes	100
	John Manning	100
	Reginald Parker	90
	Henry Davies	80
	John Barnard	80
	Jeremiah Slipper	80
	Charles Lunnage	80
	James Cooper	70
	Isaac Lestourgeon	60
	William Aldridge	170
	John Tuck Hayne	120
	Thomas Rosseter	120
	Thomas Uwins	120
	Thomas Beardsley	160
	John Newton	120
	George Armstrong	50
	Isaac Pilleau	120
	Thomas Pollard	150
	William Holdsworth	120
	William Thomas	120
	Peter Bagwell	110
	James Southey	110
	William Penn	110
	John Laverick	110
	Francis Bradley	100
	John Poore	100
	John Cotton	100
	Robert Best	100
	Thomas Daniel	90
	Francis Fleming	90

Office	Name	Salary (£s per annum)
Accountants Office	James Pengal	90
	Walter Fardinando	90
	Robert Bicknell	60
	John Bell	60
	Charles Stuart	60
	John Stevenson	60
	Harry Hulley	60
	Henry Malpas	50
	Isaac Cooper	50
	John Rawson	50
	William Wigson	50
	Thomas Gribble	50
	Charles Farrer	50
	Richard Ellis	50
	Richard Post	50
	James Milner	50
	William Lens	50
	Thomas Hutchings	50
	John Lodge	50
	Richard Goodwin	50
	Francis Symondson	50
	Edward Bentley	50
	Thomas Andrews	50
	Thomas Millington	200
	John Oldisworth	140
	Robert Browning	100
	William Bibbins	80
	Charles Douglas	80
	William Cooke	70
	Joseph Bateman	60
	William Dawes	50
	Thomas Burford	50
	Richard Gale	50
	William Kimin	150
	Daniell Gross	130
	Daniel Turner	130
	William Reeves	120

Continued on next page

Office	Name	Salary (£s per annum)
Accountants Office	Samuel Tomkins	120
	John Fisher	110
	William Kerry	110
	Charles Richardson	100
	William Walton	100
	William Yates	80
	William Kingdon	60
	William Newcombe	60
	James Drinkwater	60
	Thomas Brennand	60
	Edward Bamford	60
	William Davies	60
	Thomas Gibbons	60
	William Pliston	60
	Roger Parry	50
	James Pilliner	50
	Benjamin Heseltine	50
	Charles Moll	50
	John Holloway	50
	Richard Bontell	50
	George Bouchier Walker	50
	Thomas Boult	50
	Joseph Feary	50
	John Edward Hinde	50
	Bowler Miller	170
	Richard Payne	160
	William Ward	150
	Abraham Vickery	130
	Charles Moorhouse	120
	Thomas Windsor	120
	Thomas Selby	120
	Samuel Gore	120
	George Hutton	120
	Thomas Crockford	120
	John Hatchett	110
	Samuel Leigh	110
	James Coxeter	100

Office	Name	Salary (£s per annum)
Accountants Office	Thomas Carpenter	100
	James Edwards	100
	Lawrence Poppleton	100
	Francis Walsh	90
	Robert Hands	90
	Thomas Nisbett	90
	John Sutton	90
	Francis Fonton	80
	Edward Martin	80
	Thomas Morrall	80
	Shadrach Shaw	70
	Enoch James	70
	William Brown	70
	John Fish	60
	Joseph Ince	60
	Edward Pears	60
	Nathaniel Hancock Towle	60
	William Aldridge	60
	John Cartlich	60
	Leonard Lazenby	60
	Samuel Shudall	60
	Thomas Aimes, jun	60
	James Mathers	60
	James Godin	60
	William Gibson	50
	John Grove	50
	Joseph Fenning	50
	John Yew Griffiths	50
	Thomas Rosseter Carter	50
	John Maydwell	50
	William Francis, elder	50
	Wade Burr	50
	John Gandon	50
	Robert Reeves	50
	William Hutchison	50
	William Kingston	50

Continued on next page

Office	Name	Salary (£s per annum)
Accountants Office	Edward George	50
	Nathan Dell	150
	Joseph Settle	130
	Thomas Francis	90
	Thomas Reid	80
	Richard Marston	50
	Joseph Poole	150
	Francis Blackbeard	150
	Henry Vonholte	130
	Thomas Pemberton	120
	John Pearce	120
	Samuel Walker	120
	John Cobb	120
	John Tilbary	120
	William Taylor	100
	Nathaniel Martin	100
	William Giles	90
	William Rosse	90
	Benjamin Corbyn	90
	Henry Priaulx	80
	Richard Frost	80
	William Blewart	80
	Wingfield Turner	80
	Joseph Sparke	80
	Samuel Bloomer	80
	Charles Norris	70
	Thomas Bateman	60
	Robert Bryer	60
	Mark Haggard	60
	John Oswald Trotter	50
	William Haydon	50
	Samuel Ripp	50
	Edmund Smith	200
	Thomas Landifield	100
	Daniel Justins	70
	Nathaniel Crawford	50
	Brian Baillie	140

Office	Name	Salary (£s per annum)
Accountants Office	Cornelius Jongma	120
	John Bowman	110
	John Burrell	100
	James Henry Cautier	100
	Thomas Patrick	100
	William Slann	90
	John Munay	90
	Francis Green	80
	Jonathan Greaves	80
	Richard Jones	70
	Robert Kimin	60
Cashiers Office	Abraham Newland	250
	Thomas Thompson	200
	Sewallis Larchin	200
	William Gardner	200
	William Jackson	200
	John Boult	200
	Owen Githing	200
	Thomas Oimes	200
	William Lander	200
	John Greenway	200
	Edward Gillyatt	140
	Thomas Torr	120
	Robert Aslett	70
	John Spindler	90
	John Clifford	170
	Jobb Jones	130
	Joseph Rickards	130
	Henry Thulkeld	110
	William Armistead	90
	Henry Foster	80
	Richard Buy	80
	John Barkley	70
	Randolph Hobman	70
	Jeremiah Kelly	70
	Peter Pineau	70
	Alexander Simpson	60

Continued on next page

Office	Name	Salary (£s per annum)
Cashiers Office	James Longman	60
	Giles Collins	110
	John Naisby	80
	John Humble	80
	William Church	180
	Thomas Mayor	110
	Joseph Bourne	110
	John Holland	100
	Richard Watkins	100
	Francis Ashton	90
	Jacob Coulthard	90
	John Clark	50
	Nicholas Pamphilion	110
	William Dunn	110
	Thomas Triquet	70
	William Johnson	90
	William Smart	60
	David Price	90
	John Penn	50
	James Pretty	120
	George Nicholls	60
	John Waldron	90
	Isaac Field	70
	Peter Vitu	130
	William Rawlins	130
	John Still	90
	Samuel Underhill	70
	John Fleetwood	60
	Samuel De La Maziere	50
	John Holden	70
	Thomas Rippon	50
	William Chapman	50
	John Cole Philipps	80
	Edward Moyes	60
	Isaac Padman	130
	Matthew Vernon	100
	Christopher Olier	90

Office	Name	Salary (£s per annum)
Cashiers Office	James Barber	60
	Richard Bridger	110
	George Vincent	110
	James Duchar	120
	William White	110
	William Goodfellow	100
	William Mullens	90
	William Wells	80
	Henry Heathcote	60
	Alexander Hooper	60
	William Garrett	70
	Samuel Hulme	50
	Nathan Sutton	50
Discount Office	John Rogers	180
	Robert Gooch	100
	William Coleman	130
	William Luccraft	120
	Thomas Tilley	120
	Edmund Lewin	110
	William Sumpter Cooper	100
	Charles Smith	70
To Attend the Exchequer	Allanson Cowper	200
	Reuben Ettie	150
	John Gimmingham	90
In the Warehouse	Samuel Etheridge	200
	Richard Walker	180
	John Sharp	140
In-Tellers	Thomas Campe	150
	Thomas Smith	120
	Thomas Jeyes	110
	Seth Ward	110
	Charles Gilmour	100
	Charles Jecks	100
	Samuel Fidoe	90
	Timothy Leach	90
	Francis Kensall	90
	James Barbut	90

Continued on next page

Office	Name	Salary (£s per annum)
In-Tellers	Thomas Higgs	90
	Watkin Griffith Williams	90
	Jeffrey Browne	80
	Riviere Knight	80
	William Wather	60
	Joseph Griffiths	70
	Thomas Buxton	80
	John Taylor	60
	Thomas Bliss	60
	Thomas Finden	60
Out-Tellers	Thomas Fugion	110
	James Tudman	100
	William Clendon	80
	William Shone	80
	Samuel Proctor	70
	Henry Ansley Purchas	70
	Richard Evans	60
	Samuel Knight	50
	Charles Beazley	50
	Thomas Douy	50
	William Cautier	50
	Josiah Knight	50
Messengers and Doorkeepers	Matthias Alcock[1]	60
	Samuel Cooper	40
Gate Porters	William Watkins	40
	John Lucas	40
House Porters	Thomas Brand	25
	John Hogg	25
	Jeremiah Booth	25
	James Flood	25
	James Elliott	25
House Keeper	Jane Watkins	50
Watchmen	Benjamin Dunnage	20
	Nathaniel Neale	20
	Joseph Moreton	20
	John Welch	20
	John Blewis	20
	Thomas Wood	20

Office	Name	Salary (£s per annum)
Watchmen	Joseph Upchurch	20
	John Gibbs	20
	James Baxter	20
	Thomas Saltwell	20
	Joseph Cole	20
	William Tanton	20
	George Lucas	20
	John Wells	20
	Francis Witherick	20
Secretary's Office	Robert Lewin (secretary)	250
	Francis Martin	200
Newly appointed staff[2]	Henry White	50
	Francis Salkeld	50
	Samuel Petit	50
	William Crell	50
	Gerard Thomas South	50
	James White	50
	William George	50
	Isaac Castell	50
	Thomas Osmand	50
	John Bredell	50
	Samuel Richards	50
	William Bridges	50

Sources: Bank of England Archives, Minutes of the Court of Directors, Book V, G4/23, fols. 368–373; Book W, G4/24, fols. 54–58.

[1] Alcock also acted as a clerk to the Committees of the Bank.

[2] The offices of the newly appointed servants were not specified in the Minutes for 1783, but from the staff list of 1784 it can be seen that Henry White, James White, Samuel Petit, Isaac Castell and Thomas Osmand were employed in the Accountants Office and the remainder of the newly appointed staff were employed in the Cashiers Office.

The first Report of the Committee appointed to inspect & enquire into the Mode & execution of the Business as now carried on in the different departments of the Bank

To the Governor, Deputy Governor and Committee of Treasury

In pursuance of the Resolution of the Court of Directors of the 13th March last ordering us to report to the Committee of Treasury to be laid before the Court our proceedings & observations on the Manner in which Business is conducted in the several Offices in the Bank.

We report, That immediately after our appointment, we proceeded to the Execution of the powers delegated to us, by applying ourselves to acquire a general knowledge of the Mode of conducting the business of the House, beginning with those Offices which lie within the department of the Chief Cashier.

It was our intention in the first instance to have formed reports on the proceedings in each of those Offices, but

in the course of our Enquiries, & before we had obtained
sufficient information for that purpose; an Object presented
itself to us of such magnitude as to determine us to submit
it to Your consideration without delay.

The Object we point at is the State of insecurity in which
all Bills & Notes passing through this House are suffer'd to
remain: first in the Discount Office; & afterwards in the Bill
Office where they are dispos'd in drawers to lie 'till due.

From the information of Mr Rogers and Mr Gooch, the
2 Chief, & one of the subordinate Clerks in the Discount
Office, we learn that all Bills or Notes brought in to be
discounted, pass progressively through the hands of 5
different Clerks, who either compute, or enter the particulars
of the Bills in different books: this operation takes up a
considerable space of time, & frequently occasions the
business of the Office to continue, 'till very late at night
before it is finished. Those Bills that cannot be entered &
delivered to the Bill Office before 5 o'clock are locked
up in the Discount Office all night; as are also on every
Wednesday all the Notes brought in that day, & which
remain in the Office, 'till they shall have passed the Court
on Thursday.

These Bills & Notes generally amount to a very large
Sum; & yet it appears, to have been the uniform custom to
leave them, to the care of each single Clerk in the Office as
may be last in waiting, who is allways one of the Juniors.

This Clerk is requir'd to place them, in an Iron Chest,
standing in a Closet in the Discount Office, which we find, on
examination, to be a small, weak, & very insecure repository;
situated moreover in a remote corner of the House, & thereby
liable to greater risk: the key of this Closet is put into a
common drawer in the Office, to which every Clerk has a
key; & the key of the Office itself, is left by the last Clerk
who retires at the Gate Porter's Lodge. It is true the key of
the Iron Chest, is carried by the same Clerk to the Chief or
Deputy Accountant's Apartments: but We are informed
is frequently delivered to a Servant, who returns it next
morning, to the first Clerk that comes to the Discount
Office; for the purpose of taking out the Bills, in order to
their being delivered over to the Bill Office.

Thus it appears, That Bills & Notes to a very large amount, do frequently remain in the sole custody of a junior Clerk of the Discount Office: That the repository, in which they are supposed to be placed by him, is weak, insecure, & ill situated: That the key of it is afterwards disposed of in a loose & careless manner: and That the Clerk who locks up the Bills at night is not the Person who receives the key the next morning: a circumstance that effectually prevents his being answerable for the contents of the Chest.

From the Discount Office all Bills & Notes discounted are delivered to the Bill Office: & here likewise we find a subject for our animadversion at least as important as the former.

From the information of Mr Church, Mr Mayor and Mr Bourne, the 3 Chief, & of Mr Holland, one of the subordinate Clerks in the Bill Office, we learn that it is now the custom in that Office, to take out every morning at 9 o'clock, from the Iron Safe in the Court Room; the Chests of discounted Bills & of those paid in on the sundry or Drawing Acco^{ts} both these are immediately unlocked, & all the Bills & Notes contained in them left exposed through the whole course of the day, not only to every Clerk in that Office (who is allowed to have free access to them); but also to many others who transact business near the place; & even to Persons unconnected with the Bank, whose occasions frequently require their being admitted into the Bill Office.

It seems exceedingly improper, that the immense Concerns usually deposited in the Bill Office, should be unnecessarily exposed for a single moment; much more that they should continue exposed throughout the whole day; & equally so that they should be intrusted to the care of one person when nothing prevents their being placed in the custody of two. We conceive ourselves justified in saying unnecessarily exposed, because the business of the Office, appears to us, to require, that the Clerks should have in their possession, at one time, those Bills only which fall due, within the two, or at most the three following days; for the purpose of examining, laying them out in Walks, & sending them for payment. The other purposes for which the Clerks may have occasion to refer to the Bills themselves, are so

few, & occur so seldom, as in our Opinion not to render
necessary, their being left open in so public an Office, for
any length of time.

The bare recital of these Facts, collected from the
examination of the different Clerks (& which appear much
stronger in the Minutes of our proceedings than we have
here stated); sufficiently evinces the necessity of altering the
present mode with respect to this very important Object.

To form a plan that may put so very large a property in
a State of Security; without at the same time impeding the
established course of business; has engaged much of our
attention: & that we might be the better enabled to offer
such an one to your consideration as we hope & trust may
prove effectual, We consulted the Chief Cashier & several of
the Principal Clerks in these Offices, with a view to discover,
whether any solid objections lay against what we thought so
essentially necessary.

To attain then this very desirable end at least as far
as the nature of the Subject will allow; We submit it as
our Opinion, That a strong Closet or Safe be provided,
contiguous to & opening only into the Bill Office; divided
into 2 Compartments for containing all Bills & Notes
not in the course of payment; as well those discounted,
as those paid in on sundry Accounts: that each of these
Compartments be subdivided into the requisite numbers
of drawers, for containing the Bills in the order they fall
due according to the days of the month, in the manner now
practis'd for discounted Bills. That in these drawers all Bills
that have more than two or three days to run do constantly
remain: & that to this Safe there be 2 Locks, the key of one
to remain with one of the 3 Chief Clerks of the Bill Office;
the key of the other with a Cashier, or any other Officer that
may be thought more proper. That every morning after the
Chief Clerks of the Bill Office, shall have received all the
Bills & Notes from the Discount Office & sorted & entered
them, according to the days they fall due; one of them do
apply to the Cashier who may be in possession of the key to
go with him to the Safe to assist in opening it; & to attend,
while he deposits each parcel of Bills in the drawer to which
it belongs: & at the same time that he take out the Bills of

the day which comes next in course, for the Clerks to lay them out in Walks ready for the Out Tellers the next day. That whenever there shall be occasion to have recourse to the Bills; which can seldom happen, one of the 3 Chiefs of the Bill Office be required to call the Cashier to attend the taking out any Bill. And that access be allowed to the Safe only in the presence of one of the Chief Clerks. That a part of this Safe be so contrived, as to open with a separate door, (likewise secured by 2 different Locks) to be allotted to the use of the Discount Office, for the reception of such Bills & Notes discounted as cannot be delivered in time to the Bill Office. That these Bills & Notes be locked up therein every night by 2 such Clerks of the Discount Office as may hereafter be determined on, with order to lodge the keys at any two places judged convenient.

By this Mode of securing the Bills & Notes the general precaution established in the Bank of locking up all property under at least 2 keys, will be complied with: & We cannot discover that the Business will be in the least impeded by it; if a few Regulations be adopted in the Mode of transacting the business in both Offices such as we shall have occasion to submit to Your consideration at a future Opportunity. If the Safe, proposed, be so constructed as to admit of a Space in front sufficiently large for 2 Persons to work at a desk; it will enable the Chief Clerks, to sort out and enter the Bills in a retired situation: a conveniency now much wanted in this Office.

> (Sign'd) S Bosanquet
> Thomas Dea
> Benj. Winthrop

Bank of England 14th April 1783
Source: BEA, M5/212, fols. 67–75.

The second Report of the Committee appointed to inspect & enquire into the Mode & execution of the Business as now carried on in the different departments of the Bank

To the Governor, Deputy Governor and Committee of Treasury

Our former Report being confined to the single Object of the Security of Bills & Notes discounted or paid into the Bank: We now proceed to state the result of our farther enquiries.

We find the Business of the Bank divided into two great departments; one under the direction of the Chief Cashier, the other of the Chief Accountant: the former alone has hitherto engaged our attention.

From the information of Mr Newland we learn that the department of the Chief Cashier is branched out into the following different Offices: the principals of which are accountable to the Chief Cashier as their Head.

The Chief Cashier's Office superintended by the Chief or second Cashier.

The Cashiers in the Hall, 8 in number, all upon equal footing as to authority.

The 6 several Cash-books for making out Bank Notes, which might be more properly termed Bank Note-books, & the Bank Post bill book, at each of which the senior acts as Head or principal.

The G or General Cash-book, under the direction of the senior Clerk.

The Drawing Office, under 2 Chiefs.

The Bill Office, under 3 Chiefs.

The 3 Clearers, of whom the senior acts as Head.

The OutTellers, in some degree accountable to the Head of the Bill Office.

The InTellers in the Hall & in the Dividend Pay Office, of whom the senior acts as Head in the Hall, the second as Head in the Pay Office.

The Warrant Office, under the direction of one Chief.

The Discount Office under the direction of 2 Chiefs.

The Clerks that attend the Exchequer.

The Clerk that attends the printing of the Bank Notes.

The Bullion Office, under one Chief.

We have examined all the Chiefs & several of the subordinate Clerks in these Offices: but shall not trouble the Committee with a minute description of the manner in which they transact their business: it may suffice here to observe that our Minute book consists of such details as we trust will prove satisfactory if more particular information be desired: Our intention in this as well as in our future Reports being only to name the different Offices, making such observations as in our opinion may tend to introduce improvements or to remedy any inconveniences in the present practice.

It is natural to imagine that our attention must have been very earnestly directed towards an Object of infinite importance in this department, we mean the whole process concerning Bank Notes from their formation for currency to their final discharge. And as it is our purpose to suggest & recommend a very material Alteration with respect to this subject, we think it necessary briefly to state the present Mode of making out & issuing Bank Notes,

as well as the Manner of keeping those deposited in the
Store in the Warehouse, & to make some remarks on the
insecurity of each.

The 8 Cashiers in the Hall are appointed to sign all
Bank Notes: we name them first as being Seniors to the
other Clerks, for in regard to this part of their business the
principal confidence seems to be reposed in the Juniors.
There are 6 books called Cash-books, in which the
particulars of all Notes are entered, (4 of these, marked
A, B, C, H, are kept in the Hall, one, marked O, in the
Chancery Office, & the other, marked K, in the Bank Note
Office), only 2 fixed Clerks are stationed at each of the
4 books in the Hall; whose business it is to receive value
or vouchers for all Notes required, to fill up the Blank
Notes, to countersign, & to enter them, & then one of the
Clerks, or as it frequently happens the Party claiming the
Notes, hands them to one of the Cashiers, (who is perhaps
at some distance from the book) to be signed: the Cashier
signs them without taking any account of what he signs, &
generally knows nothing concerning the value received. The
Clerks at each book have a box or drawer open before them
on the Desk with compartments for the blank Notes of different values, which are delivered to them every morning
by the Cashiers, to whom they account, at 5 o'clock in the
evening, for the number they have received; when those
that remain unused are counted & returned into the Warehouse, where the Stock of blank Notes is kept.

This Mode of issuing Bank Notes is in our apprehension
attended with very considerable risk, in as much as
there is more danger in trusting to the fidelity & care of
a greater number of Junior & inferior Clerks, than of a
smaller number of Senior & superior ones: Convinced of
the truth of this observation, there appears to us a strange
perversion in this business of making out Bank Notes:
for surely the Trust (& great indeed it is) was intended to
be placed in the Cashiers, Men who from their Age, their
length of service, & other circumstances that have probably raised them to such a station of confidence, may be
supposed to deserve it: whereas in the present practice, the
sole reliance is on the honesty & vigilance of the entering

Clerks, each separately entrusted, not barely with a sum of money, but with the power of creating it to allmost any amount; & this under so little controul that notwithstanding every precaution hitherto adopted, opportunities still occur every day similar to that which enabled Clutterbuck to perpetrate the fraud he lately committed: for in fact there is no effectual check on the Clerks at the Cash-books for the value of the Notes they fill up & issue, before the books are examined the next day in the Accountant's Office: besides, at dinner hours from one to three o'clock, one of the Clerks is allways absent, & then the Book & all the Blank Notes are left in the charge of a single person, unless an additional Clerk be sent from another Office, which is occasionally done to some but not to all the books. Farther, on a holiday, only one of the Clerks attends, & tho' another is furnished from some other Office, yet at dinner time, one of these is absent for two hours. From all which it appears, that blank Notes to a very large Amount, are frequently left for a length of time, in the sole custody of a single Junior Clerk, with the power to fill them up, to countersign them himself, & to procure the signature of a Cashier, who signs without knowing any thing of the occasion on which the Notes are issued or whether Value has been received for them. This we state without any design to impute negligence to the Cashiers, for according to the present mode, it seems impossible that with any view to dispatch, it should be otherwise, but that they must depend on the fidelity & exactness of the entering Clerks. The situation of these Clerks in the Hall with the drawers of blank Notes open before them, is another circumstance of danger, as many Persons totally unconnected with the business of making out Bank Notes have frequent access to them by intruding where they have no right to come: an abuse often complained of by the Cashiers & Clerks who nevertheless find it impossible to prevent it. It is needless to insist on the glaring impropriety & risk that must attend the blank Notes being thus exposed; their importance, as containing allmost every feature of a compleat Note, cannot be more significantly pointed out than by adverting to a late Resolution of the Court of Directors, ordering payment of one that had been lost or stolen, tho' filled up & signed with fictitious names; a Resolution principally grounded on the detriment that must ensue to the currency of this paper, if the Publick were absolutely required at their peril to be acquainted in every instance with the names & signatures of the different Clerks.

We now proceed to state our objections to the manner in which the Store Notes are kept in the Warehouse for the purpose of paying Dividend Warrants & for supplying the Clerks who attend the Exchequer. The present practice is, when Notes are brought down from the Cash-books to increase the Store, they are distributed among the Cashiers to be signed by them, in parcels, tyed loosely of 50 Notes each: as soon as compleated, the Cashier who has the charge of the Warehouse collects the parcels, & observes whether the Number on the uppermost Note of each parcel is right; but does not count over the Notes, presuming that the Cashier who has signed & tyed them up has allready done it & without any farther certainty of having got the whole Number at first made out, he deposits them in the Warehouse, & adds them to the Account in the book kept there. These Store Notes are placed in a cupboard with two locks, of which one of the keys is kept by the Cashiers, the other by the InTellers, & any one Cashier with any one InTeller may have at all times access to them, a circumstance that precludes all possibility of charging any particular person, in case of deficiency. There is a standing Order that an account shall be taken every day of these Notes by one of the Cashiers in rotation, but the manner in which this Order is complied with actually lessens rather than increases the security of the Deposit; for alltho' the Cashier is obliged to call an InTeller to assist in opening the Cupboard; yet as it does not appear to be the custom for the InTeller to attend during the whole time the Cashier is looking over the Notes, it follows that in his absence they are left in the possession of the Cashier alone.

Farther; the Mode of taking the daily account is greatly defective; it is done by telling over the unbroken parcels as containing 50 Notes each, & the number of Notes in those only that appear to be broken, by which method if any one of these parcels was wrong at the time of depositing, or if

any embezzlement of any Notes should happen afterwards
it would be impossible to know where to fix the fraud, as
the deficiency could not be discovered untill the parcel from
which the Note had been taken should come into use, which
perhaps, might be a month after they were made out. In
either case, it would be difficult to ascertain whether the
deficiency arose from the Negligence of the Cashier who
signed the Notes; of him who collected them to deposit in
the Warehouse; or from a Fraud committed afterwards.
The Sum of Bank Notes compleat & ready for currency
usually kept in the Store fluctuates from 100,000 to 300,000
Pounds Stg; a sum much too large ever to be entrusted to a
single Person, unless obliged to account for the balance in
his hands every evening.

In order to avoid the Dangers & remedy the Inconveniences
that have been stated in this Report we are encouraged
to offer a plan for the conduct of the Business of Bank
Notes, which we flatter ourselves will be found if not quite
perfect, at least sufficiently so as to answer in a higher
degree than the present mode, two great & principal
Objects; the Security of the Bank; & the Accommodation of
the Publick. We confess we should with greater diffidence
have proposed an Alteration which is intended to supersede
a practice of many years standing if there had not been
various instances of losses & inconveniences attending
the latter, & if notwithstanding the conviction of our own
Judgement our opinion had not been corroborated by
those of Mr Newland, Mr Thompson, & most of the other
Cashiers.

The plan which with great deference we recommend
to the consideration of the Committee of Treasury, is, that
of issuing to the Publick ready made Bank Notes in the
manner practised in the Dividend Pay Office & at the
Exchequer, & of banishing from the Hall the Cash books
now kept there & the blank Notes attendant on them. For
this purpose it will be requisite to increase the Store in the
Warehouse to 500,000 Pounds Stg, a sum which from the
information of the two Chief Cashiers we think we are
well founded in asserting need never be exceeded. For the
particulars of the proposed Mode of keeping the Store

& issuing these Notes we refer to the plan itself hereto
annexed by way of Appendix.

The Difference between the Sums of 500,000 Pounds
Stg & that now usually kept in the Warehouse, cannot, in
respect to the confidence that must necessarily be placed
somewhere, be urged as an objection of weight against the
mode now offered, when it is considered that regulations
are proposed with respect to the Class of Men who shall
ever have access to the Store, nor can any argument be
adduced from a supposition of the Temptation being
stronger in the one case than in the other that will not
more effectually prove that ready made Notes should
never be kept as a Store at all, than that the difference
of the Sums is of any moment in regard to the danger of
Embezzlement: but when it is superadded that by the
proposed plan the Blank Notes will be exempted from the
very imminent danger they stand exposed to at present, a
circumstance of itself sufficiently alarming to require an
immediate alteration of practice; & that the Publick will
be accommodated on demand without the delay they are
now subject to, a consideration not to be overlooked as it
may have a tendency to increase the Circulation of Bank
Notes—we can entertain no doubt of the plan now offered
obtaining the approbation of the Committee of Treasury.

As it is proper to mention in this Report every material
Circumstance respecting the formation & issuing of Bank
Notes wherein we think any improvement can be made, or
risk avoided, we cannot help expressing our surprize that
for so many years (we believe ever since the establishment
of the Bank), it has been the custom to send the Paper &
Copper plates to the Printer's house, for the purpose of
printing the Blank Notes; the plates are carried thither &
brought back every day by Mr Barber the clerk appointed
to have charge of them. From the mode of conducting the
business are described by him we conclude that the Blank
Notes must necessarily be exposed to considerable hazard
but without his information we should certainly condemn
the practice of suffering the plates to be ever taken out
of the Bank, if there were a possibility of printing off the
Blank Notes within it. We need not particularise the danger

that both the Paper & plates must be subject to, from the moment they leave the Bank to that of their return, & we apprehend that it will be perfectly easy to avoid all future risk by causing the Notes to be printed within this House.

(Sign'd)
S Bosanquet
Thomas Dea
Benj. Winthrop

Bank of England
the 29th July 1783
Source: BEA, M5/212, fols. 155–167.

The third Report of the Committee appointed to inspect & enquire into the Mode & execution of the Business as now carried on in the different departments of the Bank

To the Governor, Deputy Governor & Committee of Treasury

Having compleated our examination into the manner of conducting the Business of the several Offices within the department of the Chief Cashier, we shall proceed to report on a matter which in our apprehension requires immediate consideration: The security of the several Offices out of the hours of business & the general care of the Gates.

From the examination of the Chief Cashier, We find that his office consists of 2 rooms; in the outer of which stands a small Iron Chest appropriated to the purpose of locking up in it every night the Keys

Of the Bullion Office,

Of the Warehouse or Treasury

& Of the Safe in the Court-room where the bills & notes are lodged every evening.

This Chest has 2 locks with 3 keys to each. The 3 keys
to one of the locks are kept in common among the 8
Cashiers in the Hall; the 3 keys to the other in the same
manner among the 10 InTellers; who all transfer them to
one another occasionally, observing only that one key to
each of the locks remains with the Cashier & InTeller in
waiting for the night, to enable them to lock the Chest when
the business is over. These 6 keys are left at night in some
or other of the Cashiers & InTellers desks in the Hall, no
farther provision being made for their security.

There are Duplicates of the keys of the Bullion Office,
Warehouse, & Safe sealed up under the seals of 3 senior
Directors, which remain constantly in another small Iron
Chest fixed in the Chief Cashier's inner Office; This Chest
has a single lock to it, the key of which is placed every
night in a Mahogany desk in the same Office; to which
desk the Chief & Deputy Cashiers have duplicate keys.
In this Chest is likewise deposited the key of the great
Iron Chest standing in the same Office, which generally
contains effects belonging to this house & to private
persons, of immense value; as it does in fact at the present
moment, in Loan receipts &, other articles, to the amount
of upwards of four millions. The hours of business being
over, the Cashiers Office is locked, & the key of it, as well
as those of the other Offices of the Bank, is hung up in the
Gate-Porter's Lodge, where they all remain exposed to the
Clerks, Watchmen, & any Intruders; the Gate porter not
being charged by particular directions, to see to the security
of them.

Thus it appears from what has been stated, that
by opening some of the common desks in the Hall, all
the keys of the small iron Chest may be got at, in which
are deposited those of the Bullion Office, Treasury & Safe
in the Court-room; & that by breaking open a wooden
desk in the Cashier's Office access may equally be had to
these several Offices by their duplicate keys, as well as to
the great Iron Chest: that is, in fact, to all the valuable
property lodged in the Bank, except what is deposited in
the Vaults. We are convinced that it never could have been
the original Practice of this house for Deposits of such

immense Value to be kept in a manner which appears to us so loose & insecure: & it is not only on this, but on many other occasions, we find reason to lament, that the 2 Chief Officers of this house, or their Deputies, are not, by the constitution of it, obliged to give their personal attendance every day untill the business is closed, & the keys of so great a trust are properly secured: a matter highly meriting the most serious consideration of the Court. However, as the evil described certainly demands a speedy remedy; We shall state a mode, which, though inadequate, considered as a compleat security, may be adopted, untill some plan of a general superintending care can be devised & rendered practicable. We propose therefore for the consideration of the Committee of Treasury,

That four of the keys to the small Iron Chest in the Outer Office of the Chief Cashier, as well as the Duplicate keys to the Bullion Office, Treasury & Safe, now kept in his inner Office, be taken away, & placed in the Safe in the Committee-room; to be used only in case of emergency.

That the two remaining keys to the small Chest in the outer Office, (being one to each lock), be in the custody of the Chief Cashier or of his Deputy during the hours of business; & be delivered, by him who leaves the Office latest, to the Cashier & InTeller in waiting for the night.

That these, (the Cashier & InTeller), be directed to see that the usual keys are deposited in the Chest, & after locking it shall carry their keys, the Cashier in waiting, his to the house of the Chief Cashier, & the InTeller, his to that of the Chief Accountant, where they are to be delivered to the Chiefs themselves or to their Deputies: but as these Officers may not always be at home to receive them into their own hands, Mr Newland has suggested, that in such case they be deposited in small Iron Chests, to be provided at the houses of the Chief Cashier & Chief Accountant, with an aperture in the lid of each, wide enough to admit of dropping in the keys. This we conceive may answer the end proposed, for as they or their Deputies will be held responsible for these keys, it will be incumbent on them to see, that they are duly deposited in the Chest every night, in case of their absence. And they must likewise see to the redelivering of them, to the respective Clerks who come for them in the morning.

That in like manner the key of the little Iron Chest in the inner Office, instead of being locked up in a desk, be taken away by the Chief Cashier or his Deputy, whichever remains latest in the Office, & be dropped into the Iron Chest at the Chief Cashier's house.

That in future the keys of the several Offices usually hung up out of the hours of business in the Gate porter's Lodge be placed in a cupboard there to be provided for that purpose, with a lock to it, & that the Gate-porter, or the Person appointed by him to attend the Gate, keep the key of it, & that without the knowledge of one of them no key shall be taken down, or access had to any of the Offices.

With respect to the Care of the Gates of the Bank, we have examined Mr Watkins, the principal Gate-porter, & without troubling you with the particulars of his information, in regard to the hours of opening & shutting them, & the care of the Keys; all which appears on our Minutes: We shall submit as our Opinion that some regulations are wanted & may very easily be adopted—such as stationing a Gate-porter constantly at the great Gate in Threadneedle Street, to attend at all hours from the unlocking of the Gates in the morning to the setting of the Watch at night. We think he might be of considerable use, for the purposes of keeping order, of having an eye on such persons as go in or out, of directing those who enquire the way to the several Offices, & of accommodating the Publick by any little services of the same nature, the want of which has frequently been complained of: & to this end it will be adviseable that he always appears when the Gates are set open with his Gown & Staff. But as it will be impossible for one Man to execute the duties of this Office, it will certainly be necessary to appoint a Deputy to Watkins, that between the two the attendance required may be given.

We are also of the Opinion, that though the keys are brought down from the Accountant's Apartm^{ts} (where they are deposited every night), & the Gates unlocked at six in the morning in Summer & at seven in Winter, yet that there is no necessity for their being open to the Publick at those

early hours, nor so late at night as is now practised, & that
orders should be given to set them open in the morning at
half past eight, & to shut them at six in the evening both
in Summer & Winter, & that the Gate porter be directed
to attend at the Gate for the admission of such persons as
may have occasion to pass before or after those hours. A
Regulation we imagine equally convenient for the Publick &
much safer for the Bank.

> S. Bosanquet
> Thomas Dea
> Benj. Winthrop

Bank of England
24th October 1783
Source: BEA, M5/212, fols. 195–202.

The fourth Report of the Committee appointed to inspect & enquire into the Mode & execution of the Business as now carried on in the different departments of the Bank

To the Governor, the Deputy Governor & the Committee of Treasury

Having in our former Reports taken notice of such Things within the department of the Chief Cashier, as appeared to require immediate attention: We now proceed to submit, for the consideration of the Court, such observations as have occurred during our examination into the conduct of business in the Offices within the department of the Chief Accountant.

This department we find divided into 15 Offices, most of them superintended by a Chief or Head Clerk viz:

The enterers of the Credits & payments of Bank Notes.

The same of the 7 days Sight notes.

The enterers, seriation, of Bills & Notes discounted.

Those of Bills & Notes discounted into the Discount Ledgers.

The Drawing Office, which checks with the Drawing Office in the Hall.

The Office of Bank Stock, & Consol^d Long Ann^y.

D^o of Consol^d Reduced.

D^o of 3 P Cent Consols.

D^o of 4 P Cent Consols, & the Short Ann^y.

D^o of 3 P Cent Ann^s 1726, & the Ann^s (for 28 Years).

The Chancery Office.

The Cheque Office.

The Writer of the Journal.

The Account of Exchequer bills kept by the Accountant General & checked by the Deputy Accountant.

The General Ledger, kept by the Deputy Accountant.

We have examined the Chiefs & most of the other Clerks in all these Offices relative to the Business of each, as well as to the Behaviour, abilities, & attendance of the Clerks themselves; but in this Report we mean to confine ourselves to such observations as we have made in the Stock & Cheque Offices, & to the suggestion of such alterations with respect to them as in our Opinion will be material improvements.

The Stock Offices being the first in point of importance, especially to the Publick, naturally claimed our earliest & closest attention, & a good deal of our time has been employed in endeavouring to ascertain how far the very frequent complaints, in regard of the delays & inconveniences experienc'd by the Publick in receiving their Dividends, are well founded, from what causes they arise, & to what degree they may be remedied. To this end, we directed our principal enquiries to the Office of 3 P Cent Consol^d Ann^s, where from the largeness of the Capital & number of the Proprietors, these inconveniences must of necessity most prevail.

The Hours from 9 to 11 in the forenoon & from 1 to 3 in the afternoon are fixed for the payment of Dividends; & from 9 to 1 for Transfers: & every Transfer ticket must be put in before 1 o'clock, or is accounted a private Transfer, & must be paid for as such. This regulation, made undoubtedly with a view to prevent the business of transferring from interfering with that of Dividends, in order that all Transfers might be over before the payment of Dividends in the afternoon commenced, is now entirely counteracted by the Brokers & Jobbers, who commonly deliver in more Transfer tickets, during the last quarter of an hour of the time allowed, than in all the preceding part of the day. The entering & executing these Transfers generally employ the greatest part of the hour between 1 & 2 o'clock (sometimes much longer), & whilst this is doing, it is the common practice of the Office to require all Persons applying for Dividends, to wait 'till the Transfers are finished on the plea that the Tickets having been put in within the time prescribed, they must be compleated before any Dividend Warrants be delivered. This interference of two different Branches of business in the hour between 1 & 2, we conceive to be the principal Source of most of the disagreements between the Publick & the Clerks, the former strenuously insisting that the time from 1 to 3 being allotted by the Bank for the payment of Dividends they have a right to be immediately satisfied, whilst the latter (however willing to accommodate them) find it impossible to comply with their demands.

Before we propose a remedy for this inconvenience, we shall proceed to state another matter which in our apprehension deserves notice. From our examination of the Clerks, we find that the method formerly practised universally throughout the Transfer Offices, of marking the non-accepted Stock on the Dividend Warrants, in order that the parties claiming their Dividends might first be call'd on to make their Acceptances, has been for some time discontinued in this Office; nor are the Jobbers now required to accept Stock, before they are allowed to re-transfer the same; notwithstanding that the words of all the Acts of Parliament which establish the Government Funds so couple the Acceptance with the Transfer as if the Transfer could not be considered as compleat without it. The reason given to us for the omission, is, that, the short time (in respect to the amount of the Capital) allowed for the shuttings previous to the Dividend, had rendered

it sometimes impossible for the Clerks to look out & mark
the non-acceptances; & it has been stated that even if this
could have been done, the delay occasioned by obliging all
persons to accept, before they were permitted to receive the
Dividend Warrants, would have been so great & inconvenient
to the Publick, that it became necessary, some years ago,
to lay aside the practise altogether. The omission, in this
Office, has been drawn into precedent, by the Jobbers in the
other Transfer Offices, & has been used as a plea, why they
should not be strictly required to make acceptances there; &
really it seems to be an unanswerable argument, that
if an acceptance be unnecessary in the great Stock of
3 P Cent Consols, it must be equally so, in those of
4 P Cents, Reduced, & other smaller Stocks.

Whether Acceptances should, in pursuance of the
words of the Acts of Parliament, be rigidly insisted on,
before Dividends are paid, or Re-transfers allowed, however
inconvenient it may prove, to the Parties, (& it has been
very forcibly represented to us by the Deputy Accountant
that the Jobbers will complain heavily if they should be
obliged to comply with that practice), is a matter we must
leave wholly to the consideration of the Court.

We have been sedulously occupied in endeavouring
to discover some means of removing the cause of
complaints arising from the interruptions in the payment
of Dividends, particularly in this Office, without at the same
time protracting the general business or producing other
ill-consequences; but of all the various Modes that have
been suggested to us, there is but one, which in our opinion
is not accompanied with great inconveniences, & as that
does not seem liable to any material objections, we now
offer it to the consideration of the Court.

The business of making Transfers & that of paying
Dividends, being entirely independent of each other, we
recommend that they be separated, & transacted in different
Offices. The two now used for the 3 P Cent Consol^d Ann^s
will, we think, in every respect answer the purpose for
this Stock, if one of them be appropriated to the purpose
of Transfers only, the other to that of Dividends. In this
case a smaller number of Clerks will be sufficient for the

Dividend branch than are now employed in that service, because the payment will continue the whole day without intermission, & they will not be subject to be called off from this peculiar business: but then a few Clerks extraordinary will be required, to have the charge of settling the disputed or intricate Accounts; of attending such Persons as may have acceptances to make; & of looking out the Warrants for claims of old Dividends: every part of which is now done by the Dividend payers themselves, to the great delay & dissatisfaction of the Publick.

If these circumstances alone be considered, it will be found that additional Clerks are wanted even at present; but if the proposed separation should take place they will unavoidably necessary, on account of the Ledgers being then fixed in the other Office. And should the Court think proper to direct that all Acceptances be required in future, the present regulation will enable the Head of the Office to carry their Orders into execution, through the assistance of these Clerks; which in our opinion cannot in its present state be effected. We may also observe, that by the proposed alteration the Transfers will certainly be carried on with more ease & be less liable to Errors than they can be in the present State of the Office: for neither the Clerks nor the Publick will meet with the interruptions they now find; from the confusion occasioned by two different Branches of business going on in the same place at one & the same time.

We have not ventured to suggest this alteration without first taking the Opinions of the Chief & Deputy Accountants, the Heads of all the Transfer Offices, & many of the most experienced Clerks, as to the practicability of the plan, who uniformly allow its tendency to facilitate the publick business of the House, to promote the ease of the Clerks, & to increase the Security of the Bank: they have expressed their wishes for its adoption, & we can discover no objection of moment to its being carried into immediate execution.

We annex, by way of Appendix, a Scheme of the requisite Alterations. They are such as may be easily effected: And by an addition of only 7 Clerks to the present number, a Regulation so extremely useful to the Publick

& conducive to the honour of the Bank may be compleatly established.

We now proceed to state some observations on the manner of keeping the Dividend Warrants in the Cheque Office, where all Warrants after payment are deposited, & where the old unpaid or Back Warrants, down to within 4 or 5 years of the running Dividend, are kept; & here we found matters deserving very serious consideration.

To obtain information in respect of the Mode of conducting business here, we pursued the method, invariably practised by us, of going into the Office, to see the process of a day's work, on the spot. And our first business was to enquire, where the unpaid or Back Warrants were kept, & what precautions were taken for their safety: our surprise was great indeed to find they were placed (to the amount of £75,000) in a wooden Cupboard under one lock, to which each of the Clerks has a key. This appeared to us the more extraordinary as the Chief Clerk informed us, that this Office was established, about 22 years ago, principally to prevent the repetition of a fraud perpetrated by one of the Clerks of this House, who by having access to these Back Warrants was tempted to forge the signatures to a large parcel of them, & afterwards to receive their amount.

With a view of keeping a Check upon this Store of unpaid Warrants, we find that all the Transfer Offices send once a year to compare these Back Warrants with their Lists, except the 3 P Cent Consol^d Office, in which the practise has been discontinued for several years. We deem it however so essential an examination that we cannot avoid recommending that Orders be given for its being constantly attended to in future.

Farther, the paid Warrants in course for sending up to the Exchequer, on settling the Exchequer Account, being extremely numerous, & necessary for the sake of reference to them to be in or near this Office, are now kept in numerical order in large boxes; but the place not being large enough to contain them all, some are in an outer room adjoining, within a low wooden partition, & others in the open Lobby, where they are much exposed to accidents. It is true that these Warrants are cancelled, & therefore the

Bank runs no risk of paying them a second time: but if any of them should be lost or destroyed, we apprehend it would raise an almost insuperable difficulty in settling with the Exchequer; where they scrupulously require every single Warrant to be produced.

But this is not the only danger this Office is subject to. From its situation over the Gate House porter's Lodges, where fires are constantly kept a great part of the year, no doubt can be made of its being more exposed to accidents from fire than any other part of the House; a consideration too alarming not to be immediately attended to, by adopting any alteration that will fix an Office of so much importance in a place of greater security.

For this purpose we recommend that the Warrant Office, now kept in the Old General Court room, be removed to its former station over the gate-way into the Room now occupied by the Officer on guard, which is large enough for the business; & that the Cheque Office be placed in the Old General Court room. This exchange will fix the Cheque in the interior part of the House, afford ample space & security for all its operations with the paid Warrants; & allow of a proper situation for erecting an Iron Safe or Chest for depositing the Back Warrants. And the present Cheque Office may be fitted up for the use of the Officer on guard.

We have consulted the Chief Cashier & Chief Accountant, who hath both concur in the propriety of the exchange of Offices, on the grounds before assigned.

S. Bosanquet
Thomas Dea
Benj. Winthrop

Bank of England
19th Feb^ry 1784

The Alterations proposed in order to separate the two Branches of transferring & paying Dividends in the 3 P Cent Consols

1st To remove the Chancery (now in the 4 P Cents) into a room adjoining to the other Chancery Office; or into a part of the Rotunda to be taken off for the purpose; or into any other part of the House thought more convenient.

2nd To remove the Office of Annˢ 1726 & 28 years (now in the 3 P Cent Consols) to the place now occupied by the Chancery in the 4 P Cent Office.

3rd To appropriate the Office of the 3 P Cent Consols nearest Bartholomew Lane, for the Transfer business only; & in some convenient part of this Office, Book cases to be placed that may contain all the Transfer books, not in immediate use, ranged in succession according to their marks, & one porter (or more if necessary) to be appointed for keeping these Books in order, of handing them to the Clerks when wanted, & afterwards of returning them into their proper places.

The establishment of Clerks in this Office to consist of 38 viz:

1 Chief
1 Second
20 Posters
16 Enterers
38

4th To appropriate the other Office of the 3 P Cent Consols, for the payment of Dividends. For which purpose the Dividend Warrants to be divided into 12 Books as nearly equal, with regard to the number of names in each, as a succession of the letters of the alphabet will admit of, none of which will exceed 6000. At each book a Clerk to be stationed for the purpose of paying Dividends from 9 to 3, without intermission or the interference of any other business.

5th Four supernumerary Clerks to be appointed, to examine & settle all disputed or intricate Accounts; to fetch from the Cheque Office any Back Warrants for old Dividends that may be claimed; to see acceptances made that may have been omitted; & in general to undertake any business that might otherwise call the Dividend payers from their Books.

The establishment of Clerks in this Office, to consist of 17 viz:

1 Chief

12 Dividend payers

<u>4 Supernumeraries</u>

17

The 6 Clerks employed in registering Wills & making out Powers, to be stationed in whichever of these Offices may be thought by the Chiefs the most convenient.

Thus, the whole number of Clerks employed will be,

In the Office for Transfers 38

In the Office for Dividends 17

<u>For the Wills & Powers 6</u>

In all 61

The present establishment is 54

Proposed increase of Clerks 7

6th Two openings for communication behind the Counters to be made, in order to facilitate recurring to the Books & prevent any obstructions to the Clerks as they pass from one Office to the other.

Source: BEA, M5/213, fols. 134–148.

The fifth Report of the Committee appointed to inspect & enquire into the Mode & execution of the Business as now carried on in the different departments of the Bank

To the Governor, Deputy Governor & Committee of Treasury

Our former Reports being in a great measure confined to the suggestion of such alterations as in our opinion would operate as very essential improvements, with respect to the accommodation of the Publick, as well as to the Security of the Bank, (& we trust that in submitting our Ideas on those subjects we have not gone beyond the line prescribed to us by the Court.)

We shall now proceed to report the result of our examinations, into the conduct & behaviour of the Clerks; an object doubtless of very great importance, & at all times highly deserving the utmost attention; but as we deem it unnecessary to descend to minuteness on this occasion, we think it will be sufficient, if we state such matters only as appear to require correction or regulation: referring those Gentlemen, to our Minutes, who may require more particular information.

To conduct with propriety, safety, & effect, an Establishment of this kind, consisting of more than Three hundred Men, who from the nature of their situation must & ought to be governed rather by gentle than by harsh means, will seldom be found so very easy in practice as it appears in theory: however, when we consider the various discordant humours & passions of Men, & the natural unwillingness to obey, where no distinct line is drawn, of Power on one side, or of Obedience on the other; we must acknowledge on the whole, that after a minute enquiry we have found no very material causes of complaint subsisting either in regard to their behaviour towards one another, or in regard to the conduct of their business. We have, notwithstanding thought it incumbent on us, to recommend in the strongest terms to the Inferiors, a due subordination to the Superiors; & a ready compliance with their orders, for we conceive that nothing will tend more, not only to the existence of harmony amongst themselves, but to the proper execution of the business of the House, than the maintenance of a considerable degree of attention in the Junior Clerks, towards the Heads of the respective Offices.

There are however some matters on which it is our duty to report & which in our opinion deserve on many accounts very serious consideration. One of them has already in some degrees engaged the attention of the Court; we mean the conduct of the Clerks in the Transfer Offices, with respect to the very general practice amongst them of transacting Business, as Brokers & Jobbers, in the Publick Funds.

We shall not endeavour to enumerate all the ill consequences that must inevitably flow from a continuance of this practice: nor need we mention the many obvious inconveniences that the Bank as well as the Publick must frequently experience, arising from the neglect of Duty & inattention to their business, which it must unavoidably introduce among the Clerks; by seducing their minds from regular employment in an easy service, & attaching them to objects inviting though dangerous, & which appears so much more immediately interesting to themselves.

The Publick, the Brokers, the Directors, all feel & have long complained of this evil; yet no steps seem to have been taken to provide an adequate remedy for it, except an Order of the Court of Directors dated the 14th Feb^{ry} 1771 which is in the following words.

Ordered

That henceforth no Servant of the Bank presume to transact any Business as a Broker in buying or selling any Stocks or Annuities whatsoever, on pain of the displeasure of this Court.

And that the said Order be transcribed & affixed at the respective Transfer Offices.

This Order we are led to imagine was considered as obsolete, or was forgotten almost as soon as made: for on examination of nearly all the Clerks in the Transfer Offices (& here we take occasion to declare that, as far as we can judge, we have experienc'd great candour in their acknowledgements on this head, &, we believe truth, in their answers to such questions as were put to them as well on this as on other subjects), the major part avowed an entire ignorance of such an Order having ever existed; others had heard of, but never seen it; & the general idea seems to have been, that if the Business of the House were properly done, they were no way culpable in endeavouring to procure Orders for transactions in the Funds, which they might either execution themselves personally, or by the interference of their friends in the Stock Exchange; & in regard to Jobbing, that no particular restraint lay on them, from their situation, as Clerks of the Bank, though many of them might abstain from that traffick on other motives.

As we are decidedly of opinion that the practice of the Clerks acting as Brokers or Jobbers is not only inconvenient & pernicious in itself, but that it may eventually lead to even fatal consequences by the powerful temptations it holds out to Men, not in affluent circumstances; we think the Court cannot too soon interpose its Authority, in order to put a stop to an evil of such magnitude. And for the effectual accomplishment of so salutary a regulation, we deem it expedient & fair, that the Clerks should be formally made acquainted with the solemn determination of the Court, to cause its former Order (or a new One, as shall be thought most adviseable) to be strictly enforced, & that Punishment, even to dismission from the Service, will be the certain consequence of future disobedience.

We are farther of the opinion that, to prevent for the time to come, the plea of ignorance on the part of the Clerks, & that the Publick may also be acquainted with this Regulation, there be painted on the Wall in some conspicuous part of the Rotunda & of each Transfer Office, Words to the following effect.

By order of the Court of Directors, the Clerks of the Bank are not permitted to act as Brokers or Jobbers in the Publick Funds.

Before we conclude this subject, we shall venture to add, that as, by far the greater part of the Clerks themselves seem very well sensible of the impropriety of this practice, especially when carried on against an express Order of the Court, & that several of them have wholly abstained from it on other considerations, we have no doubt, but that with some little attention & perseverance on the part of the Directors, this Evil may be wholly remedied.

Another matter which we have thought it our duty to enquire into, is, that of the Fees & Gratuities receiv'd by the Clerks from the Publick. Our Minute books contain the information we have collected on this head, but we desire it to be understood that we annex very different ideas to the words, Fees & Gratuities. Under the former we class such small sums as are receiv'd for private Transfers, for registering of Wills, for making out Powers of Attorney, for Bonds, Affidavits, & Powers, & generally all such as form their publick notoriety & fixed rates may not unreasonably be supposed to have obtained the sanction of the Court of Directors, as required by the 11th Bye Law. By the latter we understand all presents given to the Clerks for doing what is, in fact, no more than the ordinary business of the House.

From the Chiefs as well as many of the inferior Clerks, in every Office, we have gathered sufficient information to justify us in asserting that the Practice, under both heads, has been carried to an extent that requires particular notice; but however desirous we are to promote the Honour & the Prosperity of the Bank, by advising such Regulations as we conceive may tend to both, we must leave to the consideration of the Court, how far the practice of receiving money from the Publick under the name of Gratuities, (expressly contrary to the Letter & Spirit of the 11th Bye Law), is an evil that can be prevented altogether: for at the same time, that we express our particular disapprobation, of the introduction & continuance of a custom, not only disgraceful in itself; but liable to occasion dissatisfaction & heart-burnings amongst the Clerks themselves, from the unequal distributions in some of the Offices; & what is a matter of much more serious consequence, to give rise to partialities & unjust preferences, towards the Publick; (& we have very strong grounds for believing that in this respect, the custom, bad as it is, has been most shamefully misused): yet we have found it so firmly established, so operating as part of the legal emoluments of Office, handed down to the Clerks from their predecessors, that we think it requires, not only solemn deliberation but an accurate & nice Judgement, to determine whether it were wiser to endeavour at abolishing the practice altogether; or to regulate it, by excluding the Chiefs from any participation, & ordering equal distributions amongst the inferior Clerks, by which means the Chiefs would become a check on the inferiors & prevent unreasonable exactions on the Publick: but in this case, it will be equitable to allow an increase of salary to the former by way of compensation.

In regard however to the Fees now established in the Transfer Offices, there is one which we think should be regulated; it has become usual to charge Five shillings for every £1000 of Scrip transferr'd the same day it is made into Stock, an imposition esteemed so heavy by the Clerks themselves, that, where the sum required to be transferred is large, they generally moderate their demand, & agree with the parties on the best terms they can: If the Publick be indulged in having these Transfers; we see no reason why they should pay in proportion to the sum: but rather think, that each Transfer should be chargeable with the payment of Five shillings, instead of half a Crown the fee of a private one; in order to prevent the practice from becoming too general.

(Sign'd)
S. Bosanquet
Thomas Dea
Benj. Winthrop

Bank of England
25th Feb^{ry} 1784
Source: BEA, M5/213, fols. 151–160.

The sixth Report of the Committee appointed to inspect & enquire into the Mode & execution of the Business as now carried on in the different departments of the Bank

To the Governor, Deputy Governor & Committee of Treasury

Having finished our enquiries into the Mode & Execution of the Business carried on in the different departments of the Bank, & having in our proceeding Reports submitted much matters as appeared to us worth of observation to the Committee of Treasury to be laid before the Court, we conceive that the object of our appointment is, as far as depends on us accomplished, & that our Commission of course draws to an end: Before however we finally conclude we shall add a few remarks, which we hope may be found of use, either as applicable to the general management of the Business of the House, or to some particular matters that in our opinion deserve very serious attention.

And first with respect to the Clerks, the number
of whom most certainly renders them an object of
considerable moment; we could wish for an establishment
of a better defined system of subordination, throughout
the House, than seems actually to exist, so as to form a
chain of obedience, from the Juniors towards the Heads of
their respective Offices; & from these towards the Chiefs
of the two great departments, in order that the Superiors
by possessing a more direct & acknowledged controul may
in some sort be held accountable for the conduct of those
immediately under them. And here we must take notice of
a practice that strikes us a very extraordinary one, which
is, that the Chiefs of the two great departments, & the
Heads of most of the Offices throughout the Bank, are the
first to quit the House, some at a certain hour; & others as
soon as their particular part of the business is over; leaving
the charge of every thing to the vigilance & honesty of the
Junior Clerks, (frequently such as are very young in Office), &
not considering it as any part of their duty to attend to the
subsequent transactions of the day. This practice, beyond
a doubt, must have crept in by degrees, for we deem it
impossible that it ever could have received the deliberate
approbation of a Court of Directors; & however Time may
have sanctified the custom, the reverse of it would have
appeared a much more natural regulation: for surely if
in any situation of Trust a compleat superintendence is
desireable, it must be more immediately necessary where
the Trust is of such infinite importance.

We therefore submit to the consideration of the
Court, what has already been touched on in our Third
Report, whether means may not be found to enable the
two Chiefs or their respective Deputies to give a more
constant attendance at the Bank, & to exercise a general
superintending care until the business of the day is closed, &
the Keys properly disposed of.

With respect to the admission of Clerks into the service,
we hope it will not be deemed improper if we recommend
to the Gentlemen in the Directors to pay great attention to
the abilities & characters of those they nominate; & at the
time of Election, to their performances: for though amongst

so great a number it cannot be expected that all shall be
equally capable, yet care should be taken not to elect such
as are apparently liable to exception. Great regard ought
also to be had to the qualifications of those Clerks who
may be removed from one department or Office to another.
These removals are commonly determined by Seniority,
which, though a fair & equitable rule to govern promotion,
generally; will not apply in all cases, nor ought it to be
resorted to where particular Talents are required.

The usage of admitting Brokers to identify the persons
of their Principals, (who transfer Stock & are not known to
the Clerks), by signing their names in the Transfer books,
is a matter well worthy the serious consideration of the
Court, as some late instances have proved this practice to be
most shamefully & dangerously abused. Unless the Brokers
become in some shape responsible for the Truth of what
they sign, so as to be held liable, in case of loss attending a
confidence in their Veracity, we do not see of what use, in
point of security, this custom can be. If as the Law stands
now they undertake nothing, (& this is a question on which
we should wish to have the best legal Opinions), we think
a remedy might be found without much difficulty, either by
introducing words purporting a special undertaking on the
part of the Brokers, or by procuring a clause in an Act of
Parliament, to subject them to responsibility.

In the course of our enquiries, we examined into the
State of the Library, where are deposited all or most of
the Books used since the institution of the Bank, with all
the cancelled Bank notes & heaps of old papers, consisting
of Files of money tickets, orders for Bank Post bills and the
like: As we are of the opinion great part of these may be
destroyed without any possible injury or inconvenience to
the Bank, & that room will be wanted for those Books and
papers which it might be thought necessary to preserve,
we submit whether it might not be proper to direct a
catalogue of the Books & papers now there to be drawn out
by some Clerks of the different Offices, and then to order
such as are apparently of no manner of use, to be burnt; &
in future to cause the Books & papers to be arranged in
regular order, marked with their contents and dates, & the

catalogue of them kept up, so as that immediate reference may be had to any of them when required.

As the best Regulations for the conduct of Men are found by length of time to lose their spring & effect, when the eye of vigilance & an immediate superintending care are removed, & as we know how impossible it is for the Committee of Treasury, from their various & important avocations in the business of the Bank, to be directly attentive to the conduct of the Clerks on every occasion, we submit whether it might not be attended with very good effects if a Committee were appointed from the rest of the Direction, for that special purpose, to sit as often as might be judged convenient, to visit and examine the different offices from time to time, to hear complaints in the first instance, in short to see that the business of the Bank, as far as regards the Servants or Clerks, were properly conducted, & to make their reports to the Committee of Treasury. We cannot but think that the establishment of such a Committee, & a proper degree of attention in the gentlemen composing it, would answer many good purposes.

Our Minute books containing the detail of all our Proceedings & particularly the examinations of the principal Clerks in the different Offices may possibly hereafter be found of some use, it may therefore be advisable to preserve them: & here we take occasion to recommend to your favour our Secretary, Mr Aslett. who has been very diligent in his Duty, & in his attendance on us, thinking him entitled to a compensation for the extraordinary trouble we have given him.

We beg leave to express our acknowledgements to the Gentlemen of the Committee of Treasury for the attention we have experienced from them, & to the Court in general for the candour with which our Reports have been received. If we could have rendered these more complete, it would have afforded us the highest satisfaction: & for having extended them so far, we trust the greatness & variety of the Objects to which our Enquiries have been directed will be thought a sufficient excuse.

When we contemplate the immense importance of the Bank of England not only to the City of London, in

points highly essential to the promotion & extension of
its Commerce, but to the Nation at large, as the grand
Palladium of Public Credit, we cannot but be thoroughly
persuaded that an Object so great in itself & so interesting to all Ranks of the Community, must necessarily excite
care & solicitude in every breast, for the wise administration
of its Affairs, but principally and directly in theirs who
are entrusted with the immediate management of them:
We deem it therefore superfluous to say a single word to
the Court with a view of inculcating a religious Veneration
for the glorious fabrick, or of recommending a steady and
unremitting attention to its sacred Preservation.

(Sign'd)
S. Bosanquet
Thomas Dea
Benj. Winthrop

Bank of England
18th March 1784
Source: BEA, M5/213, fols. 172–179.

Manuscript Sources

BANK OF ENGLAND ARCHIVES

Accountant's Discount Office Rules and Orders, 9A312/1.
An Account of the Architectural Progress of the Bank of England (c. 1857), 13A84/2/19.
The Bank Picquet: Its function and history, 1963 17A100/1.
Britannia and the Bank, 1694–1961, ADM 30/59.
Clerks and their securities, M5/700.
Committee for Building Minutes, M5/748.
Committee for Examining Candidates, M5/406.
Directors Annual Lists, M5/436.
Directors' nominations, 1756–1809, M5/686.
Establishment Department: House Lists, E20.
Establishment Department: Salary Ledgers, E41.
Freshfields Papers relating to Bank staff, F6/68.
General staff lists, ADM30/12.
Governor's Diary—James Sperling, M5/450.
Governor's Diary—Samuel Beachcroft, M5/451.
List of porters and watchmen with details of their wages and allowances, 1805, M6/117.
List of Staff Receiving Pensions, E46.
Memorandum book of Samuel Bosanquet, 1783–1791, M5/471.
Memorandum regarding the introduction and continuance of the King's Guard, M6/19.
Minutes of the Committee for House and Servants, 1744–1787, M5/376.
Minutes of the Committee of Inspection, M5/212–213.
Minutes of the Committee of the Treasury, G8/2–3.
Minutes of the Court of Directors, G4/5, 22–24.
Old Book of Orders for Porters and Watchmen, M5/607.
Orders of the Court and Committee of Inspection for the Discount Office Hall, C29/43.
An outline of the history and working of the inscribed stock system, AC4/5.
Petition of Mr Gould, 6A31/1.
Petition of Nathaniel Gary, 6A31/1.
Petition of Peter Saffree junior, BEA 6A31/1.
Petition of Robert Beachcroft, 6A31/1.
Petition of Stafford Briscoe, 6A31/1.
Register of clerks in business, M5/691.
Rules necessary to be well understood for the true transacting of business, AC7/1.
A short history of the development of the system of transfer of British government
    stocks by instrument in writing, AC4/1.
Transfer books, AC28/4245–4288; AC28/6445–6487.

BRITISH LIBRARY

Liverpool Papers, Volume XXIII, Add. MS. 38212

LONDON METROPOLITAN ARCHIVE

LMA, MS 11936/253/376126
LMA, MS 11936/276/417355/359
LMA, MS 11936/341/526365
LMA, MS 11936/399/634968
LMA, MS 11936/427/740354

Primary Sources

Anon., *The Ambulator; or the Stranger's Companion in a tour round London* (London, 1774).

Anon., *The Art of Stock-Jobbing: A poem in imitation of Horace's Art of Poetry, by a Gideonite* (London, 1746).

Anon., *Considerations on the Expediency of raising at this Time of general Dearth, the Wages of Servants that are not Domestic, particularly Clerks in Public Offices* (London, 1767).

Anon., *Genuine and Impartial Memoirs of Francis Fonton, late of the Bank of England* (London, 1790).

Bank of England, *The names and descriptions of the proprietors of unclaimed dividends on Bank stock, which became due before the 10th October 1780, and remained unpaid the 30th September 1790* (London, 1791).

Bramah, Joseph, *The Petition and Case of Joseph Bramah . . . Inventor of the PATENT LOCKS for the Security of Life and Property* (London, 1798).

Cobbett, William, ed., *The Parliamentary History of England, from the Earliest Times to the Year 1803*, 36 vols. (London, 1806–1820).

Collier, John Dyer, *The Life of Abraham Newland Esq. Late Principal Cashier at the Bank of England* (London, 1808).

Fielding, John, *A Brief Description of the Cities of London and Westminster* (London, 1776).

A Gentleman of the Bank, *The Bank of England's Vade Mecum; or sure guide; extremely proper and useful for all persons who have any money matters to transact in the hall of the Bank* (London, 1782).

Hartley, David, *Considerations on the proposed renewal of the Bank Charter* (London, 1781).

Lamb, C., 'The Superannuated Man', in *The Last Essays of Elia*, with an introduction and notes by Alfred Ainger (London, 1883), pp. 259–266.

Malton, T., *A Picturesque Tour through the Cities of London and Westminster* (London, 1792–1801).

Mortimer, Thomas, *Every man his own broker: Or a guide to Exchange-Alley* (London, 1762).

The Old Lady of Threadneedle Street, vols. 1–83.

Palk, Deirdre, ed., *Prisoners' Letters to the Bank of England, 1781–1827* (London, 2007).

Parkes, Joseph, *A History of the Court of Chancery* (London, 1828).

Pickett, William, *An apology to the Public for a continued Intrusion on their Notice with an Appeal to the free and independent Proprietors of Bank Stock, demonstrating that it is highly proper for them to examine into the State of their Affairs* (London, 1788).

Preston, S. H., 'Unclaimed Stocks, Dividends, and Bank Deposits', *Chambers's Journal of Popular Literature, Science and Arts*, 8 (1891), pp. 21–24.

Price, R., *An appeal to the nation on the subject of the national debt* (London, 1772).

Sinclair, John, *History of the Public Revenue of the British Empire* (London, 1789).

Smith, Adam, *An Inquiry into the Nature and Causes of the Wealth of Nations* (Oxford, 1976).

Vallance, R. and Hampden, J., eds., *Charles Lamb: Essays* (London, 1963).

Secondary Sources

Abramson, Daniel M., *Building the Bank of England: Money, Architecture, Society, 1694–1942* (New Haven, CT, 2005).

Acemoglu, Daron and Robinson, James A., *Why Nations Fail: The Origins of Power, Prosperity and Poverty* (London, 2013).

Acres, W. M., *The Bank of England from Within*, 2 vols. (London, 1931).

Allen, Robert, *The British Industrial Revolution in Global Perspective* (Cambridge, 2009).

Anderson, Gregory, *Victorian Clerks* (Manchester, UK, 1976).

Andreades, A., *A History of the Bank of England* (London, 1909).

Anon., *Drummond Bankers: A History* (Edinburgh, 1993?).

Armstrong, W. A., 'The Use of Information about Occupation', in E. A. Wrigley, ed., *Nineteenth Century Society: Essays in the Use of Quantitative Methods for the Study of Social Data* (Cambridge, 1972), pp. 191–253.

Ashworth, William J., *Customs and Excise: Trade, Production, and Consumption in England, 1640–1845* (Oxford, 2003).

Aylmer, G. E., 'From Office-Holding to Civil Service: The Genesis of Modern Bureaucracy', *Transactions of the Royal Historical Society*, 30 (1980), pp. 91–108.

Banner, Stuart, *Anglo-American Securities Regulation: Cultural and Political Roots, 1690–1860* (Cambridge, 1998).

Barker, Hannah, *The Business of Women: Female Enterprise and Urban Development in Northern England, 1760–1830* (Oxford, 2006).

Barker, Hannah and Green, Sarah, 'Taking Money from Strangers: Traders' Responses to Banknotes and the Risks of Forgery in Late Georgian London', *Journal of British Studies*, 60 (2021), pp. 585–608.

Bartrip, P.W.J., 'British Government Inspection, 1832–1875: Some Observations', *The Historical Journal*, 25 (1982), pp. 605–626.

Batt, D., 'The 1783 Proposal for a Readymade Note at the Bank of England', *Financial History Review*, 29 (2022), pp. 72–97.

Beattie, J. M., *Policing and Punishment in London, 1660–1750: Urban Crime and the Limits of Terror* (Oxford, 2001).

Bell, A. R., Brooks, C. and Taylor, N., 'Time-Varying Price Discovery in the Eighteenth Century: Empirical Evidence from the London and Amsterdam Stock Markets', *Cliometrica*, 10 (2016), pp. 5–30.

Berry, Helen, 'Polite Consumption: Shopping in Eighteenth-Century England', *Transactions of the Royal Historical Society*, 12 (2002), pp. 375–394.

Binney, J.E.D., *British Public Finance and Administration, 1774–92* (Oxford, 1958).

Black, Iain S., 'The London Agency System in English Banking, 1780–1825', *London Journal*, 21 (1996), pp. 112–130.

Black, Iain S., 'Spaces of Capital: Bank Office Building in the City of London, 1830–1870', *Journal of Historical Geography*, 26 (2000), pp. 351–375.

Booker, John, *Temples of Mammon: The Architecture of Banking* (Edinburgh, 1990).

Boot, H. M., 'Real Incomes of the British Middle Class, 1760–1850: The Experience of Clerks at the East India Company', *Economic History Review*, 52 (1999), pp. 638–668.

Boot, H. M., 'Salaries and Career Earnings in the Bank of Scotland, 1730–1880', *Economic History Review*, 44 (1991), pp. 629–653.

Borsay, P., 'A Room with a View: Visualising the Seaside, c. 1750–1914', *Transactions of the Royal Historical Society*, 23 (2013), pp. 175–202.

Bowen, H. V., *The Business of Empire: The East India Company and Imperial Britain, 1756–1833* (Cambridge, 2006).

Bowen, H. V., '"The Pests of Human Society": Stockbrokers, Jobbers, and Speculators in Mid-Eighteenth Century Britain', *History*, 78 (1993), pp. 38–53.

Bowen, H. V. and González Enciso, A., eds., *Mobilising Resources for War: Britain and Spain at Work during the Early Modern Period* (Pamplona, Spain, 2006).

Bowman, W. D., *The Story of the Bank of England: From Its Foundation in 1694 until the Present Day* (London, 1937).

Brantlinger, Patrick, *Fictions of State: Culture and Credit in Britain, 1694–1994* (Ithaca, NY, 1996).

Brewer, John, *The Sinews of Power: War, Money and the English State, 1688–1783* (London, 1994).

Broz, J. Lawrence and Grossman, Richard S., 'Paying for Privilege: The Political Economy of Bank of England Charters, 1694–1844', *Explorations in Economic History*, 41 (2004), pp. 48–72.

Burns, Arthur and Innes, Joanna, eds., *Rethinking the Age of Reform: Britain, 1780–1850* (Cambridge, 2003).

Capie, Forrest H. and Wood, Geoffrey E., *The Lender of Last Resort* (London, 2007).

Carlos, Ann M., Maguire, Karen and Neal, Larry, 'Financial Acumen, Women Speculators and the Royal African Company during the South Sea Bubble', *Accounting, Business and Financial History*, 16 (2006), pp. 219–243.

Carlos, Ann M. and Neal, Larry, 'Amsterdam and London as Financial Centres in the Eighteenth Century', *Financial History Review*, 18 (2001), pp. 21–46.

Carruthers, Bruce G. and Epseland, Wendy, 'Accounting for Rationality: Double-Entry Bookkeeping and the Rhetoric of Economic Rationality', *American Journal of Sociology*, 97 (1991), pp. 31–69.

Caselli, Fausto Piola, ed., *Government Debts and Financial Markets in Europe* (London, 2008).

Chamley, C., 'Interest Reductions in the Politico-Financial Nexus of Eighteenth-Century England', *Journal of Economic History*, 71 (2011), pp. 555–589.

Checkland, S. G., *Scottish Banking: A History, 1695–1973* (London, 1975).

Churchill, David, 'Security and Visions of the Criminal: Technology, Professional Criminality and Social Change in Victorian and Edwardian Britain', *British Journal of Criminology*, 56 (2016), pp. 857–876.

Clapham, J. H., 'The Private Business of the Bank of England, 1744–1800', *Economic History Review*, 11 (1941), pp. 77–89.

Clapham, Sir John H., *The Bank of England: A History*, 2 vols. (Cambridge, 1944).

Clark, G., 'The Political Foundations of Modern Economic Growth: England, 1540–1800', *Journal of Interdisciplinary History*, 26 (1996), pp. 563–588.

Cockayne, Emily, *Hubbub: Filth, Noise and Stench in England* (New Haven, CT, 2007).

Conlin, Jonathan, ed., *The Pleasure Garden, from Vauxhall to Coney Island* (Philadelphia, 2006).

Conway, Stephen, *War, State and Society in Mid-Eighteenth-Century Britain and Ireland* (Oxford, 2006).

Conway, Stephen and Torres Sánchez, Rafael, eds., *The Spending of the States: Military Expenditure during the Long Eighteenth Century: Patterns, Organisation and Consequences, 1650–1815* (Saarbrücken, Germany, 2011).

Cookson, J. E., *The British Armed Nation, 1793–1815* (Oxford, 1997).

Cope, S. R., 'The Stock-Brokers Find a Home: How the Stock Exchange Came to Be Established in Sweetings Alley in 1773', *Guildhall Studies in London History*, 2 (1977), pp. 213–219.

Cope, S. R., 'The Stock Exchange Revisited: A New Look at the Market in Securities in London in the Eighteenth Century', *Economica*, 45 (1978), pp. 1–21.

Corfield, P. J., 'Class by Name and Number in Eighteenth-Century Britain', *History*, 72 (1987), pp. 38–61.

Cox, Gary W., *Marketing Sovereign Promises: Monopoly Brokerage and the Growth of the English State* (Cambridge, 2016).

Cruikshank, Dan, and Burton, Neil, *Life in the Georgian City* (London, 1990).

Dale, Richard, *The First Crash: Lessons from the South Sea Bubble* (Princeton, NJ, 2004).

Davidson, Jenny, *Hypocrisy and the Politics of Politeness: Manners and Morals from Locke to Austen* (Cambridge, 2004).

Deacon, John, 'The Story of St. Christopher-Le-Stocks', *The Old Lady of Threadneedle Street*, 58 (1982), pp. 76–78.

de la Escosura, Leandro Prados, ed., *Exceptionalism and Industrialisation: Britain and Its European Rivals, 1688–1815* (Cambridge, 2004).

Dempster, G., Wells, J. and Wills, D., 'A Common-Features Analysis of Amsterdam and London Financial Markets during the Eighteenth Century', *Economic Inquiry*, 38 (2000), pp. 19–33.

Deringer, William, *Calculated Values: Finance, Politics and the Quantitative Age* (Cambridge, MA, 2018).

Desan, Christine, *Making Money: Coin, Currency and the Coming of Capitalism* (Oxford, 2014).

Dickson, P.G.M., *The Financial Revolution in England: A Study in the Development of Public Credit, 1688-1756* (London, 1967).

Dincecco, Mark, *Political Transformations and Public Finances: Europe, 1650-1913* (Cambridge, 2011).

Dome, Takuo, *The Political Economy of Public Finance in Britain, 1767-1873* (Abingdon, UK, 2004).

Emden, Paul H., 'The Brothers Goldsmid and the Financing of the Napoleonic Wars', *Transactions (Jewish Historical Society of England)*, 14 (1935-1939), pp. 225-246.

Erickson, Amy Louise, 'Married Women's Occupations in Eighteenth-Century London', *Continuity and Change*, 23 (2008), pp. 267-307.

Feaveryear, A. E., *The Pound Sterling: A History of English Money* (Oxford, 1931).

Finn, Margot, *The Character of Credit: Personal Debt in English Culture, 1740-1914* (Cambridge, 2008).

Finn, Margot, 'Men's Things: Masculine Possession in the Consumer Revolution', *Social History*, 25 (2000), pp. 133-155.

Froide, Amy, *Silent Partners: Women as Public Investors during Britain's Financial Revolution, 1690-1750* (Oxford, 2017).

Fynn-Paul, Jeff, ed., *War, Entrepreneurs and the State in Europe and the Mediterranean, 1300-1800* (Leiden, 2014).

Gallagher, John, *Learning Languages in Early Modern England* (Oxford, 2019).

Gatrell, Vic, *City of Laughter: Sex and Satire in Eighteenth-Century London* (London, 2006).

Gauci, Perry, *Emporium of the World: The Merchants of London, 1660-1800* (London, 2007).

George, M. Dorothy, *London Life in the Eighteenth Century* (Chicago, 2000).

Gilmour, Ian, *Riot, Risings and Revolution: Governance and Violence in Eighteenth-Century England* (London, 1995).

Giuseppi, John, *The Bank of England: A History from Its Foundation in 1694* (London, 1966).

Goetzmann, William N. and Rouwenhorst, K. Geert, eds., *The Origins of Value: The Financial Innovations That Created Modern Capital Markets* (Oxford, 2005).

González Enciso, A., *War, Power and the Economy: Mercantilism and State Formation in 18th-Century Europe* (Abingdon, UK, 2017).

Graham, Aaron, *Corruption, Party and Government in Britain, 1702-1713* (Oxford, 2015).

Greig, Hannah, '"All Together and All Distinct": Public Sociability and Social Exclusivity in London's Pleasure Gardens, ca. 1740-1800', *Journal of British Studies*, 51 (2012), pp. 50-75.

Gutteridge, H. C., 'The Origin and Historical Development of the Profession of Notaries Public in England', in *Cambridge Legal Essays Written in Honour of and Presented to Doctor Bond, Professor Buckland and Professor Kenny* (Cambridge, 1926), pp. 123-137.

Hancock, David, *Citizens of the World: London Merchants and the Integration of the British Atlantic Community, 1735-1785* (Cambridge, 1995).

Harding, Richard and Solbes Ferri, Sergio, coords., *The Contractor State and Its Implications, 1659-1815* (Las Palmas de Gran Canaria, Spain, 2012).

Harling, Philip, *The Waning of Old Corruption: The Politics of Economical Reform in Britain, 1779–1846* (Oxford, 1996).

Harling, Philip and Mandler, Peter, 'From "Fiscal-Military" State to Laissez-Faire State, 1760–1850', *Journal of British Studies*, 32 (1993), pp. 44–70.

Harris, Andrew T., *Policing the City: Crime and Legal Authority in London, 1780–1840* (Columbus, OH, 2004).

Harrison, Mark, 'The Ordering of the Urban Environment: Time, Work and the Occurrence of Crowds, 1790–1835', *Past and Present*, no. 110 (1986), pp. 134–168.

Hay, Douglas, 'War, Dearth and Theft in the Eighteenth Century: The Record of the English Courts', *Past and Present*, no. 95 (1982), pp. 117–160.

Haywood, Ian and Seed, John, eds., *The Gordon Riots: Politics, Culture and Insurrection in Late Eighteenth-Century Britain* (Cambridge, 2012).

Heller, Benjamin, 'The "Mene Peuple" and the Polite Spectator: The Individual in the Crowd at Eighteenth-Century London Fairs', *Past and Present*, no. 208 (2010), pp. 131–157.

Hewitt, Virginia, 'Beware of Imitations: The Campaign for a New Bank of England Note, 1797–1821', *The Numismatic Chronicle*, 158 (1998), pp. 197–222.

Hill, B. W., 'The Change of Government and the "Loss of the City", 1710–1711', *Economic History Review*, 24 (1971), pp. 395–413.

Hoppit, Julian, 'Compulsion, Compensation and Property Rights in Britain, 1688–1833', *Past and Present*, no. 210 (2011), pp. 93–128.

Hoppit, Julian, *Risk and Failure in English Business, 1700–1800* (Cambridge, 1987).

Hopwood, Anthony G., 'The Archaeology of Accounting Systems', in N. Macintosh and T. Hopper, eds., *Accounting, the Social and the Political: Classics, Contemporary and Beyond* (Amsterdam, 2005), pp. 73–84.

Horwitz, H., 'The Mess of the Middle Class' Revisited: The Case of the "Big Bourgeoisie" of Augustan London', *Continuity and Change*, 2 (1987), pp. 263–296.

Humfrey, Paula, ed., *The Experience of Domestic Service for Women in Early Modern London* (Farnham, UK, 2011).

Hyde, Ralph, ed., *The A to Z of Georgian London* (London, 1981).

James, John A., 'Panics, Payments, Disruptions and the Bank of England before 1826', *Financial History Review*, 19 (2012), pp. 289–309.

Jeacle, I., 'The Bank Clerk in Victorian Society: The Case of Hoare and Company', *Journal of Management History*, 16 (2010), pp. 312–326.

Joslin, D. M., 'London Private Bankers, 1720–1785', *Economic History Review*, 7 (1954), pp. 167–186.

Kadens, Emily, 'The Last Bankrupt Hanged: Balancing Incentives in the Development of Bankruptcy Law', *Duke Law Journal*, 59 (2010), pp. 1229–1319.

Karslake, J.B.P., 'Early London Fire-Appliances', *The Antiquaries Journal*, 9 (1929), pp. 229–238.

Keir, David Lindsay, 'Economical Reform, 1779–1787', *Law Quarterly Review*, 1 (1934), pp. 368–385.

Kelly, Morgan, Mokyr, Joel and Ó Gráda, Cormac, 'Precocious Albion: A New Interpretation of the British Industrial Revolution', *Annual Review of Economics*, 6 (2014), pp. 363–389.

Kerridge, Eric, *Trade and Banking in Early Modern England* (Manchester, UK, 1988).

King, W.T.C., *A History of the Discount Market*, with an introduction by T. E. Gregory (Abingdon, UK, 2016).

Klein, Lawrence E., 'Politeness for Plebes: Consumption and Social Identity in Early Eighteenth-Century England', in Ann Bermingham and John Brewer, eds., *The Consumption of Culture, 1600–1800: Image, Object, Text* (London, 1995).

Knight, Roger and Wilcox, Martin, *Sustaining the Fleet, 1793–1815: War, the British Navy and the Contractor State* (Woodbridge, UK, 2010).

Kosmetatos, Paul, 'Last Resort Lending before Henry Thornton? The Bank of England's Role in Containing the 1763 and 1772–3 British Credit Crises', *European Review of Economic History*, 23 (2019), pp. 99–328.

Krausman Ben-Amos, Ilana, *The Culture of Giving: Informal Support and Gift-Exchange in Early Modern England* (Cambridge, 2008).

Kroeze, Ronald, Vitória, André and Geltner, G., eds., *Anticorruption in History: From Antiquity to the Modern Era* (Oxford, 2018).

Kynaston, David, *Till Time's Last Sand: A History of the Bank of England, 1694–2013* (London, 2017).

Lane, Frederic C., 'Double Entry Bookkeeping and Resident Merchants', *Journal of European Economic History*, 6 (1977), pp. 177–191.

Langford, Paul, *A Polite and Commercial People: England 1727–1783* (Oxford, 1998).

Langford, Paul, *Public Life and the Propertied Englishman, 1689–1798* (Oxford, 1991).

Langford, Paul, 'The Use of Eighteenth-Century Politeness', *Transactions of the Royal Historical Society*, 12 (2002), pp. 318–321.

Lemmings, David and Walker, Claire, eds., *Moral Panics, the Media and the Law in Early Modern England* (London, 2009).

Linebaugh, Peter, *The London Hanged* (London, 2006).

Lovell, Mike C., 'The Role of the Bank of England as Lender of Last Resort in the Crises of the Eighteenth Century', *Explorations in Entrepreneurial History*, 10 (1957), pp. 8–21.

Macdonald, James, 'The Importance of Not Defaulting: The Significance of the Election of 1710', in D'Maris Coffman, Adrian Leonard, and Larry Neal, eds., *Questioning Credible Commitment: Perspectives on the Rise of Financial Capitalism* (Cambridge, 2013), pp. 125–146.

Mackenzie, A. D., *The Bank of England Note: A History of Its Printing* (Cambridge, 1953).

Major, Emma, *Madam Britannia: Women, Church, and Nation, 1712–1812* (Oxford, 2012).

Makepeace, M., *The East India Company's London Workers: Management of the Warehouse Labourers, 1800–1858* (Woodbridge, UK, 2010).

Markham, Jerry W. and Harty, Daniel J., 'For Whom the Bell Tolls: The Demise of Exchange Trading Floors and the Growth of ECNs', *Journal of Corporation Law*, 33 (2007–2008), pp. 865–939.

Marshall, P. J., *The Making and Unmaking of Empires: Britain, India and America, c. 1750–1783* (Oxford, 2005).

McGowen, Randall, 'The Bank of England and the Policing of Forgery, 1797–1821', *Past and Present*, no. 186 (2005), pp. 81–116.

McGowen, Randall, 'From Pillory to Gallows: The Punishment of Forgery in the Age of the Financial Revolution', *Past and Present*, no. 165 (1999), pp. 107–140.

McGowen, Randall, 'Managing the Gallows: The Bank of England and the Death Penalty, 1797–1821', *Law and History Review*, 25 (2007), pp. 241–282.

McKinlay, A. and Wilson, R. G., '"Small Acts of Cunning": Bureaucracy, Inspection and the Career, c. 1890–1914', *Critical Perspectives on Accounting*, 17 (2006), pp. 657–678.

Michie, Ranald C., *British Banking: Continuity and Change from 1694 to the Present* (Oxford, 2016).

Michie, Ranald C., 'Friend or Foe? Information Technology and the London Stock Exchange since 1700', *Journal of Historical Geography*, 23 (1997), pp. 304–326.

Michie, Ranald C., *The Global Securities Market: A History* (Oxford, 2006).

Mirowski, P., 'The Rise (and Retreat) of a Market: English Joint Stock Shares in the Eighteenth Century', *Journal of Economic History*, 41 (1981), pp. 559–577.

Mitch, David, 'Education and Skill of the British Labour Force', in R. Floud and P. Johnson, eds., *The Cambridge Economic History of Modern Britain*, vol. 1, *Industrialisation, 1700–1860* (Cambridge, 2004), pp. 332–356.

Mitchell, B. R., with Phyllis Deane, *Abstract of British Historical Statistics* (Cambridge, 1962).

Mokyr, Joel, *The Enlightened Economy: An Economic History of Britain, 1700–1850* (New Haven, CT, 2009).

Morgan, E. V. and Thomas, W. A., *The Stock Exchange: Its History and Functions* (London, 1969).

Mulcaire, T., 'Public Credit: Or the Feminization of Virtue in the Marketplace', *PMLA*, 114 (1999), pp. 1029–1042.

Muldrew, Craig, *The Economy of Obligation: The Culture of Credit and Social Relations in Early Modern England* (Basingstoke, UK, 1998).

Muldrew, Craig, 'Interpreting the Market: The Ethics of Credit and Community Relations in Early Modern England', *Social History*, 18 (1993), pp. 163–183.

Murphy, Anne L., 'Clockwatching: Work and Working Time at the Late-Eighteenth-Century Bank of England', *Past and Present*, 236 (2017), pp. 99–132.

Murphy, Anne L., 'Demanding Credible Commitment: Public Reactions to the Failures of the Early Financial Revolution', *Economic History Review*, 66 (2013), pp. 178–197.

Murphy, Anne L., 'Financial Markets: The Limits of Economic Regulation in Early Modern England', in Carl Wennerlind and Philip J. Stern, eds., *Mercantilism Reimagined: Political Economy in Early Modern Britain and Its Empire* (Oxford, 2013), pp. 263–281.

Murphy, Anne L., 'Learning the Business of Banking: The Recruitment and Training of the Bank of England's First Tellers', *Business History*, 52 (2010), pp. 150–168.

Murphy, Anne L., *The Origins of English Financial Markets: Investment and Speculation before the South Sea Bubble* (Cambridge, 2009).

Murphy, Anne L. '"Writes a Fair Hand and Appears to Be Well Qualified": Recruiting Bank of England Clerks at the Start of the Nineteenth Century', *Financial History Review*, 22 (2015), pp. 19–44.

Neal, L., 'The Integration and Efficiency of the London and Amsterdam Stock Markets in the Eighteenth Century', *Journal of Economic History*, 47 (1987), pp. 97–115.

Neal, L., *The Rise of Financial Capitalism: International Capital Markets in the Age of Reason* (Cambridge, 1990).

Nicholson, Colin, *Writing and the Rise of Finance: Capital Satires of the Early Eighteenth Century* (Cambridge, 1994).

North, Douglas C. and Weingast, Barry, 'Constitutions and Commitment: The Evolution of Institutions Governing Public Choice in Seventeenth-Century England', *Journal of Economic History*, 49 (1989), pp. 803–832.

O'Brien, Patrick K., 'Mercantilist Institutions for the Pursuit of Power with Profit: The Management of Britain's National Debt, 1756–1815', LSE Working Papers in Economic History, 95/06 (2006).

Ogborn, Miles, *Spaces of Modernity: London's Geographies, 1680–1780* (New York, 1998).

Paul, Helen J., *The South Sea Bubble: An Economic History of Its Origins and Consequences* (Abingdon, UK, 2011).

Pearson, R., *Insuring the Industrial Revolution: Fire Insurance in Great Britain, 1700–1850* (Aldershot, UK, 2004).

Phillips, Nicola, *Women in Business, 1700–1850* (Woodbridge, UK, 2006).

Pollard, Sidney, *The Genesis of Modern Management: A Study of the Industrial Revolution in Great Britain* (Cambridge, MA, 1965).

Poovey, Mary, *A History of the Modern Fact: Problems of Knowledge in the Sciences of Wealth and Society* (Chicago, 1998).

Preda, A., 'In the Enchanted Grove: Financial Conversations and the Marketplace in England and France in the 18th Century', *Journal of Historical Sociology*, 14 (2001), pp. 276–307.

Pressnell, L. S., *Country Banking in the Industrial Revolution* (Oxford, 1956).

Purvis, J. S., 'The Notary Public in England', *Archivum*, 12 (1962), pp. 121–126.

Reitan, Earl A., *Politics, Finance, and the People: Economical Reform in England in the Age of the American Revolution, 1770–92* (Basingstoke, UK, 2007).

Reynolds, Elaine A., *Before the Bobbies: The Night Watch and Police Reform in Metropolitan London, 1720–1830* (London, 1998).

Roberts, R. and Kynaston, D., eds., *The Bank of England: Money, Power and Influence, 1694–1994* (Oxford, 1995).

Rogers, Nicholas, *Crowds, Culture and Politics in Georgian Britain* (Oxford, 1998).

Rosenhaft, Eve, 'Hands and Minds: Clerical Work in the First "Information Society"', *International Instituut voor Sociale Geschiedenis*, 48 (2003), pp. 13–43.

Roseveare, Henry, *The Treasury, 1660–1870: The Foundations of Control* (London, 1973).

Roxburgh, Natalie, *Representing Public Credit: Credible Commitment, Fiction and the Rise of the Fictional Subject* (London, 2016).

Rubini, Dennis, 'Politics and the Battle for the Banks, 1688–1697', *English Historical Review*, 85 (1970), pp. 693–714.

Rudé, G.F.E., 'The Gordon Riots: A Study of the Rioters and Their Victims', *Transactions of the Royal Historical Society*, 6 (1956), pp. 93–114.

Samuel, Roy Edgar, 'Anglo-Jewish Notaries and Scriveners', *Transactions (Jewish Historical Society of England)*, 17 (1951–1952), pp. 113–159.

Saunders, Ann, *The Royal Exchange* (London, 1991).

Sayers, R. S., *Lloyds Bank in the History of English Banking* (London, 1957).

Schnabel, Isabel and Shin, Hyon Song, 'Liquidity and Contagion: The Crisis of 1763', *Journal of the European Economic Association*, 2 (2004), pp. 929–968.

Schwartz, L. D., *London in the Age of Industrialisation: Entrepreneurs, Labour Force and Living Conditions, 1700–1850* (Cambridge, 1992).

Schwoerer, Lois G., *Gun Culture in Early Modern England* (Charlottesville, VA, 2016).

Sgard, Jérôme, 'Bankruptcy, Fresh Start and Debt Renegotiation in England and France (17th to 18th Century)', in Thomas Max Safley, ed., *The History of Bankruptcy: Economic, Social and Cultural Implications in Early Modern Europe* (Abingdon, UK, 2013).

Shammas, Carole, 'Tracking the Growth of Government Securities Investing in Early Modern England and Wales', *Financial History Review*, 27 (2020), pp. 95–114.

Shaw-Taylor, Leigh and Wrigley, E. A., 'Occupational Structure and Population Change', in Roderick Floud, Jane Humphries and Paul Johnson, eds., *The Cambridge Economic History of Modern Britain*, vol. 1, *1700–1870* (Cambridge, 2014), pp. 53–88.

Shepard, Alexandra, *Accounting for Oneself: Worth, Status and Social Order in Early Modern England* (Oxford, 2015).

Sherman, S., *Finance and Fictionality in the Early Eighteenth Century, Accounting for Defoe* (Cambridge, 1996).

Shoemaker, R., *The London Mob: Violence and Disorder in Eighteenth-Century England* (London, 2004).

Smith, Kate, 'Sensing Design and Workmanship: The Haptic Skills of Shoppers in Eighteenth-Century London', *Journal of Design History*, 25 (2012), pp. 1–10.

Soll, Jacob, *The Reckoning: Financial Accountability and the Rise and Fall of Nations* (New York, 2014).

Supple, B., *The Royal Exchange Assurance: A History of British Insurance, 1720–1970* (Cambridge, 1970).

Sussman, N. and Yafeh, Y., 'Institutional Reforms, Financial Development and Sovereign Debt: Britain, 1690–1790', *Journal of Economic History*, 66 (2006), pp. 906–935.

Sutherland, L. Stuart, 'The Accounts of an Eighteenth-Century Merchant: The Portuguese Ventures of William Braund', *Economic History Review*, 3 (1932), pp. 367–387.

Sutherland, Lucy S., *The East India Company in Eighteenth-Century Politics* (Oxford, 1962).

Tait, Jackson, 'Speculation and the English Common Law Courts, 1697–1845', *Libertarian Papers*, 10 (2018), pp. 1–18.

Thomas, Keith, 'Age and Authority in Early Modern England', *Proceedings of the British Academy*, 62 (1976), pp. 205–248.

Torrance, J., 'Social Class and Bureaucratic Innovation: The Commissioners for Examining the Public Accounts, 1780–1787', *Past and Present*, no. 78 (1978), pp. 56–81.

Torres Sánchez, Rafael, ed., *War, State and Development: Fiscal-Military States in the Eighteenth Century* (Pamplona, Spain, 2007).

Tullett, William, 'The Macaroni's "Ambrosial Essences": Perfume, Identity and Public Space in Eighteenth-Century England', *Journal for Eighteenth-Century Studies*, 38 (2015), pp. 163–180.

Tullet, William, *Smell in Eighteenth-Century England: A Social Sense* (Oxford, 2019).

Vickery, Amanda, *Behind Closed Doors: At Home in Georgian England* (New Haven, CT, 2009).

Wallis, Patrick, 'Labour Markets and Training', in R. Floud, J. Humphries and P. Johnson, eds., *The Cambridge Economic History of Modern Britain*, vol. 1, *1700–1870* (Cambridge, 2014), pp. 178–210.

Walsh, Claire, 'Shop Design and the Display of Goods in Eighteenth-Century London', *Journal of Design History*, 8 (1995), pp. 157–176.

Wennerlind, Carl, *Casualties of Credit: The English Financial Revolution, 1620–1720* (Cambridge, MA, 2011).

Whittle, Jane, 'Enterprising Widows and Active Wives: Women's Unpaid Work in the Household Economy of Early Modern England', *The History of the Family*, 19 (2014), pp. 283–300.

Whyman, S. E., *Sociability and Power in Late-Stuart England: The Cultural Worlds of the Verneys, 1660–1720* (Oxford, 2002).

Wright, B., *Insurance Fire Brigades, 1680–1929: The Birth of the British Fire Service* (Stroud, UK, 2008).

Wright, J. F., 'The Contribution of Overseas Savings to the Funded National Debt of Great Britain, 1750–1815', *Economic History Review*, 50 (1997), pp. 657–674.

Yamamoto, Koji, *Taming Capitalism before Its Triumph: Public Service, Distrust, and 'Projecting' in Early Modern England* (Oxford, 2018).

Yamey, B. S., 'Accounting and the Rise of Capitalism: Further Notes on a Theme by Sombart', *Journal of Accounting Research*, 2 (1964), pp. 117–136.

Unpublished Works

Mockford, Jack, '"They Are Exactly as Bank Notes Are": Perceptions and Technologies of Bank Note Forgery during the Bank Restriction Period, 1797–1821' (unpublished PhD thesis, University of Hertfordshire, 2014).

O'Byrne, Alison F., 'Walking, Rambling and Promenading in Eighteenth-Century London: A Literary and Cultural History' (unpublished PhD thesis, University of York, 2003).

Paul, Tawny, 'Credit and Social Relations amongst Artisans and Tradesmen in Edinburgh and Philadelphia, c. 1710–1770' (unpublished PhD thesis, University of Edinburgh, 2011).

Sweeting, S., 'Capitalism, the State and Things: The Port of London, *circa* 1730–1800' (unpublished PhD thesis, University of Warwick, 2014).

Walcot, Clare, 'Figuring Finance: London's New Financial World and the Iconography of Speculation, circa 1689–1763' (unpublished PhD thesis, University of Warwick, 2003).

Online Sources

Bank of Montreal, 'The Bank Messenger Had a Great Deal of Responsibility', accessed 2 May 2020, https://history.bmo.com/bank-messenger-great-deal-responsibility.

BNP Paribas, 'A Bygone Job—The Bank Messenger', accessed 2 May 2020, https://history.bnpparibas/dossier/a-bygone-job-the-collection-man/.

Hitchcock, Tim, Shoemaker, Robert, Emsley, Clive, Howard, Sharon and McLaughlin, Jamie, et al., *The Old Bailey Proceedings Online, 1674–1913*, www.oldbaileyonline .org.

Hitchcock, Tim, Shoemaker, Robert, Howard, Sharon and McLaughlin, Jamie, et al., *London Lives, 1690–1800*, www.londonlives.org.

OXFORD DICTIONARY OF NATIONAL BIOGRAPHY (ODNB)

Cannon, J., 'Savile, Sir George, Eighth Baronet (1726–1784), Politician', *ODNB*, accessed 5 May 2018, https://doi.org/10.1093/ref:odnb/24736.

Fry, M., 'Dundas, Henry, First Viscount Melville (1742–1811), Politician', *ODNB*, accessed 6 January 2018, https://doi.org/10.1093/ref:odnb/8250.

Lindsey, Christopher F., 'David Hartley (1731–1813), Politician', *ODNB*, accessed 7 January 2018, https://doi.org/10.1093/ref:odnb/12495.

Winterbottom, Philip, 'Henry Drummond (c. 1730–1795)', *ODNB*, accessed 6 January 2018, https://doi.org/10.1093/ref:odnb/48025.

INDEX

Note: Page numbers in *italics* indicate figures.

[269]

A NOTE ON THE TYPE

———◆———

THIS BOOK has been composed in Miller, a Scotch Roman typeface designed by Matthew Carter and first released by Font Bureau in 1997. It resembles Monticello, the typeface developed for The Papers of Thomas Jefferson in the 1940s by C. H. Griffith and P. J. Conkwright and reinterpreted in digital form by Carter in 2003.

Pleasant Jefferson ("P. J.") Conkwright (1905–1986) was Typographer at Princeton University Press from 1939 to 1970. He was an acclaimed book designer and AIGA Medalist.